METTERNICH AND HIS TIMES

Nothing is easier than revolution. . . . What is splendid and difficult is to avoid the shock, to guard against upheaval. To sail and reach port, to endure and make others endure, that is the miracle.

Charles Maurras: *Le Chemin de Paradis*.

METTERNICH
AND HIS TIMES

by

G. DE BERTIER DE SAUVIGNY

Translated by Peter Ryde

DARTON, LONGMAN & TODD

LONDON

DARTON, LONGMAN & TODD LTD
29A GLOUCESTER ROAD
LONDON S.W.7

Printed and bound by W. & J. Mackay & Co Ltd, Chatham

Contents

List of Plates

Acknowledgement

We are indebted to Eyre & Spottiswoode (Publishers) Ltd. for permission to adapt three maps from *History of Europe* by H. A. L. Fisher.

Foreword to the French Edition

A century has elapsed since the year of Metternich's death; it is a good moment to wipe some of the dust off the statue bequeathed to us by generations of historians. Indeed, if certain 'historic' figures sometimes appear to us a little artificial, unreal, dusty, perhaps it is precisely because of the number of studies they have inspired. In the end one sees them only through a screen of glossaries, commentaries and appraisals. In order to give them back their original splendour one need only return to the source, jumping at one bound over all the works to which they have given rise. By virtue of this direct contact the man reappears, as he saw himself, as his contemporaries saw him, pulsating with life, an element of substance in real surroundings, much more varied than the traditional effigy. Let us hope that a similar impression will be gained from the following pages which are made up almost entirely of Metternich's own writings, the majority of them hitherto unpublished or little known.

The character and limitations of the present work are explained by the manner in which it was born. When several years ago I plunged into the archives of the State chancellery in Vienna, my plan was to assemble documents with a view to making a study of Metternich and France from 1815 to 1848. This project has not been abandoned and I hope that one day it will be completed. But with thousands of documents passing before my eyes, I could not resist the temptation to take a note at the time of passages here and there which had a more general bearing and which perhaps, if I had not taken that precaution, would have been thrust back into the dungeons. Thus, little by little, there grew up, beside my main documentation, a selection of texts corresponding after a fashion to an intellectual survey of the great statesman. Naturally these gleanings could only be completed by materials drawn from other manuscript and printed sources. The result of that work is by no means a new biography of Metternich —some excellent ones already exist, by no means a new history of his political work—such an undertaking is beyond our scope at the moment, nor yet a new 'interpretation'—too much controversy has already obscured the picture, but simply a kind of fundamental index of the motive forces, of the images, of the general and particular notions which governed his daily activities: an introduction to the routine functioning of the political thinking-machine that was Metternich.

If one considers the position occupied by that statesman in his time, it may be permissible to think that this new approach will be of some service to the diplomatic history of the nineteenth century as well as to the history of political theory.

G. de B. de S.

Foreword to the English Edition

A translation of the present work appeared the more useful because the historiography on Metternich in English is markedly less plentiful than that in French and still less than that in German. The English edition of the *Mémoires et Documents* of the prince de Metternich is only half the size of the German and French editions. The essays of Woodward [1] and Viereck [2] come more into the category of 'historical interpretation', while the more positive work of Kissinger [3] is only concerned with a limited aspect of Metternich's work, that of his part in the coalition against Napoleon. Apart from these there exist only more or less romantic biographies.

At a time when questions raised by relations between States are being discussed, and when problems raised by nationalist agitation are again coming to the fore in a violent manner, it is worth making available to students of history and of political science, and to the ever increasing number of persons occupied with international relations, a work which allows them to become familiar with the personality and mind of Metternich otherwise than through ready-made clichés.

I have taken advantage of this translation to respond to certain criticism which had been raised at the time of the first edition, and to include in the work the results of some supplementary research, notably from the private archives of the Chancellor which are preserved in Prague, and from the files of the Public Record Office in London. The main addition is that of the chapter on the idea of alliance which did not form part of the French version. But elsewhere there is hardly a chapter in which some new quotation or correction is not to be found. Copious additions have been made to the chapter on Great Britain.

My hopes will be completely realized if this little introductory work helps to rouse the interest of more young English-speaking historians in research into, and study of, this aspect of international relations at the beginning of the nineteenth century, a period of history in which there remain, in spite of appearances to the contrary, so many questions to be cleared up.

G. de B. de S.

[1] E. L. Woodward. *Three Studies in European Conservatism*. London, 1929.

[2] Peter Viereck. *Conservatism Revisited*. New York, 1949.

[3] Henry A. Kissinger. *A World Restored: Metternich, Castlereagh, and the Problem of Peace*. London, 1957.

The Career of Metternich

1771	*Jan. 8*	Marriage of Franz Georg von Metternich-Winneburg, count of the Germanic Holy Empire, to Marie-Beatrice de Kagenegg.
1773	*May 15*	Birth of their eldest son Clemens-Wenceslaus-Lothar, at Coblenz.
1788	*Nov.*	Enters Strasbourg University.
1790	*Oct. 6*	Present at the coronation of the Emperor Leopold in Frankfurt.
1790–		Studying law at Mainz University.
1792		
1792	*July*	At Frankfurt. Present at the coronation of the Emperor Francis II (*see note on p. xviii*).
1792–		With his father, the Austrian Emperor's representative in Brussels.
1793		
1794		Accompanies the vicomte Desandroins on a special mission.
1794	*Oct.*	First visit to Vienna.
1794	*Nov.–*	In Bohemia seeing to the family estate of Königswart.
1795	*Mar.*	
1795	*Sept. 27*	Marries Eleonore von Kaunitz, granddaughter of Marie-Thérèse's Grand Chancellor.
1798	*Dec.–*	At the Congress of Rastadt, with his father who is representing the Austrian Emperor.
1799	*Apr.*	
1801	*Feb.*	Appointed Emperor's representative at the Court of Saxony, at Dresden.
1803	*Jan.*	Appointed Emperor's ambassador in Berlin.
	Dec.	Arrives in Berlin.
1805		Negotiates a treaty of alliance between Russia, Austria and Prussia.
	Oct.	First meeting with the Czar Alexander I.
1806	*May*	At the request of Napoleon appointed ambassador to France.
	Aug. 4	Arrives in Paris.
1808	*Dec.*	Journey to Vienna.

1809	Jan. 1	Return to Paris.
	Apr.	Rupture between France and Austria. Metternich held as hostage.
	July 2	Exchanged with French diplomats near Pressburg.
	Aug. 4	Appointed Conference Minister and Minister of State.
	Sept. and Oct.	Negotiation of the peace signed at Vienna on October 14.
	Oct. 8	Appointed Minister of the Imperial Household and of Foreign Affairs.
1810	Mar.	Accompanies the archiduchesse Marie-Louise to Paris and stays there until October.
1811–1812		Internal reorganization of Austria.
1813	June	Interviews with Alexander I at Gitschin and with Napoleon at Dresden; gets armed mediation by Austria accepted.
	Aug. 10	Austria rejoins war against France.
	Oct. 18	Present at the battle of Leipzig.
	Oct. 20	Raised to the dignity of Austrian prince.
	Oct.–Nov.	At Frankfurt.
	Dec.	At Freiburg and Basle.
1814	Jan.	At Langres.
	Feb.	At Bar-sur-Aube.
	Mar.	Signature of the Pact of Chaumont. At Dijon.
	Apr. 10	Arrives in Paris.
	May	Negotiations of the first Treaty of Paris.
	June	Journey to England.
	July 18	Return to Vienna.
	Nov. 3	Opening of the Congress of Vienna, organized and presided over by Metternich.
1815	Jan. 3	Signing of a secret treaty of alliance with England and France, to frustrate the plans of Russia and Prussia.
	Mar. 8	Renewal of the military alliance of Chaumont against France.
	June 9	End of the Congress of Vienna.
	June 21	At Heidelberg. Learns the result of the Battle of Waterloo.
	July–Nov.	In Paris. Negotiating peace treaties with France and the Quadruple Alliance.
	Nov. 26	Leaves Paris.

1815	*Dec. 4*	Arrives in Venice.
1816	*Jan.–Apr.*	In northern Italy.
	July	Receives the estate of Johannisberg, near Mainz.
1817	*June–Oct.*	In northern Italy and Tuscany.
1818	*July*	At Carlsbad, talks with the Russian Minister Capo d'Istria.
	Aug. 11	Death of his father.
	Aug. 29–Sept. 11	At the Diet of Frankfurt.
	Sept. 12–22	First stay at Johannisberg.
	Oct. 1–Nov. 23	Congress of Aix-la-Chapelle. Beginning of his liaison with the comtesse de Lieven.
	Nov. 24–26	Journey to Brussels.
	Dec. 11	Return to Vienna.
1819	*Mar.–July*	Accompanies Emperor to Rome and Naples.
	July 28	Meets King of Prussia and his Minister Hardenberg at Teplitz.
	End of Aug.	Carlsbad Conferences with the principal German Ministers.
	Nov. 25	Beginning of the conferences of Vienna to reinforce the Germanic Confederation.
1820	*May 6*	Death of his daughter Clementine.
	May 15	Signing of the final act of the Vienna conferences.
	End of May–June	In Bohemia: Prague, Königswart, Carlsbad.
	July 15	Learns of Neapolitan revolution.
	July 20	Death of oldest daughter Marie, comtesse Esterhazy.
	Oct. 19–Dec. 25	Congress of Troppau, suppression of Italian revolts.
1821	*May 25*	Appointed Court Chancellor and Chancellor of State.
	End of Oct.	Interview with King George IV of England and his Minister Castlereagh.
1822	*End of Aug.–Sept.*	Conferences in Vienna with Allied Ministers.
	Oct.–Dec.	Congress of Verona for Spanish problems.
	Dec. 16–25	In Venice.
1823	*End Sept.–Oct.*	Accompanying Emperor for an interview with Czar at Czernowitz, taken seriously ill at Lemberg.
1824	*June 5–July 28*	At Johannisberg. Negotiations with German States at Frankfurt to renew Carlsbad decisions.
	Aug.	Taking the waters at Ischl, in Upper Austria.
1825	*Mar. 14–Apr. 21*	In Paris.

1825	*Mar. 19*	Death of his first wife, Eleonore.
	May 7–July 4	In Milan.
	July–Aug.	Waters at Ischl.
	End of Sept.–	At Pressburg for the Diet of Hungary.
	Nov. 15	
	Dec. 1	Death of the Czar Alexander.
1826	*Feb.*	Buys the estate of Plass in Bohemia.
	July	In Bohemia.
	Aug. 12–Sept. 8	At Johannisberg.
1827	*Mar.*	Opening of London conferences on Greek affairs.
	July	Austria practically isolated by Treaty of London between Russia, England and France.
	Aug. 21–23	Interviews with King of Prussia at Teplitz.
	Nov. 5	Marries Marie-Antoinette de Leykam.
1828	*May*	Beginning of Russo-Turkish war.
	Aug.–Sept.	At Waltersdorf, near Vienna.
	Nov. 28	Death of his mother.
1829	*Jan. 7*	Birth of his son Richard.
	Jan. 17	Death of his second wife Antoinette.
	Aug.	At Königswart and Plass.
	Sept.	At Linz.
	Nov. 30	Death of his eldest son Victor.
1830	*May–June*	At Johannisberg.
	July 27	Interviews with Nesselrode at Carlsbad.
	Sept.	Recognition of the July Monarchy in France.
	Oct.	At Pressburg for coronation of the heir-elect the archiduc Ferdinand, as King of Hungary.
1831	*Jan. 30*	Third marriage to Mélanie de Zichy-Ferraris.
	Mar.	Military intervention by Austria in northern Italy against revolutionary movements.
	Aug.–Oct.	At Baden and Schönbrunn during cholera epidemic in Vienna.
	Nov. 15	Treaty of London consecrating the independence of Belgium.
1832	*Feb.*	Conflict with France on the subject of the occupation of Ancona.
	June	Persuades Diet of Frankfurt to pass six decrees against liberal movement.
	June 9	Death of his faithful colleague, Friedrich von Gentz.
	July 22	Death of the duc de Reichstadt.
	July 26–Sept. 16	At Baden.

1833	*June 11–Aug. 4*	At Meidling and Königswart.
	Aug. 7–17	Interview with King of Prussia at Teplitz.
	Sept. 4–20	Interview with Czar Nicholas I at Münchengrätz.
	Oct. 15	Signing of the Berlin Convention. Alliance of three absolutist monarchies.
1834	*Jan.–June*	Conference of German Ministers in Vienna.
	July 5–Sept. 1	At Baden.
	Nov. 20	Birth of his son Lothaire.
1835	*Mar. 2*	Death of Emperor Francis II (*see note on p. xviii*), who is succeeded by the incapable Ferdinand I.
	Sept. 20–Oct. 4	Interview at Teplitz with Czar Nicholas I.
	Oct. 4–11	In Prague.
1836	*June*	Visit of Louis-Philippe's sons to Vienna.
	Aug. 5–Sept. 14	In Bohemia.
1837	*July*	In Salzburg and Munich.
	July 22–23	Interview with King of Prussia at Teplitz.
	Aug.	At Plass and Königswart.
1838	*July 18–23*	Interview at Teplitz with Czar Nicholas I and King of Prussia.
	End of Aug.–end of Oct.	Journey to northern Italy and Tuscany.
1839	*June*	Attending the Diet of Hungary, at Pressburg.
	End of Aug.	Serious illness.
	Sept. 10–Oct. 23	Resting at Johannisberg, leaving handling of affairs to his colleague Ficquelmont.
1840	*Mar.–Apr.*	Working on his *Mémoires*.
	June 7	Death of King Frederick-William III of Prussia.
	July 15	Signing of treaty of London between three Continental Powers and England, over Eastern problem.
	July–Sept.	At Plass and Königswart.
1841	*July–Aug.*	At Königswart.
	Sept.	At Johannisberg.
1842	*Aug.–Sept.*	At Johannisberg.
1843	*May*	At Diet of Pressburg.
	July–Aug.	At Ischl and journey to Bohemia.
1844	*Aug. 22–Sept. 17*	In Trieste.
1845	*Aug.*	Interviews at Stolzenfels with Queen Victoria of England and King Frederick-William IV of Prussia.
	Sept.	Journey to Bohemia.
	Dec. 30	Interview with Czar Nicholas I and in Vienna.

1846	*Jan.*	Metternich responsible for creation of Academy of Sciences in Vienna.
	Mar.	Troubles in Galicia.
	July–Sept.	In Bohemia.
	July 29	Visit of King of Prussia to Königswart.
	Nov.	Annexation of Cracow by Austria.
1847		Metternich has new residence built for himself in Vienna, on the Rennweg.
	Nov.	War of Sonderbund in Switzerland.
1848	*Jan.*	Riots in Milan. Revolution in Sicily. Unrest in northern Italy.
	Feb. 27–29	Revolution in Paris.
	Mar. 13	Riot in Vienna. Resignation of Metternich.
	Mar. 14	Flight from Vienna.
	Mar. 24	Arrival in Dresden.
	Apr. 20–Sept. 14	In London.
	Sept. 15	Moves to Brighton.
1849	*Oct. 11*	Arrives in Brussels.
1851	*June 8*	Leaves Brussels for Johannisberg.
	Aug. 6–7	Receives visit from Bismarck.
	Sept. 24	Back in Vienna.
1854	*Mar. 3*	Death of his third wife, Mélanie.
1859	*Apr. 20*	Visit from Emperor Francis-Joseph.
	June 11	Metternich dies in Vienna at the age of 86.

NOTE ON HOLY ROMAN AND AUSTRIAN EMPERORS

The title *Holy Roman Emperor* was renounced in 1806 by Francis II who thereby became Francis I, *Emperor of Austria* (as from 1804). For the sake of clarity, however, the author has retained the designation Francis II throughout this book.

Part I

THE WIZARD OF VIENNA

CHAPTER ONE

The Man

1. Round a Portrait

IN THE pages that follow we shall be doing little more than listening to him. Such was the lot of all those who approached him during his lifetime, and thus no doubt it will always be, for in few statesmen has action been better identified with the written or spoken word. But before turning to what he said let us take a quick look at the man himself.

Lawrence's well-known portrait showing him in 1819 at the age of 46 and at the height of his career outlines the dominant features of his physical and moral personality. A German, unmistakably, and of good breeding; above the average in height, with blue eyes, fair hair showing a tendency to curl, and a fresh complexion. A well-balanced constitution. He has seldom known illness. Occasionally 'one of those wretched attacks of catarrh or rheumatism stretch [him] on the sickbed, always for nine or thirteen days'. (*Mémoires*, IV, p. 19) Then, too, he used to suffer from inflammation of the eyelids and in his later years from a suggestion of deafness. But, after all, to have defied a tubercular infection that was to carry off his first wife and three children, to marry three times and at the age of 58 to enjoy life like a young man, to get through a prodigious amount of desk work day after day for forty years, to endure without flinching the trials and reverses he was called upon to face, and on top of all that to live to be 86, gives indisputable proof of a fine, strong mechanism and one predisposed to optimism. An optimist, indeed, the man who can write one day in August from his castle at Johannisberg:

To finish all one has to do, to overcome all the difficulties arising from it, to be wonderfully fit, to breathe a pure, soft air and to live in a heavenly place, these make up the bright side of life. (to Floret, Aug. 1, 1824. *Staatskanzlei. Interiora* 82)

An optimist, too, the Minister who can declare:

I have long experience of the world's affairs and I have always observed that no matter is so easily settled as that which appears to present insuperable difficulties. (to the comtesse de Lieven, Jan. 31, 1819, p. 170)

An aristocrat, too, and the pen of the Russian diplomat, Meyendorff, comes to the help of Lawrence's brush:

I was struck by the prince's distinguished appearance. I found a kind of stiff grace shining through his polished manners and the cynical expression of features on which calm and dignity had made their imprint. Curly hair, aquiline nose, well-shaped mouth, high forehead, raised eyebrows, these form a handsome unity the harmony of which is slightly disturbed because one of his pale blue eyes is fixed. When he laughs his face, generally calm and unrevealing, becomes over-excited and almost misshapen. His half-open mouth forms a huge arc; his eyebrows separate as they rise unevenly towards his forehead (there is a Mephistophelian touch about this grimace), and his voice, usually a drawl, becomes plaintive and whimpering as soon as he stops being serious. (quoted in Grunwald, p. 162)

The man whom liberal legend wished to turn into a sinister tyrant and a gloomy pedant appeared to all those who made his acquaintance a perfectly amiable gentleman, approachable and by no means bigoted.

'You like Metternich when you leave him', wrote the Genevan envoy, Pictet de Rochemont (to Turrettini, Oct. 28, 1815. *Correspondance Diplomatique de Pictet de Rochemont*, II, p. 181); and the British ambassador, Lord Stewart: '. . . although you may be hurt by his *légèreté* and *inconséquence*, you never can be really angry with him from his personal amiability and kind manner'. (to Castlereagh, Jan. 27, 1821. F.O. 7/160)

Even more surprising, those who had to suffer under the repressive Austrian system have sometimes paid tribute to the humaneness of their persecutor. In this context nothing makes more curious reading than the *Memoirs of a State Prisoner*, by Andryane, a book much less well known today than that of his companion in misfortune, Silvio Pellico. Andryane, a young liberal-minded Frenchman, was involved in the anti-Austrian conspiracy of 1820 in Lombardy. He was, like Pellico, sentenced to *carcere duro* and underwent more than ten years' imprisonment at the Spielberg. Thanks to the representations made by his sister on his behalf to the Emperor Francis and to Metternich he was released in 1832. Her letters, reproduced in that book, tell in detail of her interviews with the Chancellor. On one occasion Metternich took the trouble to read over with her the appeal she was to present to the Emperor, pointing out in the nicest way what she should put in and leave out in order to touch his master's heart or to avoid his displeasure. In a word he was so kind and sympathetic that she admitted on leaving him 'that a gentle and devoted friend could not have gone farther in care and attention'.

We may note here that Metternich could with advantage take a benevolent line when he had unscrupulous subordinates ready to put his policy into effect and a master capable of taking upon himself responsibility for the most odious measures of repression. It might also be said that it was not difficult for a man of his experience to take advantage of the *naïveté* of an emotional young woman. More difficult to reject is the evidence of Confalonieri, the leader of the conspiracy, an unwavering and far-sighted patriot and one of the heroes of Italian independence. After sentence of death had been commuted to life imprisonment, the Emperor, always obsessed by the desire to penetrate the workings of secret societies, had ordered Metternich to speak to the condemned man himself and to extract some information from him in exchange for a promise of clemency. Confalonieri shortly afterwards told Andryane how Metternich acquitted himself of this disagreeable task:

The Prince showed the tact and good taste that one would expect
from an exceptional person who good-naturedly undertakes a
mission the outcome of which is already known. In accordance
with the Emperor's wishes he was able at one and the same time
to satisfy his sovereign and to show respect to the prisoner. I owe
him this testimony but it prompts me to say: 'Pray Heaven that
our destiny is not dependent on this man alone.' (Andryane,
Mémoires, II, p. 62)

What lies behind the façade? Is he intelligent? But what is
intelligence? One can only suggest that Metternich possesses most
of the attributes of it: memory, the ability to analyse and co-
ordinate, ease and aptitude of expression, vast culture and far-
reaching curiosity, tact and intuition in the handling of men. In
this last respect the most implacable of his enemies do him
honour. It is certainly no mean performance to have been able
to win the respect of such widely differing personalities as the
Emperors Francis and Napoleon, the Czar Alexander, Castlereagh, and Guizot. A perfect courtier with a quick, well-chosen
repartee. 'You are indeed young,' Napoleon once remarked to
him, 'to represent the oldest monarchy in Europe.' 'Sire, my age is
the same as Your Majesty's at Austerlitz.'

An exceptional memory enables him to recapture every detail
of a conversation with the very expressions used. The person
addressed, when confronted with the account of the conversation,
generally had to admit the accuracy of it. Besides, Metternich
himself says:

When it is a question of facts I really have a good memory. I have
only to transport myself in thought to the middle of events and
all the facts, down to the secondary details, come clearly before
my eyes. (*Mémoires*, III, p. 330)

I was born with an appetite for learning and I have always
looked upon life as a school. (to Hübner, May 15, 1853)

In the sphere of politics and contemporary history it was inevitable that Metternich should, by the very position he occupied,

become in time the best-informed statesman in Europe. It is not trumpet-blowing when he writes:

> Impartiality is a sham, a word without meaning, unless it be backed by real knowledge. This condition of any judgment I am not lacking in. (to Sir Travers Twiss, Mar. 10, 1857)

Metternich's curiosity extends far beyond the field of his daily activities:

> It seemed to me that my true vocation lay in the cultivation of science, in particular of the exact and natural sciences which attracted me more than the others. (*Mémoires*, I, p. 21)

> During my years at the university I completed, along with my other studies, the greater part of the medical course. I rose above all the sordidness and lived in the hospitals and anatomy rooms; I only abandoned this study when I no longer had time for it. (to the comtesse de Lieven, Mar. 1, 1819, p. 224)

This grounding enabled him in 1832 to intervene actively in the discussions of a congress of learned men, and to repeat for the benefit of Marshal Marmont a lecture by the physician Baumgartner on the subject of a new system of acoustics.

What of his reading?

> I have a bad habit of reading for half an hour—or an hour—before going to sleep, but as a rule I read nothing that touches on my work. My spare time is taken up with scientific literature, discoveries, travel and even simple narratives. Novels I never look at unless I am persuaded that they are classics having some literary value. The ordinary novel does not interest me; I find it always inferior to my own experiences. Powerful situations strike me as exaggerated and I cannot resist looking at the last page, in which the characters marry or get killed, at the same time as I look at the title. Then nothing is left but to say *Amen*, and the novel is finished for me. (*Mémoires*, III, p. 315)

At least five languages are at his disposal in his reading. 'To work twelve hours a day is my lot, four of them in German, four in French, one each in Italian and Slav, and two in Latin.' (marquis de Villeneuve: *Charles X en Exil*, p. 17) To these must be added English, which presents no difficulty. He surprises the Viennese poet Grillparzer by reciting from memory the hundred or so verses of the epilogue of Byron's *Childe Harolde*.

A lover of the fine arts, that goes without saying. From France and Italy he sends for pictures, engravings, furniture, trinkets. But the truth is that his taste in material things is not of the most enlightened, judged by modern criteria. For example, instead of acquiring some genuine antiques in Italy he prefers to order from a mediocre sculptor in Rome bad copies of the too well-known piece of statuary of the Campo Santo in Genoa. The author of these lines had the opportunity of visiting in 1959 the castle of Königswärt (Kynšvart), where the Chancellor's collections are preserved. He was surprised to find only bric-à-brac indicating curiosity rather than artistic discernment.

Among all his souvenirs one deserves mention: a luxurious wash-basin of the Empire period. Used by Napoleon on the isle of Elba, it was passed on to his son, and the duc de Reichstadt on his death-bed bequeathed it to the Chancellor as a mark of esteem and gratitude. A pity that some learn of the relations between Metternich and the Eagle only through the dramas of Edmond Rostand!

Being a good German, Metternich is sensitive to musical emotions and he lets himself go on this subject with an almost romantic openness:

> Nothing affects me like music. I believe that after love, and above all with it, it is of all things in the world the one that makes me a better human being. Music excites and calms me at the same time. It has the same effect on me as something remembered, it takes me outside the narrow framework in which I live. My heart unfolds; it embraces at one and the same time the past, the present, and the future. Everything comes to life: trouble and enjoyment that is past, thoughts and pleasures to which I look forward with yearning. Music rouses me to gentle tears. It draws my sympathy on to myself, it does me good and it hurts me which in itself is good. (to the comtesse de Lieven, Dec. 20, 1818, p. 74)

Anyone who loves music in this way could not be insensitive to nature's charms. The following lines were written in February 1820:

> I really hunger and thirst for my garden on the Rennweg. For a whole month I have been unable to visit it. It is true that my rooms are filled with the finest blooms from my greenhouses, but it is not only flowers that delight me. I need fresh air and sunshine. (*Mémoires*, III, p. 335)

More touching, perhaps, are these few lines written to his daughter by the elderly exile in Brussels in 1850:

> Blossom-time will soon be here again. There is no denying it, flowers that belong to me give me more pleasure than those that do not. Go to the villa when the lilac is in flower and give it my greetings. (quoted by Breycha-Vautier, 'Metternich à Bruxelles' in *Revue Générale Belge*, Oct. 1957, pp. 46–47)

Might it not almost be the voice of Joachim du Bellay?

What of Metternich's heart? It is a subject which might have been rather difficult to uncover before the publication, in 1909, of the celebrated love-letters addressed to the comtesse—later princesse—de Lieven. Anyone who glances through them is left in no doubt: behind the public figure always showing off there lives a man with a kind, sensitive heart, who suffers and is happy like anyone else. No one was more aware of this dualism than he:

> I have a reserve fund which I expend on words, actions, and calculations. From this fund I draw material which I transform into memoirs and protocols. My real capital—that which supplies my needs and forms the basis of my happiness—is kept separate. I only like one of these pieces of property, the other I detest. One is yours as much as it is mine, the other belongs to my country, to my position, to my duties as a statesman. I will never ask you to share that. (to the comtesse de Lieven, Nov. 15, 1818, p. 3)

It is well known that the wife of the Russian ambassador in

London was not the only one to appear in Metternich's love life. Before her two other great Russian ladies, the Princess Bagration and the duchesse de Sagan, had possessed his heart; and three Frenchwomen: Marie-Constance de Caumont la Force, the duchesse d'Abrantès, and Caroline Bonaparte, the future Queen of Naples; not to mention that gentle and romantic Austrian who sent him, before she died, a casket containing the ashes of her love-letters and a broken ring. Loves which do not give evidence of a very strict morality, but loves that were in no way unrefined. We have only to read the language in which Metternich evoked the first of these attachments:

> I made the acquaintance at this time (in Mainz) of a young woman of my age, an exquisite creature full of charm, good taste and wit. She belonged to one of the great families of France. I loved her with all the enthusiasm of youth and she loved me with all the simplicity of her heart. We both wanted what neither of us dared to admit. I lived only for her and for my studies. She had nothing else to do but to love me. This relationship lasted more than three years and had for me the invaluable advantage of turning me away from the indiscretions of bad taste that are so common at that age. When we were together we gave each other assurances of love and the future stretched such a long way before our eyes that we put off the sequel to so much love until a more opportune moment. (to the comtesse de Lieven, Dec. 1, 1818, p. 41)

If to these extra-conjugal amours are added the Chancellor's three wives, whom he loved sincerely and made happy, we can hardly deny him a gift for attracting and deserving affection. This sort of feminine plebiscite is the best guarantee of the quality of a man's heart.

From 1822 at the latest Metternich is entirely with his family. Nor did he conceal from his friend his deep love of home:

> I left my wife and children with much sorrow. You have no idea how good and comfortable my home is. (to the comtesse de Lieven, Mar. 8, 1819, p. 236)

A good son, too, entirely devoted to his parents, especially to his mother, to whom he likes to describe himself as 'the gentle friend of his dear old mama'. He himself was idolized by his children and brought them up with tender, active solicitude. The testing of his character struck again and again at this specially sensitive point. Within a few years merciless consumption took from him his daughter Clementine, aged 13; his elder daughter Maria, the Princess Esterhazy; and his son Viktor, an admirably gifted young man. The letters he wrote during Clementine's illness are really moving, and these were his emotions at the time of Maria's death in July 1820:

> My grief is that of a man who still has great duties to perform. I must forget that I am a father. I must stifle that voice which nature herself has such difficulty in silencing. I throw myself into my work like a desperate man flinging himself against the enemy batteries. I no longer live to feel but only to act. The burden imposed on me by Providence is heavy indeed and more than one would collapse under it. How I loved that child! And her love for me was greater than that for a father. For many years she was my best friend. I had no need to confide in her, she guessed my thoughts. She knew me better than I knew myself. She thought nothing, said nothing which I would not have thought or said in her place. I constantly felt the need to bless and to thank her for belonging to me and for being what she was. I have suffered an irreparable loss. (*Mémoires*, III, pp. 360–1)

At the end of 1827 Metternich married quite a young girl, Marie-Antoinette von Leykam. Great was the astonishment, amounting almost to scandal, in high Viennese society. The young bride was 33 years younger than her spouse and did not belong to that privileged circle which considered itself *la crème de la crème*. But there is no denying that it was a love match. Then fourteen months later the little princess in her turn was taken from him. Metternich broke the news to his old friend the duc de Caraman:

> I have lost all that remains of my happiness. You, *mon cher duc,*

who knew this creature, knew how perfect she was, how un-spoiled in her behaviour and pure in her thoughts, how generally sweet natured, you will understand better than most the grief to which I am exposed. Time will soften the blow, no doubt, but it can never heal the wound . . . I did all that was required of me. I was present at the most heart-rending scene of all. I witnessed the last sigh of the person who by all the laws of nature should have been the one to bless the memory of me. In death she looked as beautiful as that Saint Cecilia which we both admired in Rome —Saint Cecilia or indeed any martyr lying beneath the table of the high altar in any church. None of her features had suffered. She was innocence asleep! Would you believe it? That sight which will remain for ever in my memory has lessened for me the horror of the catastrophe. . . . (Unpublished letter, Jan. 26, 1829. Arch. de Mme Firino-Martell)

Friendship keeps its place beside love. It occurs rarely and ever more rarely as the man who is placed above others grows old, but it is constant and even charming in respect of old colleagues like Gentz and Floret. Witness this note addressed to the latter from the castle of Plass in July 1820:

Viktor brought me your letter. It is up to you, my dear friend, to come and find me here or at Königswärt . . . But consider in this matter only yourself, your strength, and your doctor. You are so sure to give me pleasure whenever you like to meet me that if I were not a stranger to egotism I would call on you to accompany me always and everywhere. (*Staatskanzlei. Interiora*, 82)

As to religious feeling, it is significant that we can read through thousands of letters or accounts of conversations and find refer-ences to God used more as a matter of style than as the expression of a deep faith. Catholicism is part of the established order and that is enough to make it respectable in Metternich's eyes:

Mistakes in matters of religion give rise to all the other mistakes. One power alone governs the moral world and every time that power is attacked the world prepares itself for shocks. That is a profession of faith to which Your Eminence has always found me faithful. (to Cardinal Consalvi, Nov. 22, 1820. Van Duerm, p. 312)

Yet there is this declaration, the sincerity of which cannot be doubted:

I steadfastly believe in God, and death holds no fears for me. (*Mémoires*, III, p. 307)

He also writes to Nesselrode on August 20, 1817:

Every day I read one or two chapters of the Bible. I discover daily in it things of beauty and I bow down before this admirable book ... Twenty years ago profound and sustained investigation of the Scriptures would have turned me either into an atheist after the manner of d'Alembert or Lalande or into a Christian after the manner of Chateaubriand; now I am a believer, I no longer examine closely. I have read and seen enough to know that reading alone does not mean understanding: that it would be rash in me to condemn what I imperfectly understand, either from ignorance or from a lack of experience indispensable to a profound critic and specially an impartial one. In a word, I believe and no longer dispute. (*Mémoires*, III, p. 59)

The man is at last taking shape through the medium of environment and his manner of living:

You have no idea how beautiful my rooms are when the sun shines into them. They face south; consequently they are pleasant and warm, and I have a job to protect my furniture from the effects of the sun. I have a good-sized anteroom, a large *salon* for people waiting to see me; and next to it is my library. This is a magnificent room lined from floor to ceiling with books in fine, open, mahogany shelves. As it is about 18 feet high, it must contain, without appearing to, nearly 15,000 books. In the centre of the room is the beautiful Venus by Canova, the pedestal of which is surrounded by a settee. Then comes my study, a large room with three windows. It contains three writing-tables, for I like to move about and I do not like to be disturbed at my desk when I want someone to write in my study. This room is filled with *objets d'art*, pictures, busts, and bronzes. You will find there some astronomical clocks and instruments of every description, for I like to devote my few hours of leisure to the study of science . . . The big table in my bedroom is covered with portfolios containing engravings, maps and drawings; besides which I also have a number of *objets d'art* arranged under glass. I am often amused at the diversion which the sight of such a varied collection of treasures causes among strangers who call on me. In this secluded spot I spend seven-eighths of my time. Why should I not surround myself here with the things I like? I do not like small rooms, especially having to work in them. In too confined a space the mind shrivels up, thought contracts, and the heart withers. (*Mémoires*, III, p. 333)

Would you like to know how I live? This is it, the whole year round. I get up between eight and nine o'clock. I dress and go to breakfast with Mme de Metternich. There I find my children and I stay with them until ten. I go to my study and work or interview people until one. If the weather is fine I go riding, returning at half-past two. I work until half-past four. I go to my salon and invariably find eight, ten, or a dozen people who have come to dine. I go back to my study at half-past six.

Nearly every day I visit the Emperor. I stay there a good while and then back to work until between ten and eleven when I move into my *salon* where social callers and strangers are assembled. I usually spend an hour in conversation with your 'children in Vienna'. I say a word to the ladies and I retire at one o'clock. Holidays, Easter, winter or summer I never change my routine. (to the comtesse de Lieven, Jan. 3, 1819, p. 104)

2. The Cult of Self

When we consider Metternich's vanity one simple allusion or a few lines is not enough. A chapter at least is needed if we are to pay proper regard to the balance of the portrait, and with all the different manifestations of this trait there is enough material to fill a book. The book, incidentally, exists. (Karl Groos, *Fürst Metternich: Eine Studie zur Psychologie der Eitelkeit*)

His is a vanity which, leaving the limits of ridicule far behind, assumes grandiose and fascinating dimensions. Like the exaggerations in architecture of the baroque or 1900 period, it takes on in time the proportions of a style. It leaves a distinctive mark on his personality, on his style of writing and on his way of thinking. Never before, perhaps, has verbal egotism been carried to such lengths. In speaking of himself Metternich is inexhaustible. He misses no opportunity: conversations, official documents, love-letters. Nothing inspires in him greater eloquence or a more felicitous turn of phrase:

> I believe that each day must add to your conviction that I am a man apart from most of my fellow men. (to the comtesse de Lieven, Mar. 15, 1819)

> My life has become a kind of apostolate . . . on every side a flock of faithful sheep await their pastor and I could not leave them with a clear conscience until I had given them spiritual consolation. (quoted by Bibl, p. 177)

> To me in Paris men become sponges eager to absorb ideas. (to the Emperor Francis, Mar. 17, 1825. *Mémoires*, IV, p. 164)

> People look on me as a kind of lantern to which they draw near in order to see their way through the almost complete darkness. (to Gentz, Apr. 11, 1825. *Mémoires*, IV, p. 158)

> The world has need of me still if only because my place in it could not be filled by anyone else. To be what I am needs an accumulation of experience, and one could as easily replace an old tree as an old Minister. (to his son Viktor, May 15, 1828. *Mémoires*, IV, p. 422)

> Throughout my long career as a Minister I have been, among those who rule, the only one capable of ruling. (to his daughter Leontine, Jan. 17, 1849. *Mémoires*, VIII, p. 422)

He is 'the perpetual thinker' (to Apponyi, July 18, 1842), 'the man of truth' (to the Consul-General of Austria in Alexandria, Apr. 25, 1843), 'a rock in the middle of a stormy sea' (to Zichy, May 19, 1827), 'the protagonist of reason' (to his daughter Leontine, Jan. 17, 1849. *Mémoires*, VIII, p. 214)

M.–B

The most flagrant flattery becomes in his nostrils the incense of justice:

> The visit which General Orloff has just paid us must have left him with a flattering impression. He said as he took leave of me, and I believe in the sincerity of his words: 'I have learned more in the ten weeks that I have spent with you than in the thirty years I spent as an observer of or a participant in the affairs of the world.' (to Ficquelmont, Oct. 13, 1830)

He ends up by imagining himself to be the centre of the world:

> What is happening to me today happens to everyone who is unswerving in thought and action. Events, like the men who take part in them, revolve round a fixed point. This movement is not exactly a circular one, it is rather in the form of a spiral. Those who follow this turning movement either end up in the centre or they swing wider until they disappear into space. (to Apponyi, Dec. 21, 1836)

Yet the same man can write with the utmost serenity: 'I have twenty defects but presumption is not one of them.' (to the comtesse de Lieven, Dec. 1, 1818, p. 43)

> I know myself thoroughly and am grateful for that knowledge. I am so strict a judge of myself that I never allow myself the same standard in the judgment of others. (to the comtesse de Lieven, Jan. 21, 1819, p. 153)

It will be seen, in the second part of this work, with what vitriolic 'indulgence' Metternich puts the statesmen of his time in their place. Besides, how could he resist the luxury of making comparisons favourable to himself?

> Nesselrode writes better than I; he is even, in my opinion, one of the best chroniclers of events; but I am a more vigorous thinker than Nesselrode, and it is thought, not grammar, that makes style. (to the comtesse de Lieven, July 19, 1819. Quoted by E. Daudet in the *Revue Hebdomadaire*, July 1899, p. 666)

Poor Nesselrode! Here is something more about him, after they had been talking together:

I had no difficulty in making him adopt several of my opinions. That which is full is easily poured into that which is empty. (to Apponyi, Oct. 13, 1830)

And how neatly little Thiers is put in his place!

I have not the genius of M. Thiers, but I am calmer than he, and if I have more experience the explanation is quite simple. I have been leader of the Cabinet for twenty-eight years whereas he is the twenty-eighth Foreign Minister in France since I first undertook that work in Austria. (to Apponyi, Aug. 22, 1836)

As for Canning, he is honoured with an altogether more elaborate parallel:

There exist in this world two types of mind: one skims the surface and does not go deeply into anything . . . the other concentrates on things and penetrates below the surface. Canning possesses the first type of mind in a high degree. I certainly have it to a much lesser extent, but I really belong, with such gifts as I have, to the second category. Canning flies, I walk. He soars to a region uninhabited by men, I take up my position on the level of human action. The resulting difference is that Canning will have on his side the romantics whereas I shall be left to the prose-writers. His rôle is as brilliant as a flash of lightning but lasts no longer. Mine is not dazzling but it preserves what the other consumes . . . Men like Canning fall twenty times and recover themselves as often; men like myself have no need of recovery because they are not subject to falls. The first play to the gallery: the second usually bore it. To the great majority of those who see me at work I must be very boring to watch but they will have to put up with it for I will not change. (to Neumann, June 23, 1826)

Immutability. That is one of the great sources of satisfaction for the statesman. 'The first moral element in me is immutability.' (to the comtesse de Lieven, Dec. 22, 1818, p. 78)

Set me down in the world of politics and you might think I was on the battlefield. I have killed many adversaries and put an even greater number to headlong flight. The reason, purely and simply, is my immense power. I keep control of my weapons in the heat of battle because I keep calm. My adversaries scatter while I remain stationary; they run through the fields, I do not move; they are breathless, I have not yet drawn breath. I am perfectly sure that in the course of my public life I have reduced to desperation more people than I have seriously angered.

My friend, you are in love at this moment with a kind of *buffer*. It has been deliberately placed where it is to stop those who run too hard in the wrong direction. They knock against it, they curse it, they swear at what they call an obstacle. The buffer appears hardly to notice the bumps it gets. There you have it, an exact description of my life. It remains unmoved for it is heavy. There is no merit in it because nothing that I do is voluntary. The good Lord made me as I am and I shall remain so for as long as it pleases Him to leave me here! At the age of 15 I was what I am now at 45. (to the comtesse de Lieven, Mar. 21, 1819, pp. 250–7)

He has been called deceitful. Not so:

My soul is strong and upright, and my words are true, always and on every occasion. (to the comtesse de Lieven, Nov. 20, 1818, p. 18)

I have two ears but only one mouth. I can listen to both sides of any question, but I can only say the same thing to different parties. (to Hummelauer, Feb. 24, 1839)

He has been called cunning. Not so:

Every time some fool is mistaken about me, he accuses me of that cunning which I detest because I despise it. (to the comtesse de Lieven, Nov. 20, 1818, p. 18)

He has been called spiteful. Not so:

Personal considerations exert no influence on my mind. They only affect me in so far as they react on my work. (to Neumann, May 30, 1843)

He is said to prefer negotiation to action. Not so:

> I consider myself stronger than most of my contemporaries because I have an invincible hatred of words and empty phrases and my instinct is always towards action. (to Gentz, Aug. 5, 1825. *Mémoires*, IV, p. 192)

In fact, if he is to be believed, he stands above worldly ambition:

> I have never wished to be what I am and have done everything in my power to prevent my becoming it, and yet there are eight or ten fools . . . who think that I have ambition. If I have any, it is ambition for good. I pay dearly for it because my heart is not in my work, and I find that it is the same with what the world calls *glory* as it is with beauty: the possession of either is more profitable to others than to oneself. (to the comtesse de Lieven, Dec. 1, 1818, p. 44)

The endlessly important source of satisfaction for Metternich is the certainty that he alone knows the truth:

> I am armed at all points. My sword is drawn and my pen is ready. My thoughts are as bright and clear as a crystal stream whereas many people these days flounder in muddy waters. (*Mémoires*, III, p. 543)

> My mind is not narrow in its conceptions. I am always either short of or beyond the preoccupations of most statesmen. I cover a much wider ground than they either want to or are capable of seeing. I cannot help telling myself twenty times a day: 'O Lord! how right I am and how wrong they are!' (*Mémoires*, III, p. 225)

This infallibility derives in the first place from his natural gifts:

> Heaven has given me excellent eyesight, accurate and sensitive hearing, and a straightforward and proper sense of touch. I see what is, I hear what is said, I feel what exists. (to the comtesse de Lieven, Mar. 21, 1819, p. 250)

Metternich believes, not without good reason, that he has the advantage of the best observation post:

As with soldiers, so it is with political observers. It is not those on the battlefield who are in the best position to judge the chances of victory or defeat, it is the observers looking down on the movements of the two armies who have a decided advantage in this respect. This is the position in which I find myself and my being withdrawn from the field of action has little effect on my faculties. A clear mind and an adequate knowledge of the situation can be a substitute for material vision. (to Apponyi, Mar. 5, 1840)

In this way nothing is obscure to him:

I suffer no illusions and I always see the strings that work the puppets while the foolish public exhausts itself looking for mechanical processes. (to Floret, Jan. 11, 1821. *Frankreich, Varia,* 93b)

In his diplomatic correspondence expressions like these keep cropping up: 'Your reports only confirm me in the judgment I formed about the position . . .' 'These dispatches afford me all the greater interest since I derive from them the certainty that I was not wrong . . .' In the end facts emerge only as humble servants to be made use of in the master's deductions:

I do not belong to that class of men who stop on the circumference to guess at what is going on in the centre of the circle. I prefer to set myself up in the centre in order to observe events on the circumference, and as soon as I do that they are of no more value to me than a simple means of control. (to Apponyi, Feb. 15, 1839)

Thanks to this 'there is no indecision in my step. I go straight to the objective and I am sure of reaching it.' (to the comtesse de Lieven, Dec. 1, 1818, p. 44)

It is therefore the duty of his subordinates to follow him blindly:

Identify yourself, *Monsieur le comte*, completely with me. Admit the truth of the propositions that I am about to expound to you and since the truth has been revealed to me let it form the basis of

our calculations and of our line of action. Do not stop to consider whether I am right or wrong; believe only in me whenever a personal doubt is raised in your mind. (to Lebzeltern,
Feb. 7, 1824)

The supernatural insight of the wizard extends to the future:

I belong to the class of men who live more in the future than in
the present. A sense of history in my make-up raises me above a
host of momentary difficulties. The future is always before my
eyes and I firmly believe that I am less likely to go wrong in
respect of it than in respect of the present. (*Mémoires*, III, p. 454)

To congratulate himself on past achievement is one more way
of proving his infallibility. For example, after the Austrian intervention in Naples:

If I may be allowed a little introspection it is confined to the
feeling that, at a time when the world was enveloped in fog, I
was never wrong, I never opposed that conviction which prevents my accepting as true what is false, as principles what are
only the subversion of them, and as solid what is often no
more than smoke. (to Lebzeltern, Dec. 3, 1821)

And this really splendid passage, taken from a report to the
Emperor:

If heaven has plainly blessed the endeavours of Austria in recent
years, it is to the immutability and uprightness of her policy that
the world owes its good fortune. Any attack on this policy is sure
to fail. Permit me to send Your Majesty from afar this assurance:
my most precious reward is the knowledge that I have never
misled my August Master. (written from Naples, Aug. 17, 1817.
Mémoires, III, p. 62)

Having arrived at this degree of certainty, the approval of the
common people is no longer needed:

In troubled times a man in my position must give up hope of
being understood. It is perhaps in the fact that he is neither
understood nor dominated that the best chance of success lies.

The reaction of evil men is thereby subdued. If a man has the intention and the will he can go forward, without support but also without hindrance. He makes headway if he is not afraid of the solitude of the desert and he sometimes ends up where he is least expected. It is only the factious who finish up by being sorry for their mistakes; honourable men profess themselves satisfied. (to the comte de Senfft, May 15, 1821. *Frankreich, Varia,* 97a)

And so abuse leaves him cold:

Insults fall on me and also on the men whom I look upon as the mainstays of a common cause. I feel honoured by the attacks launched against us by the mob. (to Vincent, July 16, 1825)

I enjoy the abuse of those on whose toes I deliberately tread. (*Mémoires,* III, p. 458)

Providence herself will see that justice is done to his adversaries:

For some years now I have made a singular observation. It is that men who are diametrically opposed to me die. The explanation is quite simple, these men are mad, and it is the mad who die. (to the comtesse de Lieven, Dec. 6, 1818, p. 56)

The judgment of his contemporaries matters little:

For some time now we have given up living as others live. Heaven and that justice which only comes with time will be our judge and our recompense. Our lives are so disturbed that we can only anticipate this recompense in our inmost feelings. (to Vincent, Dec. 9, 1820)

Posterity will judge me. Her voice is the only one whose favour I seek, the only one to which I do not remain indifferent, and yet it is the only one I shall never hear. (*Mémoires,* III, p. 341)

Such a superabundance of arrogance, such an abnormal development of the ego is not without its psychological problem, for genuine pride is usually more sober in its manifestations and a really superior intelligence is the first to recognize its own limitations. It cannot altogether be explained by the lack of restraint that is attributed, not without justification, to the Germanic character. Metternich himself suggests two other reasons in his writings. The first bears the date September 1821, the very moment when his vanity is most unbridled:

> I go forward as though I felt sure of being able to control the course of events. The least boastful man is obliged, in certain circumstances, to assume a self-confidence which would normally be a sure sign of conceit, that most ridiculous of weaknesses. (*Mémoires*, III, p. 477)

In this way the continual pose would become a process of government, a kind of incantation intended to fascinate his master as much as his colleagues, and to keep them in a state of submission to his will. By frequently playing this game, might he not in the end succumb to it himself?

There is another hypothesis. Could not all this boasting represent a kind of compensation for something lacking in the soul itself? A way of combating deficiencies vaguely felt and to which these boastings bear silent witness? Cannot this be read between the lines in the following remark? 'It is certainly no easy thing to fulfil one's responsibility and to satisfy one's conscience. But the day I showed myself *afraid* of doing so, I should do nothing but make mistakes.' (to his mother, Sept. 3, 1829. *Mémoires*, I, p. 231) And so, in order not to do anything stupid and like the small boy passing the cemetery at night, Metternich whistles and whistles. Firmness, boldness, impartiality, composure, infallibility —he is the more anxious to attribute these qualities to himself because subconsciously he is painfully aware of a deficiency in them.

In support of this interpretation we might point to many passages in his correspondence indicating the very opposite of confidence and vanity. He often confesses himself to be incapable of seeing his way clearly, to be 'lost in the fog' or 'in a maze'.

He is perfectly aware of his limitations:

> I have the feeling of being in the middle of a web I am spinning (after the fashion of my friends the spiders whom I like because I have so often admired them) . . . A web of this kind is a pleasure

to behold. Delicately woven, it can stand up to slight pressure but not to a gust of wind. (July 23, 1821. *Mémoires*, III, p. 473)

Discouragement and listlessness frequently break through:

The rôle of Cassandra is a sad one to play and good advice benefits only those who can take advantage of it, or, in other words, those who do not need telling how to conduct affairs of state. (to Esterhazy, June 16, 1829)

My life has coincided with an abominable time. I came into the world too soon or too late. At the present time I do not feel I can accomplish anything. Earlier, I would have shared in the rejoicing of the time; later, I could have helped in the work of reconstruction. Today I spend my time shoring up crumbling edifices. I should have been born in 1900 with the twentieth century before me. (Oct. 6, 1822. *Mémoires*, III, p. 369)

Some of the evidence shows Metternich as less composed, less resolute than he cared to show himself. When he learned of the revolution of July 1830, in Paris, he collapsed at his desk. His doctor was called at once and found him with his head in his hands groaning: 'My whole life's work is destroyed.' (in Bibl, p. 207) We owe to Louis Veuillot the following picture drawn by the princess Metternich. One evening, at a time when the Sonderbund war in Switzerland was going badly, the old Chancellor was taking the air with her in his garden. He said with a sigh: 'I would like to die and be spared the misfortunes which are bound to follow. My rôle is finished, and so is the rôle of all human wisdom. The reign of violence has begun and the world is lost because right, no longer supported by strength, will become merely an object of derision.' 'He wept', said the princess, 'without attempting to conceal his tears; never before has he given way so much to his own misfortunes. He was not weeping at the defeat of his own wisdom but because justice had been overcome.' (L. Veuillot, *Oeuvres complètes*, XXXIV: *Mélanges*, p. 359) Could it be that the imposing 'rock of good order' was, after all, only a stage rockery made of papier mâché?

3. Style

A technical analysis of Metternich's style has never been attempted. Would there be any interest in it? Would our knowledge of the man be increased by an interpretation of some of his mannerisms as a writer? For example, when he wishes to signify by a number the idea of several or many, why does he always use the figure twenty, and never thirty-six, a hundred, or a thousand? Whatever the answer may be, in dealing with a man a great part of whose life was spent blackening paper, some general thoughts on his style will not be out of place. He himself has told us how he worked:

> I generally write in two hours what it takes my copyists five hours to prepare. The result is that both my handwriting and my style show signs of the haste imposed on me by necessity. Nine times out of ten I am quite ashamed of myself when I go over what I have written. (*Mémoires*, III, p. 455)

> It often happens that as I write I leave out a verb or a noun. It is a very bad habit. I employ in my study someone whose special duty it is to make good these deficiencies. As he has been engaged on this work for ten years he knows my thoughts. However, sometimes he fails to guess them and then he refers to me. (*Mémoires*, III, p. 381)

As to style, he explained his ideals to Varnhagen von Ense:

> Above all I seek clarity of expression, the precise and appropriate thought presented calmly and dispassionately. Any exaggeration is harmful: that is why I shun and detest superlatives. Every superlative is a mistake, it distorts the sentence. I also banish from my style the use of florid expressions. Clarity is the only eloquence permissible in politics. It is true that in certain instances this clarity finds better expression in an image and that is why I make frequent use of them. When, on reading through what I have written, I come across an obscure passage I follow the advice of an old hand, Baron Thugut. I do not

attempt to replace it by a happier turn of phrase, I simply cut out anything that is not absolutely essential to the line of thought, and more often than not what remains exactly expresses what I am trying to say. (quoted by Grunwald, p. 178)

'If only he did it more often!' The sigh escapes from anyone who has been obliged to plough through the endless corre-spondence and memoranda stored away by 'the God Terminus of the chancelleries', as Albert Sorel calls him. Folder after folder, through thousands of dossiers there flows with the relentlessness of a natural phenomenon the grey, unchanging flood of this handwriting. Uncontrollable prolixity. On December 2, 1840, for example, Metternich wrote to King Leopold of Belgium what he chose to call a 'concise reply': fourteen large pages!

He was not the last person to realize the soporific effect of his prose:

Do you know what lies ahead for us? Endless discussions, the devil's own chicanery, interminable tedium. But leave it to me; there will be two of us taking part [Capo d'Istria and himself] and knowing how to bore myself, I am just as capable of killing an adversary by the sheer weight of boredom. (to Zichy, May 21, 1822)

Anyone who has glanced through the volumes of documents published by the Chancellor's son will know that Metternich makes use of two distinct styles: one for diplomatic documents, correct but frequently diffuse and loaded with stereotyped formulae: the other for private correspondence, often lively and stimulating, recalling that art of conversation which he practised so skilfully, being a true product of the eighteenth century.

To give an example of the first:

I should consider myself failing in the duty which my conscience dictates to me if I did not expressly establish the principle that support today for what is called the Greek cause, inasmuch as it rests on the uncertain foundation chosen for it by the malcon-tents, would be the signal for trouble which it would be im-possible to stop, and also that the triumph of this cause which has its origin in rebellion would turn into positive defeat for those principles which the Powers have hitherto been successful in defending with such great constancy and with such glorious success . . . etc.

Pages and pages of prose like this! Enough, indeed to destroy a man with boredom. The fact is that many of these productions come from the pens of colleagues who had more or less assimilated their master's style.

Happily there are to be found here and there diamonds with a cutting edge to rouse the attention.

Talking in 1828 of British policy in the Greek affair:

> England, in the final analysis, only bestirs herself to avoid having to take any action. She only contemplates going forward in order to go back. (to Apponyi, May 9, 1828)

Commenting on the famous 'balcony scene' between Louis-Philippe and La Fayette, on July 31, 1830:

> A kiss is little enough to ask for the destruction of a republic. But do you think it is possible to bestow such power on all kisses in future? (to Général Belliard. *Mémoires*, IV, p. 23)

His inspiration is never better employed than when it is in the service of scorn or irony. Thus, in 1840, in connection with the nationalist reaction in Germany to the warlike policy of Thiers:

> M. Thiers likes to be compared to Napoleon. As far as Germany is concerned the resemblance is perfect and the palm is even awarded to M. Thiers. He needed only a short time to bring that country to the point which it had taken years of oppression under the Emperor to reach. (to Apponyi, Nov. 8, 1840)

Finally, speaking of a political lawyer, whose name incidentally is not given, Metternich says to Veuillot:

> I have seen him. He seems to me to be a little heap of dung. You might say he was born of dung as Venus was born of sea-spray. (L. Veuillot, *Oeuvres complètes*, XXXIV, p. 346)

Metternich, as we have seen, makes free use of imagery and metaphor. The effect is sometimes bewildering:

> In the middle of this labyrinth, we shall remain shut up in our-selves. On several occasions we have not hesitated to stand out like a rock beset by a stormy sea: we have acquired the habit of withstanding the waves and we have seen them spend them-selves against us without any bad effect on our essence. We are now going through that experience again. To pursue the com-parison, I will admit to you, *Monsieur le comte*, that I do not fear the waves, and that, speaking for myself, I should be invulnerable to all attack if I could feel sure that the whole of Europe were not undermined by hidden fires, for nothing can resist the effects of the earthquake. An excess of evil may lead to good, and per-haps the political storm which is rumbling at this moment will have the effect of consuming harmful matter. (to Zichy, May 19, 1827)

A labyrinth, a rock, waves, a mine, an earthquake, a storm, a fire—all in ten lines! M. Prudhomme could have taken lessons at Vienna.

Frequently, however the image is an ingenious one:

> If it is possible for conquering armies to burn behind them those boats by which they effected a crossing, it is by no means the same with politicians. They cannot burn the words they have uttered. They can obliterate them by action, but then they remain a prey to the inevitable difficulty of finding themselves in contradiction with themselves. (to Apponyi, Mar. 6, 1840)

> France . . . knows now how to manage a revolution. Her educa-tion is complete. She is like a working-class coquette at a students' ball, she knows their ways better than a woman who is attending one for the first time. (to L. Veuillot, Jan. 1850. *Oeuvres complètes*, XXXIV, p. 357)

> The moral position of the Cabinet in London in the eastern affair seems to me to resemble that of a man who starts up from his sleep at the sound of a tumult, and who at the moment of waking feels obliged to enter into a discussion the salient features of which escape him. (to Lebzeltern, Mar. 14, 1826)

This last feature of Metternich's style introduces us to a little-known aspect of his talent: humour. A sense of humour that is sometimes a trifle heavy, *nimis germanicum*, but undeniable.

Three examples will suffice but many more could be found. (see, for example, *Mémoires*, III, pp. 199–200, 349, 373; IV, p. 290; VI, pp. 70, 207, etc.):

> There are a crowd of Englishmen staying here . . . I hear them twenty times expressing *prodigious* astonishment at finding that I am not a man of 70. Among them is an elderly lady covered with wrinkles and flowers who wishes to assure me that I must be my father for, she said, 'I remember having read your name in the gazettes more than twenty years ago.' I assured her that I was born a Minister. (to the comtesse de Lieven, Mar. 20, 1819, p. 255)

> As I was passing through the capital of Upper Styria (Judenburg) I received there a deputation of magistrates. Every magistrate in the world is always complaining. The burgomaster of Judenburg having apparently nothing else to complain of accused the mice of ruining his fields. 'Have the mice been causing damage for long?'—'Great Heavens,' said the burgomaster, 'ever since the French!'—'What do you mean, ever since the French? Did they have mice with them?'—'No, not exactly, but they pitched camp outside the town; the wretched fellows ate nothing but bread and dropped it all over the fields. All the mice in Styria have since moved in.'

> I believe that the scourge of mice has never, since the world began, been explained in this way. There must have been, at the time of the Pharaohs, a French camp in Egypt . . . (to the comtesse de Lieven, Feb. 10, 1819, pp. 238–9)

> There arrived last night a courier from Petersburg bringing at the same time dispatches for Gol[ovkine—Russian ambassador in Vienna]. This morning he came to communicate them to me. He is a great bore, this Gol of yours. Merciful heaven, what sentences he uses!

> After giving me a one-hour peroration designed to show to what extent his confidence in me was unlimited, he assured me 'that he did not think he could furnish me with more convincing proof of

the strength of this feeling than by reading me a dispatch of the first importance, of an importance all the greater because it bore the stamp of the age, an age that bore the stamp of great events, an age that was governed by vast conceptions of human genius and which was at the mercy of shifting minds, minds of different quality, minds at the mercy of changes, and changes governed by the spirit of the age, of men, and of parties; that, finally, in order to entrust to me his thoughts, his whole thoughts and nothing but his thoughts he believed it to be his duty to attempt to characterize the age by a concrete and apt definition. Consequently, he thought he was saying well when he said that the present was a philosophical and philanthropic era, but that in that philanthropic and philosophical era, the present moment, that very moment as ever was, was *climacteric*.'

'I understand you wonderfully well, *Monsieur le comte*!'

'I dared to flatter myself that you would! I appreciate the force of your judgment, the wisdom of your principles, the uprightness of your intentions, the honourableness of your thoughts, the uniformity of your views which result in uniformity of action, in uniformity of fact, in wisdom in your measures, in indivisibility of actions, yes, *indivisibility*—I like the word because it forms the basis of the thinking of the Emperor, my August Master! Now, let us to business!'

Life, my friend, is too short for such harangues! . . . Two or three times in the course of the 24 hours after a climacteric conversation with Gol, I have the feeling that I am verbose, confused, and not a little inflated. The mind can become swollen like a limb and needs time to rid itself of a poison. (to the comtesse de Lieven, Mar. 2, 1819, p. 228)

We must agree that it would be difficult to find a more lively satire of the chancellery style which Metternich, more than any other person, helped to popularize.

CHAPTER TWO

The Principles

1. States and Governments

'I AM a kind of titular professor of fundamental truths,' Metternich wrote in the evening of his life. (to Hübner, Jan. 26, 1850. Quoted by Breycha-Vauthier in the *Revue Générale Belge*, 1857) Yet how wrong it would be to expect to find easily in that mass of writing the elements of a complete system of political philosophy! We know that H. von Srbik was not dismayed by the task, and that he thought he had discovered 'one of the most extensive and coherent plans ever conceived by a statesman'.

It has been more usual to question the soundness of this admiration, and bearing in mind that the system devised by Metternich coincided perfectly with the political interests of Austria at the time, to conclude that all this theoretical verbiage was just a smoke-screen covering a policy that was realistic and in a subtle way opportunist. Good sport has also been made out of the contradictions in his utterances; not all of them, incidentally, if they are replaced in the context in which they were spoken are as irreconcilable as they appear at first sight to be. In this connection the French ambassador Sainte-Aulaire makes some shrewd observations which a fairly long acquaintance with Metternich enables us to endorse whole-heartedly:

> Whether from flexibility of mind or from a calculated desire to conceal his real thoughts, it often happened that without shifting his ground he would speak much good and much ill of the same person, would approve and condemn the same course of events.

These contradictions . . . might on some occasions not even de-
tract from his sincerity. Completely detached from passion and
prejudice throughout his long career as a Minister, he has
acquired vast learning. He knows the strength and weaknesses of
his contemporaries; he has studied world affairs from every angle,
and when he appears to be contradicting himself it is often simply
that he is turning over in his mind the various considerations
which influenced his judgment one way or the other before he
had reached a decision. (*Souvemirs*, p. 149)

Again we fall back for support on his own repeated assertion
that there was no such thing as the *Metternich System*. It must,
however, be clearly understood what this word *system* stood for
in his mind, namely an ideological construction having no
foundation in reality:

Supporters of this imaginary development no doubt thought
that they had invented something magnificent in giving the
name of the *Metternich System* to those *laws* which alone form
the basis of all progress from bad to good and from good to
better. It is in the nature of political systems to be easily brushed
aside by other systems; with things it is different. If I had stood
for a system, it would have disappeared with me from our
Empire and from Germany. Such has not, it seems to me, been
the case. (*Mémoires*, VIII, p. 298)

There is no point in spending much time on what is, after all,
only a difference of words. Does anyone really imagine that a
statesman of his calibre would be lacking in a master plan?
Metternich will not have it that he created any *system*, but he
admits—and misses no opportunity to glory in it—that he is
solidly anchored to *principles*:

We are not living in a century of prescience . . . and in any age
similar to this the only effective guide for men working for the
good of a cause lies in the daily application of principles and rules
which are the fruit of human experience in every age. (to
Vincent, Sept. 2, 1825)

And what does a principle mean to Metternich?

For any proposition to be called a principle, it is absolutely essential that it should be capable of application equally and without distinction to every aspect of a problem, because truth, the source and foundation of any principle worthy of the name, can in any circumstance only remain the same. (to Neumann, April 9, 1833)

The usefulness of principles thus understood is developed in a rather surprising allegory:

In the passes of the High Alps, the track leading to the top is marked for the traveller by guide-posts placed at intervals. These posts are stakes twenty feet high sticking out of the snow. The snow may block the way, in which case the traveller must stop, and if he keeps his eye on the guide-post it will prevent his falling down a precipice . . . Principles operate in the sphere of morality in the same way as these guide-posts. They are not the destination but they mark the way to it. (to Sir Travers Twiss, Jan. 25, 1849)

The value and strength of those principles derive from the fact that they are only the reflection of things themselves, the expression of those immutable laws by which these things are governed:

It has certainly never been questioned that society and the advance of society are subject to fundamental laws just as definitely as physical forces are subject to other laws differing in many respects from those that function in society and the sphere of morality but less in conflict with them than is generally supposed. (to Lebzeltern, Dec. 15, 1819)

Let us try, then, to disentangle and set in order these principles so dear to Metternich. The task is made easier by our professor's tiresome habit of labouring his point, so that there is little danger of failing to grasp a single one of his pet theories even for those who cannot flatter themselves with having read everything that flowed from his pen. Success is not achieved, however, without a laborious process of refinement: it is necessary to get rid of all verbiage, of anything practical or to do with methods, of anything that is only put forward to meet the needs of a particular case, and anything which clearly presents a contradiction. What remains after this sifting is neither substantial nor exceptional, and one is often tempted to find an intellectual kinship between Metternich and the great La Palice.

Associations, property, landed aristocracy, city guilds, these are the social foundations of the State:

> Associations and, it follows, the instinct of association are one of the essential conditions of humanity. This instinct forms the basis of society and of the life of States at every stage of their development. What, indeed, are States but associations of people created with a view to seeking by the action of their united strength the attainment of a common goal? (Opinion expressed in the State Conference of 1845. *Mémoires*, VII, p. 140)

A country which by legislation crushes the ownership of property inevitably destroys itself as a social entity:

> They manage better in England. There the State is stable because the family endures. The family endures because property is not carved up. (to L. Veuillot, *Oeuvres complètes*, XXXIV, p. 341)

> France, consisting today of exclusively democratic elements, is incapable of producing an aristocracy: any effort by her government towards that end would be useless, and the only end towards which, in my opinion, it might strive with a better chance of success, would be to re-create the *guilds*, which are the foundations of aristocracy. (to Apponyi, Jan. 3, 1838)

The meaning of the last sentence would remain something of an enigma if light were not shed by another text devoted to the rôle of the *bourgeoisie* in towns. 'They are', says Metternich, 'one of the manifestations of this spirit of association; a spirit which, by the way, leads to egotism and tends to create States within the State, so that it needs careful watching.' (*Mémoires*, VII, p. 97)

A contradiction? No. Metternich considers that in a society

which has already become democratic a middle-class corporate system in towns can, in the absence of an aristocracy and for the time being, re-establish a kind of hierarchy, a buffer class between those in power and the masses:

> When this intermediary is suppressed and supreme power is exercised directly over what we call the people, that makes a terrible tête-à-tête and one abounding in cruel surprises. (to L. Veuillot. *Oeuvres complètes*, XXXIV, p. 340)

As to nationalities, Metternich does not admit that they can form the basis of a State. The idea that community of language and of race could create a community of interests strong enough to give rise to a State appears alien to his outlook. Discussing the position of the Greeks in 1829:

> What do we mean by the *Greeks*? Do we mean a people, a country, or a religion? If either of the first two, where are the dynastic and geographical boundaries? If the third, then upwards of fifty million men are Greeks: the Austrian Empire alone embraces five million of them . . . the Emperor, our August Master, will never consent that the Greeks, his subjects, should consider themselves at the same time to be citizens of the new Greece. In this respect he can only follow the rules of public justice which prevent him from considering his Milanese and Venetian subjects as members of an Italian body politic, or his Galician subjects as belonging to a kingdom of Poland. Long experience has taught us to realize that in racial denominations there may lie elements of trouble between empires and bones of contention between people and governments. And what a powerful and ever hostile weapon such denominations become in the hands of those who overthrow, or seek to overthrow, the existing order! (to Esterhazy, Sept. 21, 1829)

The existence and stability of States is based first and foremost on moral factors: popular consent, the idea that power comes from above, and especially religion:

> In every case the idea and existence of majorities provides the

essential condition of internal repose and of sufficient armed strength to protect them from without as well as from within. In both pure and mixed monarchies it is in the obedience of the majority that the assurance of public security lies. (*Mémoires*, VII, p. 54)

Every society is based on religion. The biggest revolution the human race has experienced was the introduction of Christianity which forms the basis of civilized society. (to Sir Travers Twiss, Dec. 7, 1848)

Christian teaching recognizes no right that does not carry a corresponding duty; for this reason it offers equal guarantees to him who commands and to those who obey. It offers a guarantee to the first in the duty of obedience that is imposed on his subordinates, and to the second in the obligation required of him who commands not to abuse his power. The carrying out of both these duties remains subordinate to responsibility to God. Does not this single maxim cover the whole foundation of social order, which is itself the only possible basis of true liberty? (*Mémoires*, VIII, p. 589)

The Catholic Church does not claim a particular form of government by its side for the maintenance of social order . . . That is a matter of indifference to it provided always that one truth be recognized and upheld . . . namely that every authority receives its power from above, that this authority derives neither from the will of an individual nor from that of a crowd, and that consequently it represents only a superior will. On this foundation rests the power of all secular authority. (*Mémoires*, VIII, p. 569)

As to the human origin of the right to govern, there is no need to look beyond a fact consecrated by time:

I have struck out from my customary diplomatic vocabulary the use of the words *legitimacy* and *divine right* . . . The words *legitimate* and *legitimacy* express an idea which is in my opinion more easily grasped by minds unaccustomed to serious discussion if it is represented by the word *right*. *Legitimacy* as a noun is used to qualify the right of succession to the throne; the same word, used as an adjective, can be applied to anything. One is the legitimate owner of a house or whatever it may be, and in the same way it expresses the idea of legal right. As for *divine right*, in a practical sense it expresses no more than a precise idea . . . the expression is used in the titles of sovereigns and yet it is not restricted to this use. The prince (*by the grace of God*) cannot object to the reply that might be given by the humblest of his subjects to an inquiry into the state of his health: 'By the grace of God, I am well.' Napoleon called himself 'by the grace of God and by the constitution of the Empire, Emperor, etc.': and there is no doubt that, had God not ordained it, he would never have been Emperor, any more than a son, naturally destined to succeed his father, whether to the throne or to his private fortune, would not be born if God did not will it. According to the logic of my thinking, I would recognize the right of any national entity or republican group to call itself a republic or sovereign people *by the grace of God*. Now words which have a general use never have a special one . . . The idea and the word right fulfils its duty much better in this respect than do those of *legitimacy* and *divine right*.

. . . The Bourbons based their right to the throne of France on historical grounds and were entitled to do so. The house of Orléans wishes no doubt to do the same. The difference between these rights comes from the difference between their points of origin and from the passage of time; one is lost in the mists of antiquity, the other is new. History teaches us that the old must give way to the new. We have evidence of it every day and it is equally certain that in discussions between rights and reality, reality triumphs over rights just so long as the latter is not supported by the power necessary to make certain of victory. As a general rule old rights carry greater weight than new ones; but when they lack force, they have less youthful vigour than new laws. . . .

In the field of controversy all rights and facts are unassailable, but it is not on this level that foreign affairs are conducted; manifestos, yes, but not battles, and everything on the political level is settled in the final analysis by battles . . . Let the King of the French look at things on this entirely practical level and he will find that in the expression 'historic right' there exists between him and the elder branch of the family only the difference that exists between the present and the past, between a beginning and an end. As a general rule the passage of time strengthens but in the end it also destroys. The whole secret is to survive and he who achieves it takes his place in history. To survive and to endure mean one and the same thing to a king . . . that is what king Louis-Philippe is doing, and if he and his successors can continue on these lines they will create for themselves quite naturally an historic right, of which the year 1830 will mark the beginning . . . (to Apponyi, Jan. 22, 1837)

The form the powers will take depends on natural factors:

Man's nature is unchanging. The primary needs of society are and must remain the same and the apparent differences could be explained by the diversity of influences exerted over different races by such natural factors as variations of climate, barrenness or richness of soil, insular or continental positions, and so on. These local variations may produce effects that extend far beyond what is required by purely physical conditions. They give rise to needs on a higher plane. They end by determining the law and by having an undoubted influence on religion. (to the Emperor Alexander, 1820. *Mémoires*, III, p. 428)

Here is an example:

Divide France into two regions according to climate and you will observe that the inhabitants of the south are as strong in their support of royalty as the northerners are feeble. Farther south again you will find a greater tendency still towards absolute government. Conscience tells men whether they are capable of governing themselves or whether they still need to be protected from themselves. (to Bombelles, Mar. 25, 1827)

Whatever the origin and nature of institutions they are incapable of standing still. They pass inevitably through a cycle. Emerging from obscurity they pass through a stage of development to perfection before declining into decadence. Conforming to the nature of man they live, like him, through infancy, adolescence, an age of strength and reason, and an age of frailty. (to the Emperor Alexander, 1820. *Mémoires*, III, p. 428)

Society does not progress in a straight line. It moves in a circle, and when we think its destination might have been reached it turns out to be the starting-point. (*Mémoires*, VIII, p. 171)

Where do monarchies and democracies stand in this cycle? Here we come to one of the most flagrant and inexplicable contradictions in the whole of Metternich's thinking. He writes to Lebzeltern on August 15, 1825:

The New World is emerging from the torpor which, for States and individuals alike, is one of the attributes of early life. The newborn society gives it the constitution of a republic, and in doing so follows the course of nature. Those republics, when they reach the age of manhood, will turn themselves into monarchies.

Yet ten years later he will be telling George Ticknor:

I have always been of de Tocqueville's opinion that democracy, far from being the oldest and simplest form of government, as is often maintained, is the last of all to have been invented and the most complicated. (*Life, Letters and Journal of George Ticknor*, II, p. 14)

Wherever the truth may lie, democracy is not, as we have had reason to suspect, Metternich's favourite regime. He frankly admits as much to Ticknor, a professor and man of letters from New England:

It is true that I do not like democracies. Democracy is in every case a principle of dissolution, of decomposition. It tends to separate men, it loosens society. I am opposed to this because I am by nature and by habit constructive. That is why monarchy is the only government that suits my way of thinking . . . Monarchy alone tends to bring men together, to unite them in compact, efficient masses, and to make them capable by their combined efforts of the highest degree of culture and civilization.

'But,' Ticknor objected, 'is not the democratic regime the one most favourable to the development of the individual?'

I admit [replied Metternich] that your country would never have made so much progress so quickly under any other system . . . for democracy, by separating men, creates every kind of rivalry and drives them forward very rapidly by means of the competition that it unlooses among them. Take a thousand people in America and a thousand in France or in this old Austria of ours, and you will find a more marked individuality among the Americans than among the French or Austrians. They will also be more curious, more distinctive, more interesting, perhaps even more effective, *as individuals*, but they will not be such an effective mass, they will not be able to make so much permanent progress. Besides, democracy is a truth in America; in Europe it is a falsehood . . . (ibid., pp. 13–14)

Kind words to an American visitor? The truth is that Metternich utterly rejects the ideological assumptions of democracy:

Two words suffice to create evil; two words which because they are devoid of any practical meaning delight the visionaries. The words are *liberty* and *equality*. The word liberty conjures up nothing in the mind; it indicates something excellent if it is in the right place, something detestable if it is in the wrong. Liberty of what? Liberty to do good (but the whole world enjoys that faculty) or to do evil? The word *liberty* is like the word *religion*. To what religion do we refer?

It is much the same with *equality*. The word can be taken to mean equality before the law or social equality. The first is perfect . . . the second is folly, a pretence devoid of practical meaning . . . Never will I be persuaded that there is equality between a fool and an intellectual, between a pauper and a rich man, or between a hunchback and a man of noble and pleasing physique. Equal before God and the law, but not from the point of view of their *social* existence. (to Sainte-Aulaire, Sept. 15, 1840. *Mémoires*, VI, p. 443)

The word *liberty* does not convey to me the idea of a point of departure, but of an actual destination. The word *order* indicates the point of departure. It is only on the idea of *order* that the idea of liberty can repose, for without the foundation of order the pursuit of liberty is no more than the attempt of a particular party to attain its end. Applied to real life this aspiration will inevitably find expression in tyranny. At all times and in all places I have been a methodical man, and I have always aimed at the establishment of genuine liberty and not of a spurious liberty. For me, tyranny, of whatever kind, has always been synonymous with sheer madness. As a means to an end it strikes me as being the most absurd that circumstances ever put into the hands of those who exercise power. (*Testament politique*, *Mémoires*, VII, p. 640)

The sovereignty of the people can only be a fictitious idea because, since the meaning of sovereignty is unquestionably that of supreme power, and since that power is incapable of being exercised by the people, it must be delegated by them to an authority *other than the sovereign*. What is there left for the sovereign except a name, whereas *the thing* passes into other hands! Pure invention! (to Sir Travers Twiss, Aug. 11, 1849)

In speaking of monarchy two expressions must be set aside as fallacious; absolute monarchy and constitutional monarchy:

The word *absolutism*, when applied to the government of a State, is a modern invention based on a derogatory and slanderous interpretation of monarchical government. The word itself is unintelligible, for the most strongly established monarchy is by no means absolute in the sense which the revolutionaries would like to ascribe to it. The throne, and the same is true of all forms of power, rests on foundations; and so the ideas of foundations and limits are inseparable from their nature. (to Apponyi, Dec. 31, 1843)

It is no less wrong to speak of constitutional monarchy 'because all forms of government rest on foundations which are equivalent to a constitution'. (to Apponyi, Apr. 19, 1844) An example: the Austrian Empire all parts of which are governed by traditional constitutions which the sovereign religiously respects.

It is not even within the monarch's power to provide a constitution:

Nothing that is part of the forces *of nature*, whether in the moral or material sphere, lends itself to *human regulations*. What would one think of a charter in which were drawn up, side by side with the rights of man, the laws of gravity, and of centripetal and centrifugal force, even if it were only in the form of a declaration giving them recognition? Between the decree of the Convention (recognition of the Supreme Being by the French nation) and those other high-sounding words like the Declaration of the Rights of Man, responsibility and irresponsibility, one is left with all too big a choice. If there is no God, nothing will be gained by declaring that one exists. If one exists, his existence does not depend on such declarations.

The mistake of thinking that certain objects can give substance to provisions of the law leads to the contraction, if not to the complete destruction, of the subject of this experiment. (*Mémoires*, VIII, p. 577)

A legislator can do no more than establish:

. . . an order of things which might give rise to a constitution thanks to the influence of time which creates and destroys, which uncovers truths and redresses errors; thanks also to the fixing of certain points of origin and to the underlining of those principles which must form the basis of a structure in which time is the sole factor.

The defining of these points of origin is equivalent to *charters*, not to *constitutions*. A charter that is based on logic and is in harmony with material conditions and with the factors that govern the existence of the State can, in the course of time, be transformed into a constitution. In the first phase of its existence it can only be a *programme* and not a finished piece of work. Now charters have this in common with all programmes, the more carefully thought out and detailed they are, the greater the number of difficulties that will be encountered by those who are called on to put them into effect. (*Mémoires*, VIII, pp. 543–4)

If, then, the expression constitutional monarchy, as opposed to pure monarchy, is not to be used, what term is to be given to those monarchical regimes in which power is shared? It is the representative system, a false and feeble system:

It is suited to the existence neither of a monarchy nor of a republic. It binds the hands of those in power without untying those of the people. It lacks proper balance because force belongs to the third authority in the social hierarchy, namely the *bourgeoisie*, and the first power in the State is driven to exert its influence by ingenuity and subterfuge. (to Apponyi, Mar. 20, 1839)

This regime is founded on the philosophical Utopia of the balance of powers, a device made popular by Montesquieu:

The division of power proclaimed as a supreme rule and as the initial or sole guarantee of a *State's* well-being is no more than a principle of disorder and ruin. There is an infinite variety of forms of government, but whether power be exercised by one or several, it becomes nothing more than anarchy in disguise the moment it ceases to be based in the final analysis on a strongly established principle of unity ... The doctrine of counter-balance, as it is understood by the publicist of M. de Pradt's school, destroys what it claims to build up, for anarchy is, above all, despotism. (Reflections on an article by de Pradt, Sept. 3, 1829, in *Frankreich, Weisungen*, 1829)

The so-called English constitution is chimerical:

Montesquieu had seen in England a balance of powers where in fact there was only an aristocracy which, in order to establish its power beside that of the throne, rigged itself out in cheap finery. This finery, beneath which aristocracy concealed its breastplate in 1688, has been taken over by modern liberalism. (to Apponyi, Feb. 15, 1839)

The British system of the division of powers between king and Parliament cannot be exported to the Continent, if only because of the need of the Continental Powers to maintain large armies. Thanks to her insular position, England does not need for her defence a military force that might endanger the independence of Parliament:

Let us imagine a King of the French, more sovereign in fact than in law, personally victorious and consequently the first man in the land, how would he deal with the opposition of the demagogues? (to Stadion, June 23, 1808. *Mémoires*, II, p. 187)

Among the evils that follow in the wake of the representative system, not the least deadly in Metternich's eyes is that of the freedom of the Press. Not that he underestimates the power of public opinion; far from it:

> Public opinion is the most powerful of mediums. Like religion, it penetrates into the darkest corners and wherever administrative measures lose their influence. It is as dangerous to be contemptuous of public opinion as it is to be contemptuous of moral principles. The latter may be able to rise again in the very place where it was intended that they should be suppressed, but with public opinion it is different. That needs special attention, tireless study and patience. (to Stadion, June 23, 1808. *Mémoires*, II, p. 187)

The more convinced he is of the power of opinion the more sorry he is that it is capable of being corrupted by an uncontrolled Press:

> Buonaparte, who was certainly not lacking in ability, told me on more than one occasion 'You see that I am strong. Well, I would not undertake to govern France for three weeks if the Press were free. . . .' What is called the freedom of the Press is meaningless, a phantasmagoria, something that cannot be established. Seductive like all heresies, it could never be satisfied with general guarantees. It desires some all to itself and it forgets that by this fact it proves how much it is in opposition to the essence of all social order. (to Apponyi, July 2, 1827)

> The most intolerable despotism is that exercised by men who never emerge from behind the scenes, who commit to combat nothing more than their pens, and whose pretensions exceed those, quite differently founded, of men who shoulder the responsibility for the present and the future. (to Apponyi, Jan. 2, 1836)

And how pretentious journalists can be!

> Worshippers of the Press do it the honour of calling it the *echo of public opinion*, and yet every article is merely the expression of its author's particular thoughts. Here (in Vienna) we see every day

a palpable anomaly. Will there ever, anywhere, be a government publication, even that of a republican government, honoured by being described as an expression of public opinion? Assuredly not. Yet there is no journalist so obscure that he does not claim for his products the honour of representing everybody's opinion. What a confusion of ideas there is here! (*Mémoires*, VIII, p. 606)

What can be done about this scourge?

I am constantly being shown that it is only possible to exert a salutary influence over the Press in preventive ways ... Repression in those matters which are stirred up by the Press will always be ineffective because it cannot touch the offence contained in what has been written. It would be like destroying the pen which was believed to have been used in the execution of some foul deed. (to Hügel, Oct. 4, 1837)

In a word, only censorship is effective, for anything else designed to produce the effect of repression would be even more contrary to the free expression of opinion. (to Apponyi, Aug. 14, 1835)

The 'anti-social' institution of the jury is lumped together with the freedom of the Press:

The institution of the jury belongs . . . to ancient Germanic times, to the days which preceded the advent of the first traces of a more advanced civilization. It was this civilization which, as it progressed, replaced the jury in those countries where it existed by regular tribunals, just as in modern times the disciplined unit has replaced the levies that used to be raised and disbanded according to requirements. England . . . which is of all European countries the one whose criminal law still bears the deepest imprint of the barbarian age, has also preserved the jury . . . That France should have made use of this institution is no doubt one of the most regrettable decisions she could have made . . . But it is the same with the jury as it is with the freedom of the Press: those countries which have the misfortune to possess them do not stand much chance of getting rid of them ... (to Apponyi, Feb. 8, 1837)

'To govern is to keep on one's feet and to go forward' (*Mémoires*, VIII, p. 581), Metternich once wrote, but in practice this art requires a judicious separation of functions and responsibilities:

> In every age and in any condition of society what is needed is *one man* with a grasp of affairs who must at the same time watch over and direct the handling of them. The most natural person to perform such a function must be, in a monarchy the king, in a republic the president. *Ministerialism* is a disease of the age, a stupidity which will crumble as foolishness always does. (to Apponyi, June 14, 1839)

> . . . *To reign* and *to govern*, two conditions inseparable from power which no one would wish to try to separate unless it were by a feeble play on words; he governs who reigns. On the other hand we are the first to recognize that it does not help, and can be dangerous, to entangle the dividing lines between government and administration. But to say that the *king must reign and not govern* is absurd; whereas to recommend sovereigns to govern without getting lost in administrative detail is to offer them good advice. (to Apponyi, Apr. 10, 1835)

The monarch must, therefore, divide the functions of state between his Ministers:

> As far as the personal responsibility of individuals is concerned I have a conviction which amounts in my opinion to a religion. It is based on the truth that however honest and capable men may be deemed to be, they should only assume personal control over certain parts of the whole functioning of the State. This condition is essential if the smooth conduct of affairs is to be ensured. (*Mémoires*, VI, p. 218)

The co-ordination of the different aspects of government is carried out in councils where discussion takes place:

> In my opinion the most intelligent formula to use in passing large-scale measures of government has always been the old French one: *Notre conseil entendu.* (*Mémoires*, VIII, p. 529)

CLEMENS WENCESLAS LOTHAR VON METTERNICH AS A YOUNG MAN

By F. Gérard

PRINCE METTERNICH

Painting by Lawrence

COMTESSE DE LIEVEN

Painting by Lawrence

PRINCE METTERNICH

Daguerrotype by Mylius

JOHANNISBERG, NEAR MAINZ

KÖNIGSWART

PLASS

STATE CHANCELLERY, BALLHAUSPLATZ, VIENNA

EMPEROR FRANCIS II

Painting by Lawrence

FRIEDRICH VON GENTZ

Painting by Lawrence

LORD CASTLEREAGH

Painting by Lawrence

GEORGE CANNING

Painting by Lawrence (detail)

THE DUKE OF WELLINGTON

Painting by d'Orsay

(Reproduced by gracious permission of Her Majesty The Queen)

CZAR ALEXANDER I

Painting by Lawrence

COUNT CAPO D'ISTRIA

Painting by Lawrence

DUC DE RICHELIEU

Painting by Lawrence

COMTE DE VILLÈLE

Since government is the same thing as co-ordination, it is necessary to establish harmony between the different powers and this is only possible by *discussion*. It is natural that there should be fear of discussion among those who, through ignorance of the truth or because they allow themselves to be swayed by their petty feelings and narrow outlook, can envisage only one thing. But in this they are quite simply deceiving themselves. (*Mémoires*, VI, p. 221)

Two hidden reefs must be avoided in the sphere of administration: excessive centralization and bureaucracy:

Bureaucracy does not move; it is by nature static. The lower strata of bureaucracy instead of carrying the upper, lean on them for support. Administration takes the place of government which disappears under a crushing load of detail. But what happens to the stratum that should be the administrative one? It undertakes the government of the State which is beyond its scope, and once that point has been reached it will in time confine its action to seeking orders from its superiors. This rising cascade of moral and material nonsense ends up by drowning the head of the State in a flood of detail and deprives the State itself of all *action*. (on the subject of Austria, Jan. 8, 1848. *Mémoires*, VII, p. 575)

As for the army, it could not replace the civil power. 'One does not govern with bayonets.' (to Apponyi, Jan. 29, 1848) When revolutionary agitation grows in Lombardy at the beginning of 1848, and certain persons in Vienna pin all their faith in the military authority, Metternich protests:

The cry goes up 'Let them govern militarily!' To govern is to govern; whether those who govern are dressed as soldiers or civilians is of no importance. In making the civil government disappear, the reserve will be put in the vanguard. Then where is a new reserve to be found? . . . Let the civil government have the courage to do its duty, and let it lean for support on armed strength but do not let it hide behind that strength. (*Mémoires*, VII, pp. 588–9)

M.–C

The activities of the government are bound to come up against the intermediary bodies, more or less coherent groups of citizens. Here one encounters again the problem of the associations but seen in a very different light from the time when their rôle in the creation of the State was being considered:

> If one studies the associations which are springing up everywhere like weeds and submits them to a calm, impartial examination, one is easily persuaded that for most of the time their purpose is contrary to the life of the body politic and that they have only the appearance of being useful assemblies. . . . Common prudence suggests the remedy. It lies in upholding and exercising that right of strict tutelage which belongs to authority . . . The supreme authority must have knowledge of the basic idea behind each association, of the ways and means it intends to adopt . . . even before it is set up. Associations should only be allowed to come into existence after they have been authorized by the government. (Opinion expressed at the State Conference, 1845. *Mémoires*, VII, p. 142)

At this point there arises the problem of the relationship between the State and the Churches. Three cases occur to Metternich:

> In the first place is the question of the Protestant creeds, lacking an ecclesiastical hierarchy, and having as their principle of unity adherence to a confession of faith. It is true that freedom of conscience is a personal question but, looked at from outside, the collectivity that results from it and which manifests itself in a cult, comes within the scope of an association and in consequence State control is justified. (to Archduke Lòuis, Aug. 22, 1848. *Mémoires*, VII, p. 139)

Secondly:

The Anglican and Russian Churches have this in common, they are State Churches. In both Empires the sovereign is inseparable from the Church. The two Churches are therefore religious and political institutions at the same time. They have this latter characteristic if only because the temporal and spiritual authorities are united in the supreme head of the State. (to Neumann, Jan 17, 1842)

Finally the Catholic Church:

Is the Church in the State or the State in the Church? Answer: since the Church considers itself to be the universal Church, it cannot be in the State, otherwise it would lose its character of universality. All things considered, neither is the State *qua* the State in the Church. [In 1844 Metternich had declared that 'the State in which this Church is dominant, is in the Church'. *Mémoires*, VII, p. 37.] It is the faithful who are in the Church, for they form an integral part of it.

If the Church is not in the State, that is to say if it is not in subjection to it, and if the State is not in the Church, that is to say in its capacity as a body politic, what common ground is there between the two institutions? Answer: the two powers must seek common ground in the respect of rights that are appropriate to both of them and in the observance of duties that are incumbent upon both of them. . . .

. . . The solution is to understand *the questions of competence* properly and to resolve them correctly. (Notes of May, 1850. *Mémoires*, VIII, pp. 514–15)

How far does the competence of the Church extend and how far that of the State? Undoubtedly within the competence of the Church belong questions of dogma and ecclesiastical discipline without which the idea of the existence of a Church would have no more value than a myth. Within the competence of the State belong secular legislation and the regime that is based upon it. Although in matters of dogma and ecclesiastical discipline the State cannot be granted the right to intervene in the government of the Church, the third sphere, known as *jura circa sacra*, remains the one in which, despite all precautions, controversy can arise between the two powers. (Report to the Emperor, Apr. 6, 1844. *Mémoires*, VII, p. 38)

The many functions of the State seem hardly to have occupied his mind.

Financial questions did not lie, at least in principle, within the province of his Ministry. Yet on several occasions circumstances induced him to get involved in them at close quarters. In 1816, for example, at the time of the big monetary reform undertaken by Stadion, he devoted several hours a day, for months on end, to the study of this matter with Gentz, and, to judge from what his colleague said, he made astonishing progress in it. (Gentz to Nesselrode, Nov. 16, 1816. *Letters and papers of the comte de Nesselrode*, V, p. 261)

He was only interested in the question of customs barriers because of their political repercussions: for example, the creation of the Zollverein. (*Mémoires*, V, pp. 517 et seq.; VI, pp. 561 et seq.)

The problem of the railways led him to define his attitude towards the intervention of the State in economic life:

> I cannot find a better parallel to the problem of the railways than that of an irrigation system in which two things have to be considered, the uses to which it can be put and the danger of its drying up. A railway brings vitality and fertility to the region through which it passes. Those areas that are not covered by it fall into decay. Railways and irrigation are indeed reckoned to be two of the most important forms of capitalist enterprise, and it is a government's duty to regulate and watch over those two aspects of them. There are two ways in which this can be done:

> Either the government itself must be responsible for the enterprises or it must hand responsibility over to share-holding companies. In the first case it must supply its own credit; in the second it must leave them to private credit (in which speculation always plays a big part).

> Generally speaking, I am against enterprises promoted by the State. They are seldom successful and when they are, the cost never fails to be greater than if it had been left to private individuals. In my opinion the State should only concern itself with ventures which might be of use to it for loftier purposes. Otherwise they should be left to private individuals; but I am referring only to those requiring considerable capital, and I would reserve

for a government the right to exercise protection and control.
(to Hummelauer, Aug. 3, 1844. *Mémoires*, II, pp. 554–5)

It is not surprising that Metternich was unaware of the social
responsibilities of the State; it was not the age for that. But it is
strange to find no reflections on the part the government should
play in intellectual and artistic life. He will content himself with
being, in a personal capacity, a patron and an enlightened amateur,
and in his Ministerial capacity, Curator of the Imperial and Royal
Academy of the Plastic Arts of Vienna.

To sum up, the principal, essential rôle of government is in
his opinion to ensure order and repose—'the first requirement of
any human society'. (to Apponyi, May 8, 1835) In other words to
restrain and to fight against revolutionary forces.

2. Revolution and Preservation

'There is only one serious matter in Europe in 1832,' Metternich
writes, 'and that is revolution.' (to Apponyi, May 14, 1832)
Again it is necessary to analyse what he means:

> There are three kinds of revolution. Those that are called palace
> revolutions break out against *persons*. Political revolutions are
> directed against *forms of government*. Social revolution attacks the
> *foundations of society*. (*Mémoires*, VII, p. 625)

It is clearly the last category which represents for Metternich
the 'serious matter'; so much so that for forty years it seems to
have acted as a magnet to his thoughts and actions. In terms of
writing that means a multitude of documents from which it
should be possible to prepare a kind of treatise or, if one can use
such an expression, a philosophy of revolution.

Let us first of all define the nature and origin of the phenomenon:

> The struggle in which society is engaged today is already an old
> one; it is eternal because of the elements involved. It is the same

struggle that can be seen in individuals between conditions of life and death in the form of good or bad health.

Health and balance are identical ideas like *repose* and *order* for without order repose is not possible. Social repose is disturbed when conflict breaks out between moral forces and when, as a result, material forces are set in motion. Those forces are not subject to discipline or restraint. Once they are let loose and are in conflict, they strike against each other until one of them is overcome. There follows a state not of *real* but *apparent repose* which even in the victorious party is only the consequence of exhaustion.

This outline covers the history of revolutions and of the many different forms they take. Old or new they only amount to episodes. They form transitional stages without creating anything definite and without changing the nature of things. They are incapable of altering anything except the shape of things, for the essential conditions of society are immutable. (*Mémoires*, VIII, p. 569)

Revolution thus defined depends on factors rooted in human nature:

The civilized world is divided into two classes: the idealists, democrats, and any kind of reformer are in opposition to the wise men who see good and evil only where they exist. The first group put themselves above all restraint. The world and civilization might not have existed before them, and past experience has little or no value for them compared with the value of those experiences that lie ahead. The second group allow time the qualities that belong to it by right. They scarcely believe in new moral experiences, and without rejecting them outright they are prepared, before passing judgment, to examine in detail what the inventors describe as so many masterpieces of the spirit of the age, that is to say of their own spirit or of their passions. (to Decazes, June 8, 1819. Quoted in G. de Bertier, *Metternich et Decazes*, p. 86)

Two elements are constantly at war in human society, the positive and the negative, the conservative and the destructive. (*Mémoires*, VII, p. 639)

Behind the ideological conflict, Metternich perceives the clash of interests:

> It is the campaign which the ambitious and the proletarians wage against the peaceful owners of property; it is the struggle of those who wish to possess against those who already do so, between those who wish to arrive and those who are already there. (to Hügel, July 16, 1833)

> Today, as in the past and for all time to come, two irreconcilable groups are in conflict in society: *those who have and those who have not.* (to King Leopold of Belgium, Jan. 1853. *Mémoires,* VIII, p. 547)

The flaw that lies at the root of revolutionary enterprise is none other than presumption:

> Religion, public morality, legislation, economics, administration —they all seem to have become common property accessible to all. Knowledge appears to be innate. Experience has no value to the presumptuous man. He substitutes for faith, which means nothing to him, a so-called private conviction and he reaches this conviction without examination and without study.

> Such methods of approach seem too trivial for a mentality that thinks itself strong enough to take in at a glance a whole set of problems and facts. Laws have no significance for him because he has had no hand in the making of them and because it would be beneath his dignity to take any notice of limitations imposed by brutish and ignorant generations in the past. *Power* resides in himself. Why should he submit to a rule that is only of use to the man who is devoid of enlightenment and knowledge? . . .

> The real aim of the idealists . . . in the final analysis is none other than to create for each individual a life entirely independent of any authority and of any will other than his own. This is an absurd idea, contrary to man's nature and incompatible with the needs of human society. (to Emperor Alexander, 1820. *Mémoires,* III, pp. 430–1)

> One can imagine that the goodwill of the multitude could easily be won over to anything which tends, in a false but facile sense,

to place the individual above the law, to open up a wide field for every kind of ambition, to sanctify every passionate aim, and to confound all reasoning. One can also observe whither the so-called *perfecting of society* (the representative system) is heading. The calm and impartial observer finds in twenty countries only piles of rubble, and, with the exception of England, he finds in return for all that destruction nothing but a promissory note drawn by a handful of feeble men or clumsy idealists, on the account of posterity's happiness.

The peace of entire generations, including their own, does not appear to enter into the calculations of those few philanthropic dreamers, but the same is not true of their associates, *the calculated liberals*. They resemble those opportunists who break into the house which they have set on fire, not to save the valuables, but to make off with them. (to Esterhazy, Mar. 23, 1820)

The earliest recognizable point of departure of the social move-ment which today covers the world is to be found in the Re-formation in the sixteenth century. (to Lützow, Jan. 2, 1848. *Mémoires*, VII, p. 571)

The evil spread to France in the eighteenth century, owing to the weakness of her governments and to the skill with which subversive ideas were disseminated:

You have only to mention a social contract and the revolution is made! In the palace of kings, in the *salons* and the *boudoirs* of a few towns the revolution was already complete, whereas it was still only being prepared among the mass of the people.

The example of England also counted for a good deal. And so the revolution broke out in France. The frightful scenes that marked it, and also the wars of aggression undertaken by the Jacobins, created at first a feeling abroad that was hardly favour-able to the propagation of revolutionary theories. But the seeds were sown none the less. The military despotism of Napoleon only favoured their growth:

His conquests removed a whole crowd of established rights, institutions and customs, severing bonds that were sacred to all nations and which had survived the years. The result of these disturbances was that the revolutionary spirit could easily cover itself, in Germany, Italy and later in Spain, with the mantle of patriotism.

The triumph of the Alliance might have ensured for the world a more peaceful future. But Louis XVIII ill-advisedly gave royal sanction in his Charter to some of the revolutionary principles, conferring on them in this way a kind of respectability. Napoleon, himself, at the time of his offensive in 1815, destroyed in a hundred days the work of fourteen years during which he had been in power. He unleashed the revolution he had succeeded in restraining. [I am here making a résumé of a lengthy elaboration in the abovementioned memoir to Alexander I. *Mémoires*, III, pp. 431–5.]

Even the return to peace proved to be favourable in a way to the development of revolutionary ideology, the movement which had come to an end on the material plane transporting itself to the moral plane. (*Mémoires*, VIII, p. 538) Thus by a strange paradox political peace and prosperity engender leisure which makes it possible for troubled minds and covetous persons to 'tamper with things'. (*Mémoires*, VII, p. 90) 'People who want *panem et circenses* do not want to be bored. They want to be ruled by a strong hand and to be *amused*.' (to Ficquelmont, Feb. 17, 1848)

In France the Revolution remained concealed:

> Static revolutions bear the same relation to other kinds of revolution as chronic disease does to inflammation. The trouble has changed its character, not because it is clearing up but because of lack of resistance in the individuals it attacks. (to the Czar Alexander, Dec. 3, 1821)

In France the combustible elements had already been consumed and so Metternich was declaring as early as 1820 that there was no danger of another outburst there. The revolution of 1830 was to serve as an illustration of the natural law that bodies which have suffered recently from certain illnesses are less susceptible to another attack than those which have never experienced illness or which recovered a long time ago from a first attack. . . . The disaster of July 1830 thus had the effect for France of a revolt crowned by a usurpation rather than of a social revolution . . . the effect, that is, of a *quasi-revolution*.

The changes wrought in the political system were, indeed, very slight and the government gained rather than lost in power. 'Never would Charles X and his Ministers have undertaken with impunity what Louis-Philippe undertakes daily.' (to Hummelauer, Dec. 25, 1834)

> It is, therefore, necessary to distinguish between those countries in which an advanced liberal party cannot do much harm and which have nothing to fear except from radicalism, and those to which a liberal revolution in velvet gloves may prove disastrous. This would be the case with Austria, Italy, and even Prussia, whereas France and Western Germany belong to the first category. In comparing revolution to a book I would say that we have reached the foreword while France has nearly, but not quite, reached the last few pages. (Remarks noted by Hübner, Feb. 21, 1848. *Une année de ma Vie*, p. 5)

History also shows us that there is a kind of inner fatality in the revolutionary phenomenon:

> Revolution, once it has taken the first step, tends to run the whole course. (to Esterhazy, Mar. 17, 1831) *'Thus far'* and *'no further'* become meaningless expressions. (to Apponyi, Feb. 6, 1834)
>
> In revolutions those who want everything always get the better of those who only want a certain amount. (to Esterhazy, Apr. 2, 1831)
>
> Moderation is fatal to factions, just as it is the vital principle of established power. To ask malcontents to be moderate is like asking them to destroy the foundations of their existence. (to Apponyi, Feb. 6, 1834)
>
> The more excitable the nation, the greater the need for revolu-

tionary movements to be sustained by the spectacle of devastation and the spilling of blood if they are to turn into proper revolutions. Rose-water revolutions (that privilege of the liberals) are not revolutions, and a partial revolt which does not turn, in the space of a few years, into a general revolution involving every class, has lost by then its source of life and action. (to Neumann, Dec. 28, 1824)

That is no doubt why revolutions so often rush headlong into a foreign war which makes possible the imposition of extreme measures at home:

When anarchy comes to a head in any great State it always leads to civil or foreign war and often to both scourges at the same time. (*Mémoires*, V, p. 57)

Political strife [is] undoubtedly the necessary consequence of revolutions running their proper course. (to Apponyi, May 27, 1836)

Thus, 'a revolution is its own worst enemy' (to Zichy, Mar. 28, 1823), and if it were not for the fear of external contagion, could be left to right itself by its own excesses, in accordance with the natural order of things:

Revolutions which are fomented in the higher levels of society spread down from the intellectual level and attack material things. Once these have been overthrown, the need for rest dampens high spirits, experience once again begins to mean something and finally comes into its own. Revolutionary elements continue to float on the surface for some time, but the under-current detaches itself and becomes purified. (to Apponyi, July 25, 1835)

What happens in practice?

When those individuals who are seeking their fortunes are reduced to trying to do so at the expense of private property, the number of persons who rally to its defence exceeds by a greater number each day those bandits who want to found their fortunes on the ruination of their neighbours. (to Hummelauer, Dec. 25, 1834)

It is not the least conservative who are the original revolutionaries:

> It is quite common to see men destroy the ladder by which they have stormed a position, and they are the ones who will defend to the bitter end what they have won by conquest. (to Apponyi, Dec. 2, 1835)

Thus somehow or other a new order is born which could never quite be the same as the old one:

> Neither the German Empire nor the old French monarchy was able to re-establish itself in 1814 . . . Whether the process be slow or rapid, the dissolution of the elements which constitute a body politic paves the way for the destruction of the State. A new regime can be created only with new elements, unformed or purified material taken from previous constitutions but still unable to take the shape of the old. (to Apponyi, Mar. 27, 1836)

Do not let us forget that revolutions are made by man. But revolutionaries cannot generally expect much from the great mass of the people. 'The masses are and always will be conservative.' (to Apponyi, Dec. 4, 1846)

> The labours to which (the masses) must devote themselves are too continuous and too positive to allow them to throw themselves into the uncertainties of abstract ambitions. The ordinary man knows that the best he can hope for is to be able to be sure of the morrow, for only then will he be repaid for the exertions and troubles of today. The ordinary man mistrusts movement, which interferes with hard work and which invariably brings fresh burdens in its wake. (to the Czar Alexander, 1820. *Mémoires*, III, pp. 436–7)

Unfortunately the masses too often allow themselves to be guided by passion, ignorance, and fear:

> They are never invulnerable to enthusiasm: the voice of the people, *which is the voice of God*, makes itself known only

through the medium of judgment, not in moments of action. At such times it is emotion and enthusiasm that prevail. (to Apponyi, Feb. 15, 1839)

People naturally want public order to be maintained, but the great majority of them no longer know where it is to be found. . . . They will accept it from any hand that appears to offer it, without examining the value of the offer. Whenever disorder is suggested as a means of achieving that end, they will not reject it. Swift and well-organized revolutions are of little value to the populace apart from staging a drama at the showing of which they form part of the audience. It is left to the actors to deal with the risks and dangers. The audience has no desire to participate, except to hiss the losers. (to baron de Werner, Aug. 23, 1830)

The people have for long failed to feel sure of being protected by thrones against the attacks of genuine zealots. Being unsure, rapid submission appears to them only too often to be the best course. (to Vincent, Apr. 8, 1821)

It is not in their ranks that the dangerous men are to be found:

The restless classes of society today are the intermediate ones for whom personal interest, ambition, and greed are everything and among whom place-seekers pursue quick and easy returns. (to Apponyi, Feb. 8, 1837)

... The dissatisfied classes are the financiers, those genuine cosmopolitans who secure their profits at the expense of absolutely any order of things, the Civil Servants, men of letters, lawyers, and persons in charge of public education.

To these intermediate classes of society others attach themselves, those who have false ambitions—their number is never large in the lower orders but is considerable among the higher ranks of society . . . perverted and lost spirits in the widest sense of the words. Their career is, therefore, usually a short one. They are the first victims of political reform and the rôle of the few who survive is generally that of humble servants despised by their inferiors who have risen to the highest offices of State. (to the Czar Alexander, 1820. *Mémoires*, III, p. 437)

One type of man Metternich specially detests:

> *Savants* . . . I do not like that breed. I could wish that for the
> good of humanity there could be learning but no learned men.
> (to the comtesse de Lieven, Apr. 24, 1819, p. 306)

> Artists are much better value. They are usually a little queer in the
> head but their hearts are sound. The contrary is true of *savants*.
> (ibid., Mar. 8, 1819, p. 235)

Yet professors, whether they be *savants* or not, are not so much
to be feared as lawyers:

> There are no clumsier conspirators than professors, individually
> or in groups. Conspiracy is only profitable when it is directed
> against *things* and not against *dogmas* . . . When *political* dogmas
> are involved they must be supported by action, but action means
> the overthrow of every existing institution and the application of
> the principle 'out of my way and let me in!' Savants and pro-
> fessors are incapable of this; it is the lawyers who are best suited
> to it. I know scarcely one savant who understands the value of
> property; lawyers, on the other hand, are for ever dealing with
> other people's property. Besides, the professors are nearly all
> theorists whereas there is nobody more practical than your
> lawyer. (*Mémoires*, III, p. 262)

There is a theory dear to the heart of the doctrinaire school
and to Guizot in particular; according to him the revolution of
1789 consecrated the inevitable victory of the middle classes over
privilege and absolute power. Metternich gives way to violent
criticism of this conception. The supporters of this system, he
says, would replace the old social hierarchy by an intermediate
class and in this way would create a new privilege in favour of
them:

> This thought, reduced to figures, presents the following formula:
> given 1, 2, and 3: take away 1 and you are left with 2 and 3.
> But what the doctrine overlooks is that in taking away the first
> figure, the second is no longer the middle one. . . . The attempt
> of the middle class to throw off the class above them and to
> prevent the class below them from rising to their level results in

that paradox . . . It is one of the diseases of our times and the tendency is by no means confined to the French *bourgeoisie* . . . What is the effect of this phenomenon? We see the upper layer (No. 1) link up with the lower layer (No. 3) and make common cause to prevent the triumph of the intermediate class. That is precisely what is happening in France and it explains why the doctrinaire school is detested by the old aristocracy as well as by the democrats.

What increases the feebleness of this doctrine is that it is incapable of giving form to its own essence . . . M. Guizot found a form for it, namely intelligence, but intelligence cannot be the prerogative of any one class, it can only be the prerogative of individuals; when applied to a class it becomes no more than a pretence devoid of any foundation . . . (to Hügel, May 31, 1837)

More than any other category of opponents the doctrinaires inspire the avenging zeal of M. de Metternich:

The doctrinaires are the least practical of men and at the same time the least able to learn from their experience. Judging everything *a priori*, they are blinded by vain theories, imbued with all that is false in German philosophy and all that is exaggerated in English philosophy, and they are, without any doubt, more dangerous than the radicals, those fools of good faith or those scoundrels so easy to unmask. (to Apponyi, Apr. 10, 1835)

Revolutionary crimes are less to be feared for their effect than false doctrines. The former provide their own remedies, for an entire population will not allow itself to be pillaged and guillotined with impunity, but the latter can, without appearing to, develop such an intensity that the basic strength of an empire may be drained away without rousing the suspicions of the masses that any danger exists, although they would recoil in horror the moment it was pointed out to them. (to Esterhazy, May 6, 1820)

Since the masses are by nature passive, revolutionary movements are bound to be the creation of active minorities:

Numerically the revolutionary faction is not the largest one. Its strength derives from its energy and from the disorder which is created in the administrative machinery of the government by repeated attacks which keep the government on their toes. By forcing on them a situation calling for exceptional measures, the faction achieves its principal object, which is to rouse general discontent quite naturally in the inert mass of the population. When waters are infested by pirates, the number of these is certainly fewer than that of the regular naval forces; but a few pirates have only to appear to paralyse commerce. (to Apponyi, Feb. 13, 1834)

Metternich believes in the existence of an international revolutionary movement mobilized into secret societies, freemasonry, *Carbonari*, and other affiliated sects:

From the beginning of time there have existed men of like disposition. . . . But now for the first time these normally rare elements are formed into a fairly compact organization from which has arisen a number of associations whose object is the overthrow of society. We have in particular the formation of a hierarchy within this anti-social body which appeared to be incapable of supporting one. Finally, we have the existence of a government which can command more obedience than most established ones, and whose relentless power to dissolve hampers and may sometimes even stop the machinery of administration, and will eventually make the preservation of order impossible. (to Apponyi, Jan. 2, 1836)

In what way can governments oppose these revolutionary activities?

The precise aim of malcontents is one and the same. It is the overthrow of everything legal . . . The principle which monarchs must oppose to this plan of universal destruction is the preservation of everything legal.

The only means of achieving this will be by allowing no innovations . . . I am convinced that it is impossible in a just and reasonable sense to preserve and to reform when the masses are on the move . . . Let governments govern, let authority face the fact that without power it is nothing. By governing it can actually improve the situation; but it must remove nothing from the foundation on which it rests. (to the Czar Alexander, May 1821. *Mémoires*, III, pp. 505–6)

Preservation does not mean reaction, a return to the past:

Only the most complete flight from reason or remarkable duplicity could accuse us of harbouring ill feeling towards any legally established institution in Europe, because we abhor measures of violence which overturn them on the pretext of reforming them. On the contrary I defend, and with equal sincerity, the widely separated institutions which control my country and the monarchical freedoms of other empires and even the existence of the republican canton of Vaud. (to Wellington, May 8, 1823)

Nor is preservation to be confused with immobility:

This maxim, 'to preserve is to act', has always served me as a line of conduct, while those who should have backed me up were confusing the duty of preservation with inactivity. (*Mémoires*, VIII, p. 235)

I have been accused by those who run of remaining still: I do not know how to be stationary except on matters of principle. I cannot be stationary in the application of principles. I can move and stop as circumstances demand, but I have never believed that a hot pace was the one best suited to governments. (to Sir Travers Twiss, Feb. 11, 1849)

Progress then, but wisely measured and prudently handled. Metternich once made use of a happy allegory to put his point of view. It was during a conversation with a Herr Krause of Dresden, a landowner on a big scale, who reported the following observation to George Ticknor:

If you had on your estate, on that high ground which overlooks the Elbe, a vast reservoir threatening at any moment to flood your rich fields and which must one day overflow, would you straightway breach the dam and let the torrent ravage your land? Would you not rather pierce it carefully and let the water flow out slowly and safely in order to irrigate your fields instead of devastating them? (in *Life and Letters of G. Ticknor*, II, p. 10)

When we come to reforms, we find a principle on which Metternich never varied:

> Useful or necessary alterations in the legislation and administration of States should only arise from free will, from the premeditated and well-informed impulse of those into whose hands God has placed the responsibility of power. (Circular of May 12, 1821. *Staatskanzlei, Interiora, Circularien*, 18)

One who was for years in almost daily contact with the Chancellor and who therefore knew him well, Caraman, the French ambassador, explains Metternich's thoughts in a similar way:

> Prince Metternich is quite convinced that in the present state of Europe it is almost impossible to lag behind without conceding anything to the leaders of progressive thought or to the needs created by recent events; but he is equally convinced that a government is only secure inasmuch as it anticipates what might be demanded, and he wishes the sovereign to make concessions without having anything taken from him.

Caraman adds:

> In the past the Emperor has pronounced so strongly against any innovation that it will need all our care and skill to detach him from this exclusive line of thought. (Foreign affairs. Diplomatic correspondence. Austria 399, Feb. 23, 1818)

Indeed, it appears that if Metternich was not always consistent with his principle of dynamic conservatism, this must be attributed in the first place to the stubbornness of his master. Another French ambassador, Rayneval, recorded this confession:

> What he (the Emperor) desires first and foremost is stability. And if I were to allow myself to be guided by any other principle than this, I would soon cease to be his Minister despite the confidence he has habitually placed in me. (ibid., 412, Jan. 25, 1830)

The first need, therefore, is to see that improvements which cannot be avoided are not introduced as concessions:

A king must never sacrifice any part of his authority. To propose it is to propose his degradation; and since in consenting to such a proposal he is betraying not only his own interest but the safety of his people, it is a crime to make it. There may be delegation of certain branches of public authority (that of making laws, for example) to bodies existing by virtue of ancient institutions or established for this purpose by the sovereign himself. But delegation is not alienation, neither is it sharing. Just as the sovereign, in entrusting to his Ministers the exercise of his executive power, preserves no less the fullness of it, so any other delegated power necessarily carries with it the condition that the foundation, the substance, and capital of power invariably remains in the hands of the sovereign. The only possible meaning of the word constitution in connection with the monarchical system is that of an organization of public powers under the supreme, indivisible and inalienable authority of the monarch . . . In any other context *constitution* is the equivalent of *anarchy*, and the so-called division of powers spells the death of monarchical government. (to Wellington, June 29, 1822. *Wellington's Supplementary Dispatches,* 2nd Series, I, p. 396)

To believe that just and reasonable measures can be introduced as concessions would be to admit that there is a clash of interests between those who govern and those who are governed, whereas the contrary is true. (*Mémoires*, V, p. 374) Therefore let governments take the initiative in remedying well-founded complaints and let them win over from the ranks of the revolutionaries all those who might otherwise be driven by hardship to take the wrong path. (quoted by Nada: *Metternich e le Riforme nello Stato pontificio*, p. IX)

Revolts have their origin in the lower orders of society. Revolutions always arise from a government's mistakes. (*Mémoires*, VIII, p. 587)

The worst evil to which any State can be exposed is lack of power. People endure despotism more easily than complete inactivity. (to Esterhazy, Mar. 7, 1820)

Firmness must not degenerate into cruelty towards individuals or into blind reaction:

> The wisdom of princes must prevent their exceeding the limits of a fair severity and giving way to that disastrous attitude of mind, the reactionary one. (to Neumann, Sept. 18, 1819)

> For a long time now order has been re-established by measures and with an ardour which make it almost more dangerous than disorder itself. The executioners are unable to destroy the human race and the scaffold is running with blood. Laws continue in existence, they destroy customs, they sweep society into catastrophes for which there are no remedies. I think that for a long time to come every government is going to lose every battle it fights against the Revolution, and those battles which they appear to have won will still have been lost. Against the Revolution every government is fighting in enemy territory. The sanction of public opinion is missing from the decrees of justice. (to Louis Veuillot. *Oeuvres complètes*, XXXIII, pp. 341–50)

Even though a high degree of indulgence may be needed, amnesty must not be confused with pardon:

> God grants no amnesty, for the very idea of such an action, inasmuch as it turns the existence of the crime into an abstraction, would be contrary to the idea of Divine justice which of necessity abhors moral evil so long as it continues to exist. The mercy of God operates only through forgiveness. There are cases in which prudence and even justice may require a sovereign authority to show clemency towards offenders. In such cases that authority would do well to state that it does not intend to associate itself with claims that cannot be justified before the tribunal of reason. (to Lützow, July 12, 1846. *Mémoires*, VIII, p. 255)

If open conflict cannot be avoided, governments will generally win because

> it is in the nature of things that ordered strength should prevail over strength that lacks order. Now there is nothing in the opponents' game that could ever find itself under the domination of an order. The day that order prevails the revolution recedes,

and its supporters, being without strength, will cease to be dangerous. (to Zichy, Nov. 27, 1824)

Revolution may triumph in a nation. If it does, neighbouring governments must work together to limit the disaster:

Material damage, once it is confined to the ground it has invaded, and is obliged to act upon itself, cannot help losing its intensity and its vigour. Like a flame which must be fed if it is to grow, the revolutionary principle, if it is shut in and deprived of the opportunity to expand, must end by consuming itself. (to Lebzeltern, Jan. 2, 1826)

To outlast an adversary, that must be the objective:

I consider that the first calculation to be made by any government in moments of great crisis must be limited to fact and to finding a way of living beyond the reach of such attacks. No invalid who is stronger than his disease is in any danger of dying. That is the whole secret of our policy. (to Esterhazy, May 6, 1820)

If monarchies disappear, it is because they give up. (*Mémoires*, VII, p. 629)

When kings can say *no*, they win their point. (*Mémoires*, IV, p. 270)

3. Relations between States

Political relations between Powers rest on two elements, one invariable, the other subject to the vicissitudes of time. The first is bound up with material circumstances such as the geographical position of States. These circumstances themselves create conditions of existence stronger and more lasting than the changing will of mankind. The second element, being the work of man, is much more directly subordinate to what is variable in his mind. (to Esterhazy, Sept. 17, 1838)

A lasting union between Powers can only be considered possible on a basis of principles which safeguard permanent interests. This is not the case with short-term interests. It is a mistake to attempt to find a basis for a permanent political liaison in such elements as the internal constitution of a country, the organic laws that govern it, or in its predominating religion. . . . States which are subjected to the representative system are not for that reason either the natural allies of each other or the implacable enemies of States under a different system. (to Apponyi, Apr. 12, 1847)

And so worthless disputes will be avoided:

It is with principles of government as it is with religious dogmas. Discussion of them is often dangerous and always a waste of time. A Cabinet must concentrate on living in peace and harmony. The surest way to achieve that desirable end is carefully to avoid subjects of discussion on which agreement is unlikely and to endeavour, equally carefully, to meet on grounds of mutual interest. (to Neumann, Oct. 31, 1832)

But in the sphere of diplomacy it is not possible to exclude these differences of opinion.

It is not in the nature of political bodies to make contact over questions having a general as well as a particular interest without some friction . . . States have, like individuals, different temperaments: a particular interest or situation will predominate in a State just as a particular passion or weakness influences individuals. These different attitudes are not slow to make themselves known, heard and felt. The same results that would be found in a family consultation should, by the same right, be found in a meeting of Powers. (to Esterhazy, Mar. 5, 1821)

It is necessary to know when to stop asking:

It is only by not exaggerating their claims that States can develop friendships, for friendship between empires is only interests wisely consulted. (to Neumann, Feb. 8, 1843)

In relations between governments Metternich recommends sticking to realities and the avoidance of sentimentality:

Words which express a sentiment are dangerous ones to use in serious matters because they say too much and because for that very reason they are liable to a variety of interpretations.

Such an expression is *entente cordiale*, which was used by Guizot in 1844 to describe the solidarity existing between France and Great Britain:

> A cordial agreement cannot exist between States any more than it can between individuals except in relation to special and therefore definable cases. Speaking generally the two words only indicate *a moral inclination*, and it is precisely such inclinations that bank the fires of passionate and bitter criticism. (to Apponyi, Aug. 29, 1844)

> In this particular case the words cover an intense rivalry and will lead to rude awakenings.

> The blows that are struck by hatred, concealing its growth behind the mask of friendship, are usually violent blows. (to Apponyi, Oct. 26, 1845)

It is true that the causes of conflict are more often material interests.

Metternich is resolutely pacifist, not only because war is contrary to the principle of repose but to a greater extent because of its uncontrollable character:

> One characteristic of war is that once it has begun laws are no longer imposed by the will of man but by force of circumstance, and another is that circumstances of pure chance become reasons, and that although one may know one's starting-point the same is not true of one's destination. (to Esterhazy, Aug. 24, 1821)

What, then, are the bases of peace?

1. The political independence of any legally recognized government, that is to say the liberty it must enjoy to adopt, in its internal affairs as well as in its foreign relations, whatever system it judges most suitable in the interests of its own preservation, security and tranquillity, without damaging the interests of others.

2. The maintenance of all existing treaties so long as they are not abolished or modified by common agreement between the contracting parties.

3. The declared resolve of the Powers to maintain, by the respect
which they show for these principles, the peaceful and enlightened relations already existing between them, and under
the protection of which the internal peace of States and all the
property which they alone guarantee, can flourish. (to Apponyi, June 3, 1831)

As with individuals, so with political bodies: they only enjoy true
independence when they are surrounded by sufficient strength
to guarantee their well-being. (to Viale Prela, Sept. 4, 1846)

Is independence compatible with customs unions? The possibility of such a union between France and Belgium, which
arose in 1842, evokes the following oracle:

Customs unions are a recent invention which can only be applied
to political bodies united by a federative link, as is the case with
the German States, the Swiss cantons or the United States of
America. Even so the federal link will by no means eliminate for
those States taking part in a customs union all the difficulties
arising from a complete loss of freedom of commercial or industrial movement. What is beyond dispute is that the difficulties
to which such a system gives rise increase in proportion to the
size and value of States and weigh more heavily on big than on
small ones. A customs union must repose on a fair distribution of
costs and profits; the only possible practical basis on which to
operate this distribution is that of population.

This basis is perfectly fair, yet it would, if applied to Belgium,
make union with any other State impossible, bearing in mind the
disproportion that exists between the production and consumption of the four million Belgians and that of an equal number of
population in any other country. The loss of freedom of movement which such a measure would mean to any weak State tied
to a more powerful neighbour—a loss which in many respects
borders on that of political independence—can only be partly
compensated by legal conditions and fundamental guarantees
such as are offered by federation. None of this applies to the
Franco-Belgian union. Nor would it apply to an Anglo-Belgian
or to a German-Belgian union. (to Apponyi, Jan. 7, 1843)

Nearly always it is concrete cases that inspire Metternich's generalizations. Greece was particularly fruitful in respect of problems involving the idea of independence.

Can a people claim the status of an independent nation simply by rising against the authority of a government?

> At what point precisely do the activities of a people who have taken arms against their government constitute legal warfare? The Greek insurrection began with a furious massacre of Turks. After this cruel start, it created, it is true, flying squadrons, flotillas, and fire-ships; it organized the pillaging of property, coastal devastation, and every kind of piracy; but did it thereby change its nature? If it were left to a foreign Power to determine the transition from a state of frenzy and violence to one of open warfare, the most criminal insurrection would only have to disguise itself in a few diplomatic and military trappings to be able to count on allies and protectors. To do that would be to privilege in advance any revolt that might break out in troubled times, for if ships and soldiers are enough to establish a revolutionary power equal in law to the power whose authority it has abjured, stability no longer exists for any nation in the world, and social peace everywhere will be at the mercy of the first faction fortunate enough to unite under its colours whatever is necessary to usurp the title of a belligerent power. . . . (to Esterhazy, Feb. 10, 1825)

Anyone with a knowledge of the history of Greek independence will recognize in this Metternich's protest against the decision of the British Government to grant the insurgents the status of belligerents. From this it was only a step to the recognition of true independence. Metternich protests against such an eventuality:

> What would happen to Europe and to civilization if the doctrine of the *divisibility of States* were ever recognized by the last bastions of international peace? How can an intelligent man put forward, or at least attempt to put forward, such a subversive doctrine? Is England ready to consider as a power equal in law to her king the first Irish club to declare itself the insurgent

government of Ireland? Is she ready to consider as legally valid any French Power which accepted the rôle of mediator simply on the strength of an invitation from the Irish Government, and to regard as just the threat of coercive measures whether that threat came from France alone or from a combination of powers? The French ambassador in London would continue his diplomatic functions unabated, would continue to enjoy his immunities, and French commerce would suffer no hindrance in English ports! There is no end to the absurdity of it!

Nevertheless, after eight years of struggle, he had to admit the impossibility of bringing the Greeks back under Turkish domination:

> It is a fact that revolutions whose origins are the most reprehensible have on more than one occasion ended in triumph, and that once this disastrous state of affairs has been reached, the most enlightened and unyielding of governments must come to terms with the best established usurpation. (to Esterhazy, Mar. 15, 1828)

Should the independence of States absolutely exclude the possibility of intervention by neighbours in their internal affairs? An immense question, Metternich admits. (to Ficquelmont, Oct. 31, 1830)

It is tempting to answer this question by a simple statement of well-known facts: the threat of intervention levelled against France by the treaty of the Quadruple Alliance, in November 1815, which was renewed at Aix-la-Chapelle in 1818; Austrian intervention in Italy in 1821 and after 1830; and the principle loudly proclaimed at Troppau and at Laybach of the right of legitimate defence to extend beyond national frontiers.

But against these facts and declarations can be set others which sound quite a different note:

> The way of foreign intervention is not capable of uniform application because revolutions often give rise to phenomena, so strange and so utterly different from anything that had been prepared for, that what is generally speaking true may in a particular case turn out to be false. (to Vincent, July 5, 1822)

The case in question was that of Spain, where Metternich wanted to avoid armed intervention by France. And so he flaunted principles directly opposed to those which he had invoked the year before in favour of military action by Austria in Italy:

> We believe that too direct an external influence intended to hasten the progress of the just cause in a State torn by revolution is more likely to hinder that cause than to help it. Similarly, we are of the opinion that if restoration is to be complete and enduring in a great State which is placed in an independent position by more conditions than one, it must be prepared and carried into effect by the country's own methods. (to Vincent, July 10, 1822)

Might not the key to this apparent contradiction be revealed by the following image which fell from the Chancellor's pen? 'Any solid mass which fails to cover a fire completely only adds to it.' (to Vincent, June 15, 1820) We appear to be coming up against one of those examples of hypocritical opportunism with which Metternich is sometimes reproached. His so-called principle on intervention appears to amount to no more than this: intervene if you are strong enough to score a complete victory, keep out if you are not sure of success.

In fact, the answer is not so simple. Metternich's doubts as to the effectiveness of foreign intervention give the impression of being well rooted in him. He is of the opinion that if Brunswick had succeeded in taking Paris in 1792, it would not necessarily have meant the end of the French Revolution. (*Mémoires*, I, p. 94)

> Nations are not disposed to accept as benefits those lessons which they are taught by force of arms. (*Mémoires*, I, p. 94)

> It is not by means of foreign cannon that revolution in a big State can be stamped out. In such circumstances, what such a State has been unable to prevent by its own strength will not be prevented by outside force. (to Apponyi, May 27, 1837)

And, indeed, Metternich declared himself firmly opposed, in 1830, to intervention by the absolute monarchies against the July Revolution in France. Yet at the same time he regretted that

Prussia did not dare to crush the Belgian revolution, and he himself did not hesitate to intervene vigorously in northern Italy. Well, then?

We can imagine that such a contradiction did not fail to rouse some discomfort in a mind that was in the habit of linking every action with an immutable principle. The result of his efforts to find a respectable synthesis can be seen in the following explanation, the theme of which recurs in very similar terms every time the question is raised:

> Reciprocity is the primary and fundamental principle of the political relations between independent States. The true independence of States rests on security. This security is the responsibility of every government. The maintenance of external peace is dependent on the sanctity of treaties and consequently on the position of the Powers responsible for observing those treaties and putting them into effect. No government can appropriate to itself the right to intervene in the legislative and administrative affairs of another independent State. Those who defend the right of political intervention do not claim to apply it to that kind of situation, and to attribute to them any such intention is to take arms against a fantasy.

> The right to intervene, of course, only extends to those extreme cases in which public order is so disturbed by violent revolutions that the government loses the power to honour the treaties which bind it to other States, and the latter find their security, or their very existence, threatened by the currents and disorders that are inseparable from all such upheavals.

> In such a state of affairs the right to intervene belongs as clearly to any government that is exposed to the dangers of being swept away in the revolutionary torrent as the right belongs to the individual to extinguish the fire in a neighbouring house in order to prevent its spreading to his own home . . . The same is true when the sovereign or legal authority of a country is at the mercy of a violent revolution and calls for help, on the strength of positive treaties or by virtue of common right, to its neighbours or to any other government which possesses the means of preventing its destruction. (to Ficquelmont, Oct. 31, 1830)

Thus the final position of Metternich on the right of intervention admits only one moral justification: the principle of legitimate defence. It admits only one judicial basis: the appeal for help from the legal government involved. He does not appear ever to have acted contrary to this line of conduct.

However powerful States are, however flourishing their internal economy, their independence is limited by the community of interests which modern civilization inevitably creates between them.

Here is an example. In 1825 strong pressure was brought to bear on the Austrian Emperor to persuade him to close a Jesuit college at Lemberg in Galicia. From a purely Austrian point of view such a move was defensible. Yet Metternich, with his eye on the internal condition of France, where the anti-Jesuit dispute was raging, thought that such suppression would encourage the opponents of the Villèle government. And so he formally advised against it:

> Although different States may, in times of peace, have an indisputable right to consider their own needs before those of any other country, this axiom is not always capable of such wide application in moments of stress and crisis. (*Mémoires*, IV, p. 240)

Turning to the sphere of principles, we must quote here, for all its length, a passage from the well-known profession of faith which Metternich put into his autobiographical essay and which appears to date from 1840:

> Politics is the science of the vital interests of States. But since no State is any longer isolated and any such State only exists in the annals of pagan history or in the abstractions of self-styled philosophers, we must never lose sight of the *society* of States which is an essential condition of the modern world. Every State has, therefore, besides its own interests, others which it shares with all the other States or with a group of them. The great axioms of political science derive from a knowledge of the true political interests of *every State*. Upon these general   interests

rests the guarantee of their existence. Conversely, particular interests have only a relative and secondary value, although day-to-day or fortuitous political events sometimes give them great importance, and attention to them constitutes political wisdom in the estimation of those who pursue a restless and limited policy . . .

One characteristic of the present world which distinguishes it fundamentally from the ancient is the tendency of nations to draw closer together and to set up a kind of corporate body resting on the same basis as the great human society which grew up at the heart of Christianity. This basis is none other than the precept formulated by the Holy Book: Do unto others as ye would they should do unto you. This fundamental rule of any human society, when applied to a State, is called *reciprocity*. In practice it determines what are called in diplomatic language *'les bons procédés'*, or in other words mutual consideration and honest dealing. In ancient times, politics shut itself away and practised absolute egotism with human prudence the only restraint upon it. The law of retaliation raised eternal barriers and provoked endless enmities between different associations. Upon every page of ancient history is to be found the principle of an eye for an eye. Modern history, on the other hand, demonstrates the principle of international community of interests and the balance of power, and furnishes the spectacle of several States together trying to withstand the domination of one State, to check the spread of its influence and to force it back into the framework of common law. The re-establishment of international relations on the basis of reciprocity under the guarantee of respect for established rights and for the plighted word, is at the present time the very essence of politics, of which diplomacy is only the day-to-day application. Between the two there lies, in my opinion, the same difference as between science and art . . .

In the face of these truths, what becomes of policies that are selfish, hedonistic or meanly ambitious? Above all, what becomes of a policy which pursues what is useful in contempt of the most elementary rules of justice, which mocks good faith and which, in a word, relies solely on vain pretensions of power or cunning? One can judge from this profession of faith how much importance I attach to policies of the size, or if it is preferred, of the quality of those practised by a Richelieu, Mazarin, Talleyrand, Canning, Capo d'Istria, Haugwitz and by so many other more or less famous figures. (*Mémoires*, I, pp. 30–32)

Often he will say: 'In an age that is so full of dangers for the very foundations and safeguards of social order, the only good policy is to pursue no policy.' (to Apponyi, Jan. 27, 1826)

Social, in his vocabulary, means the opposite to *political*. It is in this sense that he must be understood when he says:

I am socialist, in the true sense of the word, by birth. I have always considered politics in the presence of social dangers to be a luxury. (to the archiduchesse Sophie, Mar. 31, 1848. *Mémoires*, VIII, p. 12)

Two things not only occupy my thoughts but absorb me completely. One is the great mass of social problems, the other usually goes by the name of politics. I put social problems first . . . (to Neumann, July 3, 1840)

It is in this sense that he one day wrote this phrase, for which no doubt he will be much forgiven: 'For a long time now Europe has had for me the value of a mother country.' (to Wellington, June 14, 1824. loc. cit., p. 239)

CHAPTER THREE

The Methods

I. The Attributes of the Diplomat

POLITICS IS a science; diplomacy, which is the application of it, an art. Metternich, the man of learning, the political philosopher, can be rather disappointing, but the diplomatic artist commands admiration. 'Unrivalled practitioner', Albert Sorel called him. Let us, then, watch him at work. The passage from the realm of theory to that of practice produces an astonishing transformation. Doctrinal rigidity gives way to the most supple realism. The god Terminus of the Chancelleries becomes 'the virtuoso of his time'. (August Fournier) 'I always considered that in matters of government inflexibility was only applicable to principles.' (to Sir Travers Twiss, Feb. 11, 1849) And again:

> In any important political issue it is necessary to draw a distinction between two elements, first the principle and then the reality against which must be set questions of propriety. (to Neumann, Dec. 19, 1841) The more resolved I am never to give way over a principle which I recognize to be just . . . the more aware I shall always be of the advantages of taking into consideration the natural order of things in order to determine and to modify the course we have to follow, according to our present needs. (to Lebzeltern, Feb. 11, 1849)

A bold paradox this: the attachment to principles which he professes will serve as an excuse for freeing himself from them in action:

> We can never give way over a principle and for this reason we

M.–D

shall always be found compliant over means. Compliance of this kind is not at all dangerous for those who know how to act. Only the abandonment of principles is really dangerous and this truth explains the adaptability in practice of men of principle. (to Apponyi, Jan. 9, 1836)

This leaves the diplomat absolutely free to vary his attitude according to his needs:

It seems to me that in politics, as in war, an offensive or defensive plan must be adapted to the characteristics of the adversary. The enemy who has no regular army to command or who would be incapable of leading one must be scouted in formations that are quite different from those needed against an enemy who follows known rules of attack and defence. You will find in this proposition the explanation of several variations in our course which must have really surprised you. (to Lebzeltern, Dec. 3, 1821)

Nothing more realistic than his attitude when confronted with problems:

I studied my right. When I was thoroughly familiar with it, I tried to uphold it or to make it prevail or to emphasize it, but always taking men, circumstances, and time into account. I made a point of never colliding with the impossible. (to L. Veuillot, Jan. 1850. *Oeuvres complètes*, XXXII, p. 360)

No banging his head against walls:

Anything that is in accordance with the laws of nature is outside human action and to try to pit oneself against such an order of things is folly and dangerous to oneself and to others. (to Hügel, Nov. 23, 1833)

No loss of control:

Ill temper is not one of my weaknesses, and those who have had dealings with me in business or pleasure would hardly deny the truth of this. I take things as they are and I do not waste a moment over recrimination or vain wishful thinking. In this way I save much time. (to Apponyi, May 6, 1840)

No trusting to luck:

> I usually base my calculations on the possibility that everything will go wrong, but not to the extent of being unable to take advantage of an opportunity to succeed, should it present itself. (to Esterhazy, Sept. 16, 1831)

No counting on good feelings:

> In politics sentiment plays such a subsidiary rôle that it is never worth dwelling on it and when in exceptional circumstances it plays an active part it becomes an evil. (to Hummelauer, Oct. 10, 1837)

> Gratitude is not an active sentiment in politics. It is a mistake to take account of it. (to Esterhazy, Mar. 18, 1841)

> To base one's conduct in an important undertaking on faith in the *moderation* of one of the contracting parties is to ask for trouble . . . to build on air, to gamble the future on one throw. (to Trautmansdorff, Sept. 10, 1829)

Not too much reliance on the help of others:

> Long experience of difficult negotiations has taught us to rely for the execution of our plans on ourselves alone and on such means as we possess. (to Vincent, Oct. 6, 1820)

On that particular question—Austrian intervention against the Italian revolutions—he is under no illusion as to the attitude of his allies:

> If we are successful, everyone will wish to share our success with us, and we, instead of giving way to petty jealousy, shall allow every man the right and the pleasure of calculating his part in something that he may neither have understood nor wanted. If we fail, our closest allies at the time will assure us that they were never of our way of thinking. It is the way with all human undertakings which offer at the same time serious chances of danger and success. (to Esterhazy, Feb. 2, 1821)

Interests and not sentiments must form the basis of a healthy policy:

It often happens that it is extremely difficult to disentangle the true from the false, but a man has one guide that rarely lets him down, namely the calculation of interest. It is the calculation we ourselves prefer to follow, and experience has shown us that it does really work. (to Apponyi, Jan. 2, 1836)

That is why Metternich is more at home with realists like Louis-Philippe:

King Louis-Philippe is essentially a practical man, and he is more so than others because he never experiences the constraint that principles impose. M. de Broglie, on the other hand, is a typical doctrinaire. Between the two it is nearly always easier to do business with men of the King's stamp. One is sure of meeting them on the line of their interests. (to Apponyi, Jan. 10, 1835)

Metternich has fewer illusions than might be expected about the value of the results he obtains. At the time of his greatest triumph when he has just established moral ascendancy over the whole of Europe at Troppau and at Laybach, when he has just crushed revolution in Italy and is publicly praising the success of Austria, he confides to one of his closest colleagues:

Immense good has just been achieved. It just gives us the possibility to go on living. Make no mistake; we are not one step removed from that possibility. (to Floret, Apr. 21, 1821. *Staatskanzlei Gross. Correspondenz*)

Finally, realism demands that there should be no clinging to untenable positions. This will happen to Metternich in the first phase of the Eastern question. Having brought all the resources of his diplomacy to bear against the emancipation of the Greeks, he will end by accepting the fact which violated his whole conception of the legitimacy of governments:

There are times in the affairs of men when the strongest will, the most legitimate resistance, is broken against an imperious necessity to which everything must submit. The statesman must take things as he finds them, leaving history to uncover the original,

fundamental mistakes which gave rise to these sad necessities.
(to Esterhazy, Mar. 15, 1828)

That is why we shall see him take the initiative himself in proposing a procedure for the establishment of the new State born
of the revolt:

> The line that we have drawn between good and evil is clear cut.
> Our reasoning and our decisions have their origin in the belief
> that the good is lost and that now the choice lies only between
> two evils. That being so, reason must lead us to prefer the lesser
> evil. (to Trautmansdorff, Mar. 18, 1828)

Another diplomatic virtue is his patience, his playing for time
which allows things to 'find their place' and gives those involved
the chance to see their way more clearly.

> I am not in the habit of fixing my thoughts on some great matter
> the extent and significance of which is still unknown, and indeed
> it is in just those really important questions that my practice is to
> wait for natural forces to arrange matters. (to Esterhazy, Aug. 17,
> 1837)

Metternich is inclined to 'sleep on questions that are extremely
difficult' (to Apponyi, Dec. 11, 1826) and not to give an opinion
straight away. His attitude towards them is that of a doctor at the
patient's bedside, ready to ward off a crisis but careful not to force
nature. (to Esterhazy, Mar. 19, 1829)

> To wait and not to judge or act in a hurry, that is the extent . . .
> of our present policy. Tomorrow shall inform us both of what we
> have to do and of those things which we were not in a position to
> decide the day before. (to Esterhazy, Mar. 19, 1829)

He also relies on the passage of time to enlighten his colleagues:

> Only experience, to which in the end the world always yields,
> can locate the truth among all the evidence. To try to hasten the
> process of time is generally a useless endeavour and often a dan-
> gerous one. (to Esterhazy, Dec. 4, 1822)

Besides, time is only on the side of those whose position is correct and sufficiently strong from the outset. It is 'a most dangerous enemy of those whose existence is only ephemeral'. (to Bombelles, Dec. 27, 1832)

> There is in existence a tremendous force, one which benefits only those who have right on their side: that force is time. To make sure of benefiting by it, it is necessary to dig in and to consolidate one's position. When confusion, which is the certain result of misguided action, comes it finds us armed and ready, and the natural consequence of such a position is to turn the enemy's retreat into a rout. (to Lebzeltern, Mar. 3, 1825)

Playing for time is not, however, to be recommended indiscriminately:

> Time cannot always be used for improving a cause that is inherently wrong. Sometimes it can affect a good cause adversely. Its benefits can, in the final analysis, supply the elements of calculation only to the Power that is strong enough to believe with complete confidence that it alone can dominate events. This does not apply to weaker Powers. (to Lützow, Oct. 12, 1821)

Conforming to these principles Metternich repeats in all manner of ways to his staff the celebrated 'no zeal' of his rival Talleyrand:

> That zeal which constantly does more harm than good and which takes hold of subordinate minds frustrated by the limits within which their activities are confined. (to Zichy, June 17, 1826)

> Calmness is more advantageous in avoiding complications than an excess of activity. (to Apponyi, June 15, 1828)

> The less Cabinets have to say to each other the more natural will be the course that events will follow. (to Thorn, Mar. 4, 1842)

> The endeavours of men generally only hinder the natural course of events: so that when what is natural corresponds to what is desirable, there must be no movement. (to Apponyi, Jan. 2, 1837)

'Tact goes farther in business than intelligence,' (to the comtesse de Lieven, Dec. 8, 1818. *Correspondance*, p. 53); 'for in politics it is men who determine events: it is therefore desirable that those who are called to direct affairs should not be inclined to be wrong about men.' (to Apponyi, Aug. 7, 1838)

> Of all the careers which political life offers to those who wish to take their place in the machinery of the State, a diplomatic career is the one that demands the most intimate knowledge of men and which at the same time offers the best opportunities of acquiring that knowledge.
>
> It demands a knowledge of men because diplomacy has nothing in common with administration in the proper sense of the word ... In the realm of government as in the realm of administration, matter comes first; men are like the workmen in a factory: they are divided into those who give orders and those who obey them. On purely moral levels there is no longer any giving of orders; it changes into *instruction*. In the diplomatic sphere it is different. Rights clash, forces are in dispute; here it is not a question of commanding and obeying. Rights are equal. The struggle consists of discussion between the representatives of different interests. A clash must be avoided and the objective must be reached. At this point, consequently, we come up against individuals with their qualities and their defects. Results are achieved through controversy. (*Mémoires*, VIII, pp. 568–9)

Few nineteenth-century statesmen have possessed to the same extent as Metternich this trump card of diplomacy: a natural result of the exceptional span of his career, but also the fruits of a deliberate attempt not to miss any opportunity of meeting the men who counted for something in Europe:

> I know the moral attitude of the Emperor Alexander as well as the line that his Cabinet will follow, voluntarily or involuntarily. I also know the minds of the two Secretaries of State, their tendencies and their moral range. Consequently nothing that comes from St. Petersburg or that arises out of the doubtful points in Russian policy is capable of surprising me. (to Lebzeltern, Apr. 6, 1817)

Among the testimonies of third persons confirming this gift of the Chancellor let us quote an unpublished one, that of the French ambassador Caraman:

> The distinctive feature of Monsieur Metternich's character is a perfect understanding of men. He subdues them with a skill that is quite individual and although he may not succeed in making them accept his views . . . they have everything to fear from him. A dangerous enemy, a cunning intriguer, stubborn in his feelings and in his actions, he shrewdly calculates dangers and opposition. He holds in his hands a thousand hidden springs which he operates cleverly, and the spreading abroad of an opinion, the establishment of a reputation, the destruction of a statesman, these are no more than games in which his politics or his conscience indulges. (*Affaires étrangères, Mémoires et documents,* France 719, May 14, 1821)

Indeed, it would require a separate study to describe the way in which Metternich set about destroying the reputation of statesmen who dared to defy him: Capo d'Istria, Pozzo di Borgo, Chateaubriand, Canning, Palmerston, not to mention lesser lights. The diabolical skill with which slander and scandal are deliberately spread about, plots hatched to ruin his adversaries in the opinion of their sovereigns, their countrymen and foreign statesmen—all that constitutes one of the most unpleasant aspects of the policy of the Austrian government and sometimes gives Metternich the odious appearance of a Basilio in silk stockings.

Nothing is more precious in human relations than trust. He who seeks it does not find it:

> It is with trust as it is with sleep which in the normal condition of men is at once a consequence of good health and a source of it, in other words cause and effect are reciprocal. (to Apponyi, Feb. 8, 1841)

A few simple rules have to be observed if one is to keep this advantage:

> Failure to honour engagements entered into is the biggest mistake a government can make. Its consequences cannot be confined to

one particular circumstance, they shake the whole position of any authority by loss of trust, which is the first means of action in politics. (to Stürmer, Jan. 21, 1846)

Avoid anything that might needlessly injure the person to whom one is talking:

> Men do not generally like their minds to be roughly handled and dominated. The wisest and most upright of men wish to give the appearance of surrendering freely. Therefore always leave that door open to them and remember, when you have written something, that one never has cause to regret a word that has been crossed out. (to L. Veuillot, *Oeuvres complètes*, XXXIV, p. 360)

> One must, if one can, kill one's opponent, but never rouse him by contempt and the whiplash. (to Apponyi, Sept. 10, 1842)

No appearance of doubting the sincerity of others. That is the advice he frequently gives to Count Apponyi, his ambassador in Paris:

> Whenever King Louis-Philippe tells you that his intentions are not being carried out by his own agents, do not believe a word of it but give the appearance of never doubting it. (May 31, 1834)

In this respect it can be said that Metternich was, broadly speaking, repaid in his own coin. His reputation for dishonesty is well established among the statesmen of his age. Talleyrand, for example, said in comparing him to Mazarin: 'The Cardinal deceived but did not lie; Metternich lies all the time and never deceives.' Like all *bons mots* this is, to say the least, exaggerated. Metternich respects a loyal man when he meets one, for example the duc de Richelieu:

> Few people understand how much advantage can be taken of cunning people; for my part I have never been afraid of them provided they have intelligence. The only adversary it is difficult to vanquish is the perfectly honest man. (*Mémoires*, III, p. 549)

There can be no doubting his sincerity when he writes: 'In any negotiation simple truth is the most formidable weapon of all.' (to Vincent, Sept. 5, 1825) That is a striking sentence, but it would be nice to know how far its author acted consistently with the theory of it. On this delicate question Sainte-Aulaire, Louis-Philippe's ambassador in Vienna, would seem to have struck the right note, because his opinion is modified:

> I often heard him proclaiming the maxim 'that we do not owe the truth to those who have not the right to ask it of us'. And having sometimes dared to press questions on him which he considered indiscreet, I found his practice to be in perfect agreement with his theory. Without the least scruple, without the slightest expression of embarrassment on his face he would affirm the opposite of what was true. Sometimes, if he was feeling in the mood and if the ingenuousness of his adversary gave him confidence, he would mystify him mercilessly. (*Souvenirs*, p. 148)

But some pages later Sainte-Aulaire adds:

> It would be a great failing in business never to believe a man because he sometimes deceives you . . . Monsieur de Metternich has a reserve of loyalty for the big occasion. When he is obliged to give a categorical answer to a clear-cut question I never found him to be Machiavellian or double-faced. (*Souvenirs*, p. 188)

The art of diplomacy being to a large extent the art of convincing people, clear and exact language is an essential instrument of it:

> In my opinion real intelligence is that which always expresses itself clearly. It must be an illumination without smoke. (*Mémoires*, III, p. 374)

> Success in matters of a delicate nature lies in a scrupulous choice of forms and words. I only recognize as useful the employment of those rules or canons which have the advantage of being expressed in perfectly clear and intelligible language. (to Lebzeltern, July 15, 1822)

> Nothing more easily causes harm than long discussions. The more diffuse they are, the less accurately and firmly are questions put,

and the greater the jeopardy in which the whole business stands, however important and interesting it may be. The right words are a real force, and the world would be a different place today, perhaps, if this truth had been universally recognized and acted upon since 1814. (to Apponyi, Feb. 20, 1826)

For this reason Metternich steadfastly refused to use the expression Holy Alliance: he would only recognize Alliance by itself. He did not like to talk of the Greek nation but only of the Greek tribes. We have seen how the term constitutional monarchy is 'deprived of all practical significance'. In regard to Germany he gave long and frequent dissertations on the difference between Bundesstaat (federal State) and Staatenbund (federation of States):

> In an age such as ours, the first care of a government must be not only to be right, but, even more important, to see that everything is called by its right name. (to Lebzeltern, June 26, 1820)

This belief pursued him to the end. A few months before his death he wrote to an English friend:

> I finished my letter to you with an appeal for a revision of the dictionaries which has a much stronger claim to be in the interest of society than a revision of the map of Europe . . . whether a plot of land belongs to A or B may after all be largely a matter of indifference to the human race, but the same can never be true of the value of words. The confusion of language is intolerable, considering what it produces, for if men are to live together in society the words they exchange must have the same significance.

This explains why Metternich insisted on maintaining the use of the French language in diplomatic relations, in spite of the efforts of British Ministers to get notes in English accepted. Every independent State would have the right to do the same, he says, and then

> confusion would reign again, and the whole purpose of modern governments in sending political agents abroad to a permanent residence would be contradicted. This purpose is none other than

the careful maintenance of harmony between nations and of the good relations established by treaty or by mutual interest. It would mean a return to the Constantinople system, in which negotiation is carried on only in Turkish and through the agency of a *dragoman* because the Turks can speak no other language.

The first effect of such a polyglot diplomacy would be to impose on every government the need to attach to its Ministers at foreign courts a swarm of interpreters or *dragomans* to translate expertly the communications of that court or of other Ministers accredited to it. It is only too easy to imagine that such renewed rivalry of language would lead to retaliatory measures on the part of other courts and would end by establishing a system of isolation in political relations. (to Zichy, Dec. 26, 1826)

Did Monsieur de Metternich, in his worst nightmares, ever foresee the Babel of the United Nations?

2. Cogs and Springs

Metternich at work. There was a time when he was said to be more occupied with going the rounds of the *salons* and *boudoirs*. As late as 1815 his faithful colleague Friedrich von Gentz despaired of the flippancy and lack of application shown by his master:

Monsieur de Metternich's manner of working makes it extremely difficult, even impossible, to get any sort of continuity in dealings with him. It is true that he is overburdened with work, but the trouble is attributable even more to his way of life, to the inefficient employment of his time, to a certain looseness in his engagements, to his tastes, his social activities, his overdeveloped sense of nonchalance and friendliness, and to a number of other details which I cannot explain. The result is that he often appears to be neglecting those things the importance of which he is the first to recognize, he is accused of double dealing because his behaviour lacks consistency, and every day he displeases people for whom he has in fact a high regard. (*Despatches to the Hospodars of Wallachia*, I, p. 149)

Metternich, it is true, will never be of the breed of statesmen who base their prestige on inaccessibility. The natural need to talk, a desire to understand men, a deep-seated *bonhomie* keeps his door open at all hours not only to his colleagues but to any stranger of note who wishes to see him. Berlioz, for example, will be admitted in 1844, much to his astonishment, at the mere mention of his name:

> The hardest thing for me [Metternich explains in 1819] is to remain alone in my study for five minutes on end. The work I do resembles, in the rhythm of its duties, that of a toll-gatherer. No sooner have I begun a piece of work than another is brought to me. A bore is shown in or an intriguer who wants to see me or to seek advice or instructions. The first are quickly disposed of; the second are deadly, for hardly more than one in twenty of them ever seeks advice in order to follow it. (to the comtesse de Lieven, Nov. 5, 1819. Quoted in the *Revue hebdomadaire*, Aug. 1899, p. 39)

In these conditions he evolved a very individual routine which he explained one day to Varnhagen von Ense:

> I cannot concentrate on one subject for two or three days on end as some of my colleagues do. A hundred other thoughts would cross my mind and I should lose sight of the essential. When a subject preoccupies me, the work goes on within me while I am engaged on something quite different. Results come to fruition amidst apparent distraction. The best ideas, the most brilliant flashes of wit occur to me during meals, during interviews or while I am travelling. When my mind has become saturated I sit down to write and the arguments hang together of their own accord. When that point is reached interruptions do not disturb me. I can take up my work at any time where I left off. (quoted by Grunwald, p. 166)

The truth is that although he may not have the appearance of working, as a bureaucrat understands it, he is, in fact, always at work in the most important sense of thinking and directing.

Besides, shortly after the Congress of Vienna a kind of change was wrought in him. A confidential letter from the French ambassador, the marquis de Caraman, provides some evidence of this. It also provides a remarkable picture of the Minister's technique:

> Metternich is no longer the man you knew, and I can best sum up what I feel about him by saying that in the past year from being a frivolous, superficial person he has turned into a statesman. You will judge for yourself when you see him but I think you will have to agree that I am not wrong. Metternich today has enlarged his horizons by hard work and reflection; he is a good judge of men because he is neither passionate nor biased; he is sufficiently subtle to uncover their weaknesses and skilful enough to take advantage of them. A particular source of strength to him is that he never loses his head and is scarcely affected by injured pride. Obstacles do not upset him, and nothing is easier for him than to change direction if he feels that the line he has taken will lead nowhere. He is specially clever at recognizing blind alleys down which others may go. He patiently lets them go and then gets ready to help them out. This gives him a very great advantage. In this way he has taken charge of Prussia and of nearly all the German States. Today he is almost their arbiter and plays the leading rôle among them. Without seeking to, he literally dominates them and has become a kind of centre to which everything turns in the end.
>
> Metternich does not allow himself to become disheartened by too much detail, he tries to keep the objective in view and if he is turned aside from it he returns to it and does not get lost. He is ingenious in thinking up something new when old methods fail, and without exerting himself unduly he achieves what he sets out to do because all the time he wants to, and this continuous pressure which he has maintained without interruption ever since he became aware of the strength of his position and of the means at his disposal has made a new man of him. The vanities and follies of this world hardly touch him now, and from this has arisen his new way of life which I believe he has no desire to forsake. (quoted in G. de Bertier, *France and the European Alliance*, pp. 59–60)

Some years later Metternich could write to Caraman:

I have not given you news of Vienna, because I am as remote
from it as though I lived a great distance away. So true is this that
I know much better what is going on in Paris and Constantinople
than in the streets of our city, so blocked with snow. (Feb. 1829.
Arch. de Mme Firino-Martell)

The Minister is certainly well backed up. The Imperial Chancellery is a heavy machine: in 1817, according to the Imperial
Almanach, it comprises ten departments divided into two sections: the political section under the direct orders of the Chancellor: the administrative section directed by the Counsellor of
State (Staats-und-Konferenzrat), Joseph von Hüdelist, who con-
trols in particular censorship and the Press. The heads of department, with the no less sonorous titles of Counsellors of Court
(Hofräte) or Counsellors of the Chancellery (Staats-Kanzleiräte),
are men experienced in their profession, capable of imitating
their master's style and of reading his thoughts. They have the
assistance of secretaries (Hofsekretäre) and writers (Hofkonzi-
pisten).

Into the orbit of the chancellery are drawn other auxiliary
services (Hilfsämte): registration and dispatch of the mail, cipher
office, printing works, archives, treasury, accounts. It was in 1819
that Metternich began to use the lithograph for the reproduction
of important documents which he wanted to send to his ambassadors or to the Allied courts. The cipher office, as distinct from
the dark-room—which will be dealt with later—was also given
the task of translating documents into foreign languages. That
was no sinecure in such a government. Latin, which was the
official language in the kingdom of Hungary, and naturally also
of the Holy See, continued to be used in Austria itself for certain
ceremonial documents such as letters of credence, full powers,
acts of ratification and chancellery letters; German was used for
correspondence with envoys attached to the Federal Diet of
Frankfurt and to the secondary German courts, as well as for

reports to the Emperor and for communications between Ministers: and Italian, which was the official administrative language in the kingdom of Lombardy and Venice, was also frequently used in relations with other principalities of the peninsula. Finally, as we have seen, Metternich retained the use of French in what he called 'general transactions', and in the notes, memoirs, etc., which were exchanged between the principal embassies in Europe, as well as in written communications with his representatives at the courts, even in Berlin. When the Foreign Office in 1817 tried to get notes in English accepted, the Ballhausplatz replied by threatening to address notes to London only in German, which made the English recoil in horror.

In addition to staff drawn from the departments, Metternich is surrounded all the time by more intimate colleagues, forming a kind of Ministerial Cabinet: made up in part of humble copyists charged with a special task, and in part of his advisers who participate in the most intellectual aspect of his work. Of these none was more precious to him than Friedrich von Gentz, that eccentric personality who had left the service of Prussia for that of Austria. Until his death in 1832 this little man with the red hair and black spectacles was to Metternich a kind of spare brain, reading and writing for him, helping him to plan memoirs, dispatches, newspaper articles, manoeuvres, following him to congresses, quite unafraid to oppose him or to speak bluntly to him, maintaining personal relations with foreign statesmen, and even being given pensions by them. Metternich wrote of him:

> A man the like of which I have not found in the course of my long public life; having a character which from the very first made him give way easily in an extreme point, but which always brought him back to a recognition of the truth. There was a special quality about Gentz's mind and that was *positivism*, driven by him, if need be, to extreme limits. That is why he never could understand jokes, which he described as being nothing but the 'negation of a truth'. Thus Gentz was the first man to succumb to practical jokes and was their sworn enemy. (to Sir Travers Twiss, Apr. 26, 1856)

In spite of all the pens at work on his behalf, in spite of his declared principle 'not to do anything which he could get some-one else to do for him', Metternich sketches with his own hand the outlines of every important diplomatic dispatch, revises those which come from his departments after he has told them what they should contain; and naturally he wishes to read himself the political reports from all the Austrian ambassadors and Ministers, also reports from the police and other sources of information. If we add to these the almost daily conferences with the Emperor, the demands made on him by court and society, appointments, and private correspondence, it becomes clear that the last criticism that can be levelled against Metternich is that of laziness. Not until 1846 does he consent to leave the personal signing of work of secondary importance to an Under-Secretary of State.

The ambassadors of His Royal Apostolic and Imperial Majesty stand naturally in the front rank of the Chancellor's assistants. Chosen for a variety of reasons they seem to come from quite different backgrounds. The Austrian monarchy is receptive and takes its talent where it finds it. We meet in her diplomacy as in her army, side by side with subjects drawn from the different possessions of the Crown, Germans of every kidney, Italians, Belgians, even Frenchmen, families from Lorraine linked to the dynasty by tradition or *émigrés* of the Revolution. All are capable and all belong to the nobility; but while in some cases aristocratic blood opened to them a career in which their ability developed, in other cases ability raised them in the social hierarchy.

Metternich applies his principle of preservation to his em-bassies, leaving the occupants where they are for as long as possible. Esterhazy—Prince Paul—for example will remain in London from 1815 to 1842; Count Apponyi, in Paris, from 1826 to 1848, and it is the same in Rome whither Lützow was sent to replace him.

Of the first of these Metternich writes: 'I treated him like a son, and he loves me like a father.' (*Mémoires*, III, p. 449) What other Minister, indeed, would have shown such forbearance in face of the extravagances of an ambassador? Quite staggering are the details concerning Prince Paul's conduct as revealed in the private correspondence of the first Secretary, Neumann, in 1818. (*Staatskanzlei. Frankreich. Varia* 99) The ambassador, in the absence of his wife, indulges 'in every kind of unseemly behaviour hardly befitting the position he occupies'. He runs up debts, stops writing to his family, and does not even reply to his wife when she tells him of the birth of a child. His Excellency has got into the habit of coming down from his room at two in the afternoon and going out immediately, so much so that when Neumann wishes to talk business with his chief, he is obliged to go looking for him in the *salons* of London . . . or elsewhere. He hangs on to letters from Vienna without replying to them, without even opening them, allowing them to accumulate in his drawers. At one period which lasted for six weeks seven important dispatches were sent, not one of which was acknowledged. In his relations with the English he was equally casual. Twice in succession he was granted an interview with the Foreign Secretary, Lord Castlereagh, over a matter of considerable importance, and kept neither of them without a word of excuse. In the same way a ball for which he had issued invitations by word of mouth, was postponed three times, without a word to the guests.

Metternich, having sent his faithful Floret to London on a mission of inquiry, will satisfy himself with sending for the guilty man and giving him a good talking to . . . then returning him to his post for a new and lengthy term. It is true that in this instance he was dealing with the brother-in-law of his dear daughter Marie. But the same kindness and forbearance are apparent in other cases. In that, for example, of General Vincent, appointed ambassador to Paris after the second Restoration. This old soldier, loyal and conscientious but melancholic and misanthropic, took it upon himself, on the grounds that he was a widower and without much wealth, never to entertain, with the result that he was completely out of touch with public opinion; added to which he made life hell for his subordinates. As early as 1819, Metternich declared that the general was not cut out for the post; yet he was allowed to stay on until 1825 to enable him to reach retiring age without being subjected to the humiliation of being unattached or downgraded to a less distinguished appointment.

We have read the letters written by the Minister to the old servant of the State, preparing him for this retirement without wounding his pride. Nothing could be more delicate and generous.

One last example: Neumann, Austrian Minister at Florence, has expressed a desire to visit Rome. Metternich replies to him:

> What do you expect me to say about the journey you wish to make to Rome? Go or do not go, according to whether you feel you can do so without doing harm to the service. You are too experienced and too trustworthy a diplomat to need advice, especially advice from 300 leagues off. I authorize you to do what you want and at whatever time you deem it possible or convenient. (Mar. 22, 1846. Arch. Plasy)

A master who could treat his subordinates in this way was, deservedly, repaid by their loyalty.

An ambassador's rôle is of all the greater importance when difficulties of communication leave him with an independence of action which modern diplomacy has long since forgotten. Thus in 1822 a letter dispatched from Vienna by special courier normally takes seven days to reach Paris; by ordinary post ten or eleven days are needed. In the direction of Constantinople it is much worse. Couriers stick in quagmires or get held up by floods; and at the first sign of cholera in the provinces through which they must travel, sanitary precautions and quarantines pin them down.

Metternich therefore knows how to trust his agents by allowing them some freedom of action within the framework of their instructions. Here is one example: Apponyi thought it his duty to change something in a communication he had been instructed to give the French Government. The Chancellor replies:

> I duly appreciated the considerations which led you, in agreement

with the Russian ambassador, to modify some of the terms of this dispatch. Since I am convinced that delicate negotiations can only be properly handled if a Cabinet allows reasonable latitude in the actions of those deputed to carry out the measures, I have no objections to raise to the changes that you have introduced into the text of these instructions. (July 6, 1831. *Mémoires*, V, pp. 181–2)

The conductor of the orchestra spares no effort in his attempts to see that his instrumentalists are thoroughly acquainted with his intentions, that they identify themselves with his thinking, and see the operation as a whole. In times of crisis each of his representatives in the major capitals receives a copy of the notes sent to the others. More often than not the ambassador in Paris is instructed to forward dispatches addressed to London or Madrid. He receives them open—*sub volanti*—and he is advised to read them before sending them on their way. Occasionally ambassadors receive a carefully elaborated appraisal of the situation, 'one of those labours', said Metternich, 'which I am in the habit of setting down on paper *absque ira et studio*'. (to Neumann, Sept. 15, 1840) At the conclusion of a long dissertation of this nature, addressed to Apponyi, we read this declaration:

What I have just written has no value except as a formal clearing of the conscience, such as I like to set down, not only in response to a feeling which is not confined to the immediate present and therefore amounts, in my opinion, to an appeal to the judgment of future generations, but also with the honourable intention of acquainting the Emperor's representative with those feelings on which our Cabinet bases its opinions. (Jan. 29, 1827)

Finally, the beginning of each year offers the opportunity for a general look-round, in which the master pronounces his oracle on different European States.

The foundation of all political action is an exact estimate of the situation and factors involved. And so the statesman's first need is information:

I am the last person in the world to indulge in fanciful calculations. I always try to make sure of something solid on which it will be possible to base a calculation. I do not believe much, but I try to find out a great deal. (to Esterhazy, June 18, 1819)

We have seen the trouble Metternich took to understand the psychology of other statesmen. That is only one aspect of the constant effort to keep himself informed. He must know everything, even details which appear trivial. After asking Count Apponyi to try to find out what were the real thoughts of Michel Chevallier, economist of the Saint-Simon school, who had sent him a work, Metternich adds:

Do not imagine, *Monsieur l'ambassadeur*, that I shall attach more importance to all this than it deserves. I draw a big distinction between what it is necessary to know and what it is necessary to dread. In so many social upheavals, one endeavour more or less does not matter much, it is only when taken as a whole that things count, and as a whole is composed of parts, we should try to understand the latter exactly and never despise them. (Dec. 21, 1836)

Dates are an example of those details which he is careful to note:

Dates must play a big part in following the course of any intrigue. A comparison of dates is the easiest way to pick up the threads, and three, perhaps only two coincidences are sometimes enough to lead to the discovery of the origin of one of the threads. (to Zichy, Jan. 11, 1822)

Metternich himself always takes care to specify the dates of the documents to which he is referring.

I like to mark these different dates for you, *Monsieur l'ambassadeur*, seeing that when affairs are being conducted at a great distance, dates play a large part in the discussion of serious issues.

Vienna, by its very position, makes an admirable listening-post:

The geographical, moral and political situation of Austria is such that we never lack information. Everybody has some matter to

clear up with us, because we are more or less situated on everybody's road. Some come to us for consolation, others for remedies, others again do us the honour of being afraid of us and
as soon as that happens they try if they can to win us over.
Finally there are those who simply want to sound us. The result
of all this is that we learn much without having to bestir ourselves. Movement is never more easily observed than from a
fixed point. (to Esterhazy, Jan. 5, 1829)

The Chancellor is also a tireless reader of papers and political
tracts. For this he has an original procedure:

> I read almost all the tracts that are published. I have read Bignon's
> pamphlet in a quarter of an hour, and M. de Pradt's in five
> minutes. I begin with the title to see what it is about, then I read
> the end to find out where we are trying to get to: finally I glance
> through five or six pages by way of a sample, and that is all I need
> to satisfy myself as to the quality of the part I have not read.
> (Feb. 17, 1821. *Mémoires*, III, p. 456)

As for newspapers, his ambassadors see to it that he gets those
of the principal European capitals. He is specially eager for all that
is published in Paris. The *Journal des Débats* has no more assiduous
reader, but he also takes an interest in the small satirical sheets.
In March 1840 he asks Apponyi to take out a subscription for
him to the *Guêpes* of Alphonse Karr, and he adds:

> Generally speaking, Your Excellency is authorized to procure for
> my benefit a copy of any publication appearing in Paris which is
> similar to the *Guêpes*. They frequently serve to throw light on the
> situation there. (Mar. 5, 1840)

In his opinion, Louis-Philippe makes a big mistake when he
boasts of not reading the French Press. Metternich will never
cease to congratulate himself on not having followed his example:

> You are aware, my dear Hübner, that I have always been a con-
> scientious reader of newspapers. I have frequently been told that
> in doing so I am wasting my time. That is not my experience.

Man cannot know everything by his own resources. If he is concerned in public affairs he must take notice of what others are
thinking and wanting. There is a great difference between supposition and knowledge and there is no quicker or better way
of acquiring the latter than by reading what people themselves
are saying. (quoted by Breycha-Vauthier in the *Revue générale
belge*, Oct. 1957, pp. 46–47)

To gather and transmit information is certainly one of the
main duties of Austrian ambassadors. One of them, that old
campaigner, Vincent, thought he had dealt with a change of
Ministry in Paris by sending the newspapers carrying the announcement. Metternich scolds him:

> This knowledge is not enough. We wish to have the opinions,
> the convictions, and the judgment of the man who is set as a
> steady and well-informed observation post among the shifting
> sands.

Furthermore, he wants the opinions of his ambassadors at
other courts:

> I therefore request you to reinforce your correspondence con
> siderably, to extend it so that it covers those subjects which may
> seem to you of lesser importance. I even ask you to accelerate it
> as much as possible and not to hold it up for lack of a Cabinet
> courier. (Jan. 3, 1822)

Vincent's successor, Apponyi, will be more painstaking, but
even he will not escape an occasional prodding:

> Be so good, *Monsieur l'ambassadeur*, as to continue to observe
> carefully and actively all that is going on round you. What are
> most valuable to us are facts. Collect these, of whatever kind
> they may be, and endeavour to inform us of them lucidly and, if
> need be, quickly. (to Apponyi, May 3, 1832)

The consuls are also made to contribute. The consul at Marseilles is congratulated on the information he has supplied not
only about French naval armaments and the military units in his

area but also concerning the morale of the country and the movements of Italian refugees.

Alongside his diplomatic staff Metternich employs private informers, who send him periodically little reports gathered from the *salons* and antechambers. In Paris under the Restoration there are in his pay the following: a certain marquis Giamboni, who was an acquaintance of Talleyrand's; the comte de Senfft-Pilsach, formerly a Saxon diplomat, who was converted to Catholicism and who had influence with ultra-royalists and some religious orders; the baron d'Eckstein, another convert and a Jew, who was well placed in journalistic circles. Later, in the days of Guizot, the confidential adviser is a certain Mr. K. . . . (Klind- worth) whose initial keeps recurring in letters. The Rothschilds also give Metternich the advantage of their admirable network of information, and their couriers, more rapid than diplomatic ones, are often the first to bring stirring or fateful news to Vienna. Thus the bankers pay in kind for the facilities provided by the Austrian Government for their operations.

Finally there are the well-wishers:

> We really have the same facilities as the police, and it is not the men who are a burden on the Exchequer who most inspire our confidence. It is those who are devoted to conservative principles and who enjoy an independent position who are the most use to us.

> Any information they fail to supply the malcontents undertake to provide, and thus the official police are rather a means of control than of positive action. (to Apponyi, Sept. 11, 1835)

The chief of this Austrian police, Sedlnitzky, was, according to the French embassy, 'completely subservient to the Chancellor'. Apart from the advantages of getting from him early news of any discovery, Metternich found in him a means of playing on the Emperor's mind. If he wished to destroy some reputation in his master's estimation, the police records would describe him as 'revolutionary', an unpardonable imputation in the eyes of

Francis II.[1] (Montmorency-Laval to Rayneval, Oct. 30, 1820. *A. E. Corr. fol Austria*, 409)

The police of certain foreign countries were also made to contribute. Those of the German States pooled their information in the commission set up at Mainz at the time of the Carlsbad conferences in 1819. In the Italian States the police were always biddable. Co-operation was often offered and accepted by the French police themselves, both in the time of Decazes and of Villèle.

Finally, Metternich raised a sinister levy on all letters, Austrian or foreign, private or official, by means of the dark-room attached to the secret cypher (*Geheime Zifferkanzlei*) office of the Chancellery, an organization which he was always seeking to perfect. Nothing could be easier than to apply this system to letters leaving or coming in to the country. The chief of the postal services had a list of persons whose contacts were to be watched. He handed the communications over to the dark-room before forwarding them to their destination. As for foreign correspondence, Austria, encouraged by her geographical position, strove to attract within her frontiers as many postal lines of communication as possible, by offering the best forwarding conditions from the point of view of cost and time. It had been easy for him to put pressure on the Italian States, and all their correspondence, with the exception of that of Piedmont, passed through Austrian hands. When in 1830 France claimed the right to free herself from this dependence and to create new postal routes through Piedmont and by sea, Metternich's vigorous reaction was significant. Once the letters were in the hands of the chancellery's *Postlogisten*—highly paid specialists—it was child's play for them to break the seal invisibly, copy them, translate them, and if need be, decode them. The head of this department boasted of having

---

[1] One example will give an idea of the detailed work of the Austrian police. I had access in the State archives of Vienna to six huge folio-size folders in which was set down alphabetically, complete with references, all available information about individuals suspected of belonging to the secret revolutionary societies in Italy between 1820 and 1824. That is nothing compared with the piles of dossiers which linger on in the archives of the *Polizeihofstelle*, in spite of the outbreaks of fire in 1926 and the bombardments of 1944 which destroyed a good part of them.

broken 85 foreign codes, among them a particularly stubborn one used by Russia, the secret of which it had taken four years to reveal. A more rapid method was used in 1833 for the French code: it was simply 'borrowed' for a few hours from the room of the ambassador's son.

Traces of this work were left in the diplomatic archives of the Ballhausplatz, where it is not unusual to come across copies of letters passing between foreign ambassadors and their governments.[1] The process was so well known that more than once Metternich did not hesitate to make acknowledgement of intercepted letters in the presence of third parties—his ambassadors, naturally, but even foreign statesmen. On these occasions he never failed to make clear, with a cold humour, that the communications had fallen into his hands *by chance*.

A curious example of this concerns Chateaubriand while he was ambassador in Rome. On May 22, 1829, the great writer expressed his dissatisfaction to his Minister at the nomination of Cardinal Albani, a professed partisan of Austria, to the post of Secretary of State. He suggested a threatening move to induce the Pope to reverse his decision. This dispatch fell into the hands of Metternich, who lost no time in sending a copy of it to his own ambassador in Rome with instructions to read it to the Secretary of State. With one stone two birds: a grateful cardinal and a discredited French ambassador.

The example is doubly interesting in that Chateaubriand, from all appearances, did not entrust such a letter to the post but to an embassy courier. What conclusion can be drawn except that

---

[1] An amusing irony of fate, for Metternich himself became the victim of the process he used against others and in a domain in which he must have been particularly sensitive, because it was correspondence between him and his mistress, the comtesse de Lieven. Yet he took precautions. A letter from her, dated September 19, 1819, arrived at Paris in the dispatches of the English ambassador, Sir Charles Stuart. It was guarded against possible indiscretions by four envelopes: the first addressed to the baron de Binder, first Secretary in the Austrian embassy in Paris: the second also addressed to him with a message from his colleague in London: 'there is no need for me to recommend this to your care, my dear friend': the third addressed to the counsellor Floret in Vienna: the fourth a plain envelope intended to be handed to the Chancellor. In spite of all these attempts to put the curious off the scent, a copy of the letter found its way into the archives of the French police, where it was later brought to light with several others by Ernest Daudet. (*A travers trois siècles*, p. 168) The French police and their dark-room could, it seems, give some points to their Austrian counterparts.

Metternich had an accomplice in the chancellery of the French embassy itself? It is not an isolated incident and in the archives of Vienna are to be found communications of this kind—confidential memoirs and the like—which by their very nature could only have been gathered from foreign embassies.

All this justifies on the whole the proud satisfaction with which Metternich wrote in 1817:

> The sort of European police which we have set up on a scale far outstripping anything that has existed before has not let us down. I am convinced that hardly any plot could be hatched against the established order without our knowing about it from the start. (to Lebzeltern, June 28, 1817)

And to Dalberg, the French Minister at Turin whom he had met earlier that year in Florence, he wrote: 'You see in me the chief Minister of Police in Europe. I keep an eye on everything. My contacts are such that nothing escapes me.' (Foreign Affairs. Political correspondence. Austria. 398)

Yet one may wonder whether a statesman does not belittle himself by assimilating his functions to those of a Minister of Police. Is there not a danger that familiarity with police methods might lead to a deformity or a shrinking of the mind? That was the subtle observation made by the British *chargé d'affaires*, Gordon, who had accompanied Metternich on his journey to Italy in 1819:

> Nothing can surpass Prince Metternich's activities in collecting facts and information upon the inward feelings of the people. With a habit of making these researches he has acquired a taste for them, which gives no repose until he finds himself ignorant of nothing that was intended to be concealed. But it may be feared that the secrecy with which this taste is necessarily indulged leads him to attach too great importance to his discoveries. Phantasms are conjured up and magnified in the dark, which probably if exposed to light would sink into insignificance, and his informers naturally exaggerate their reports, aware that their

profit is to be commensurate with the display of their phantasmagoria. (Gordon to Castlereagh, July 17, 1819. P.R.O., F.O.
7/141)

It is not enough to keep a watch on the opinions of others, it is
also necessary as far as possible to orientate them. Metternich may
well detest journalism, but he is obliged to take account of it and,
better still, to make use of it himself. The Ballhausplatz is a work-
shop of political articles. Among those engaged in it are Josef von
Pilat, the romantic Friedrich Schlegel, Adam Müller, and above
all the invaluable Gentz, whose place was taken by a former professor of Berlin University, Karl Jarcke. Metternich enjoys wield-
ing the pen himself and more frequently still sketches the outline
of the articles he wishes to see published.

The Austrian newspapers are under his control. The tedious
Oesterreichische Beobachter is his recognized organ in which news
from home and abroad and inspired comment appear together
with official announcements:

> Every day the editor of this journal, Josef-Anton Pilat, comes to
> the Chancellery and, after receiving the master's orders, settles
> down in the antechamber to write the article for the next day,
> the text of which is immediately submitted to the Chancellor.
> (Sir H. Wellesley to Lord Dudley, Jan. 14, 1828, P.R.O., F.O.
> 7/204)

The *Wiener Zeitung* and the *Wiener Jahrbuch der Literatur* are
addressed to the intellectuals: their editors draw on the Chancellery budget and can make no objections to the suggestions that
come from higher up.

A more subtle way is to work on the foreign Press. The
Journal de Francfort, published in French and widely circulated in
every European country, serves as a syndicating agent. An
article appearing in this organ can later be reproduced in the
journals of Milan, Paris, Berlin, Brussels, and London without the
stigma that attaches to a governmental handout. Metternich
finances this paper and makes full use of its influence. On one or

two occasions, for example at the time of the Carlsbad conferences, he approaches the French Government to get them to
insert extracts from the *Journal de Francfort* and from the *Observateur autrichien* in the *Moniteur*. More often it is money that does
the trick, for it is not so very difficult to find discreet intermediaries to sell themselves. In October, 1820, Metternich boasts:
'Anyone who picks up a copy of the *Journal des Débats* will read
me without knowing it. For hardly a week passes without my
sending an article to that journal.' (*Mémoires*, III, p. 370) This
occurred, however, at a moment when the *Journal des Débats* was
agitating in favour of the Right. Later Metternich treated it as a
'disgusting rag' (to Lebzeltern, Aug. 11, 1824) which 'in the end
developed criminal tendencies'. (to Vincent, Oct. 25, 1824)

The London Press is also called in to help. The Chancellor
writes to Esterhazy on Jan. 31, 1822:

> Please try to get the enclosed article inserted in the *Morning
> Chronicle*, but on the strict understanding that its origin is never
> revealed. If you achieve this, send me the paper in which it
> appears, and accompany it with an open dispatch showing that
> even in London its contents are taken for a sham. You can send
> the dispatch by ordinary post.

From this last remark it can be seen that Metternich is relying
on the dark-room to further his little scheme.

Five years later he has the opportunity of explaining to the
same Esterhazy his strategic plan for a campaign conducted
against British opinion. After congratulating him on getting
several articles into the *Morning Chronicle*, he adds:

> Please do not be satisfied, *mon Prince*, with having made a start.
> The important thing to grasp is a proper division of responsibility
> between the London embassy and the Cabinet here. This is to be
> found in the following general rule: the publication of any
> *commentary* must be decided *by us*; the contradiction of state
> ments put forward as facts by mistake, in bad faith, or out of
> spite, should be regarded as the *common responsibility of both
> parties*. It is not unusual to see facts or assertions, the falsity of

which is strikingly obvious, given an airing in certain papers; other assertions conceal a venomous meaning. Such deviations from the truth can be usefully contradicted only at their point of origin. Attacks against articles that are absurdly false wear the critics out. Consequently such articles should be left to fall into oblivion, as they quickly will if they are not disturbed. The more serious assertions must be contradicted and the controversy gains weight if it is conducted by pens that are genuinely independent. There remains the question of grave accusations. These should be *drawn attention to* in London and *thundered against* in Vienna. Good disclaimers in the English Press give us real opportunities.

Metternich supplies him with several paragraphs which might be used as material for articles, and adds:

We for our part will lose no opportunity to get even powerful commentaries published, but the choice of them must be left entirely to us, for we alone are in a position to judge the effect that such publications will have in those places where it is necessary for us to produce it.

The effect to be produced, in other words the influence to be exerted over the minds of those who are at the head of affairs— it is precisely by these means that diplomatic battles are prepared and waged. It remains to be seen, with the help of a few examples, how this manoeuvre is carried out.

3. Diplomatic Strategy

How does Metternich react to the first shock of an unforeseen event, the Neapolitan revolution of 1820, for instance?

This is fine news, *mon cher comte*! I confess that at this very moment I know that I have a head and two arms and that one is silent and the others are still. That is how I embark on all important affairs. . . . To stand firm, to remain calm and not to lose one's head are the duties of everyone who has a task to perform. (to Zichy, July 15, 1820)

The next step is to light up his lantern:

> It is not our way to begin with a judgment. On the contrary we do not allow ourselves to form one until the problem becomes in our opinion sufficiently clear. (to Vincent, July 10, 1822)

Therefore care will be taken to wait until events sort themselves out and the sources of information have been checked:

> In moments of crisis a Minister is never far from going astray when he allows himself to form a judgment based on the information of one isolated subordinate. (to Zichy, Apr. 12, 1820)

It is essential also to know the reactions of other governments. A quite remarkable 'special' letter, addressed to Paul Esterhazy, explains Metternich's method of working:

> A question comes in from Petersburg, or it may be from Paris or London. I seize it and on it base my reasoning for or against. This reasoning I pass on to the three embassies and the replies I receive show me in what material and moral light the coalition Cabinets see the details of the problem. Once that point has been reached I can co-ordinate, direct and criticize my own actions. I can oppose in one direction and lend support in another. I can modify my language and adapt it to suit my hopes and my doubts as well as my fears. If you do not confront the English Minister with my own words I am deprived of the advantage I am looking for. The same thing happens if you do not reply in detail to the communications which I send you and which you will have passed on to those Ministers. I feel paralysed and general expressions of opinion, however satisfying they may be in themselves, do not fulfil their object [. . . .]

> Being in the habit of speaking perfectly frankly to you, I will tell you where the fault lies. There is not enough bite in your approach to the English Ministers. You know that I do not belong to the *violent* school of foreign Ministers, but I calculate positions. . . . We must speak firmly and insist on replies that are no less precise. . . .

Therefore speak, *mon cher Prince*, but when you speak use our own words and insist on their being approved or rejected. I appreciate that you may encounter certain difficulties with the Duke (of Wellington) and Lord Dudley: in the former little faculty for grasping the finer points of a matter and in the latter a deplorable butterfly-mindedness, but if you find difficulty in getting an audience between the pair of them, try the following method: write out short extracts from my pieces and put them in the form of demands. Insist on replies to numbers 1, 2, 3 . . . this always succeeds and often persuades those on whom it is practised to make an effort to read with care the document of which, in the first place, they were only given the bare bones. (Feb. 12, 1828)

A few rules will help in the interpretation of the mass of information that has been assembled. In addition to that of 'the calculation of interests', referred to above, there is this one:

In the judgment which I permit myself to form on the ways of men and even of governments, I start always from one simple rule of calculation. I am convinced that anything that is good in itself must be capable of being expressed clearly and precisely. The moment I come across words that are not very clear or that are positively wrong, I am left with the conclusion that they are either *mistaken* or *deceitful*. (to Zichy, Mar. 8, 1823)

This first phase, a time for gathering information and for reflection, cannot be prolonged without risk:

Whenever men who are responsible for important matters of State allow themselves to wait for fate to lead them, things go wrong just as they do in the case of the ship that leaves the setting of its course to chance. (to Wellington, June 14, 1824)

Meditation more or less conscientiously pursued becomes crystallized in the end into a plan of action:

I do not always sleep equally well. When a thought takes hold of me to the exclusion of everything else I often wake up. When that happens I may spend as much as an hour lying in one position and puzzling it out. It is then that I feel the full weight of the burden I am bearing and it seems beyond my strength. Difficulties and complications assail me, but I always end by hearing a voice inside me rising up against every obstacle. I then imagine myself getting bigger and I end up by feeling immense. The fact is that during those hours when the soul is undistracted by outside influences everything runs to extremes. Exhausted, I go off to sleep again and on waking the next morning I find that a plan has taken shape in my head. This plan is not the product of my brain but is in some way born of itself. (Aug. 20, 1820. *Mémoires*, III, p. 367)

Premeditated action must be carefully calculated in accordance with the objective:

We consider it to be a general rule that however important a measure may be, however necessary and even urgent, there must always be a proper balance between the object aimed at and the means by which it is to be attained . . . It is possible for immense benefits to be sought at a price beyond their real value. To tackle the most formidable evil with exaggerated remedies is to invite the bitter regret of having substituted for calamities to which events outside our control have given rise others for which we are solely and directly responsible. (to Vincent, May 15, 1825)

And so:

On those occasions when the natural order of things comes to the assistance of a government's policy, wisdom should dictate that the government limit its activity to encouraging and supporting this natural force. (to Apponyi, Mar. 2, 1826)

But prudence must not be confused with timidity:

In any situation where each of the possible lines of action is fraught with difficulty, the strongest line is the best. (to Vincent, Jan. 30, 1823)

Any plan conceived in moderate terms must fail when the circumstances are set in extremes. (to Vincent, Dec. 2, 1822)

Also, if a plan is to be practical it must be broad and resilient enough to be capable of adaptation to unforeseen circumstances:

> In a moment of crisis, the clever navigator must know how to take in sail and to vary his canvas according to the needs of the moment. Any plan which descended to details would in most cases be in danger of going wrong, just as nothing would be more false and dangerous . . . than the absence of any overall plan. (to Zichy, Apr. 12, 1820)

This method has another advantage:

> When we are called upon to handle important matters we tackle them vigorously, and for this to happen it is necessary that the course we are following should not only be clear in the eyes of the Cabinet but should also be made clear in the eyes of the public.

> The most effective means of achieving that is to define frankly the overriding principle concerned and at the same time to assess accurately those factors which should ensure its success. (to Neumann, Sept. 28, 1840)

Finally, in some cases abstention becomes necessary:

> Whenever those facts are lacking which are necessary to indicate the really effective remedy, or when the most suitable one can be seen but cannot be applied because our hands are tied, our principle is to refrain from action and to hand over to others in a better position a responsibility which we are not prepared to shoulder. We leave it to time to procure for us the information we need. (to Neumann, Mar. 30, 1842)

When we turn to action, the important thing is to get off to a good start:

> I believe that success and defeat, happy solutions and dangers are, in any matter, directly linked with the points of departure. In what is unavoidable, the provisions of men and of Cabinets must be limited to determining this point of departure and to seeing to it that mistakes, false pretensions, and isolated ambitions do not cause it to be lost sight of or cause action to deviate from its original objective. (to Wellington, May 8, 1823)

The diplomatic offensive is launched by a discussion aimed at gaining the approval of his partners. Metternich believes in the power of reason, which is, needless to say, always on his side. One comes across many observations in his correspondence like this: 'The evidence of reason being entirely on our side, our triumph was bound to follow'. (to Esterhazy, May 20, 1818) 'He thinks he can bring the rest to his way of thinking.'

> Strong in my conscience and in the uprightness of my views, and knowing how to rise above considerations of human respect whenever I think that I may serve the cause of good, I do not spare those who do not deserve to be spared. I am persuaded that even if I do not succeed in making a Cabinet change its mind, I can at least, by speaking the plain truth, stop its progress down the slippery slope. This method has already succeeded more than once in my dealings with Russia and we have by no means exhausted the uses of it. (to Lebzeltern, Jan. 19, 1824)

These exchanges of view, these discussions, normally follow two parallel paths: on the one hand, conversations with the ambassadors of the Powers at Vienna, relayed by them to their respective governments; on the other hand, correspondence sent to the ambassadors of Austria which serves as texts for their conversations with foreign Ministers.

With the ambassadors of other nations Metternich establishes himself at the earliest opportunity on terms of open friendship. He receives them as often and for as long as they wish. Conversations begun in council are sometimes continued in the *salon*. The marquis de Caraman reveals that the two of them used to talk interminably until past midnight in the Chancellor's garden during the summer. Metternich opens his dispatches in his presence, reads him passages from them as they pass through his hands. If there is too much of it or if there is something else requiring to be done he instals the ambassador in a corner of his office where he can study at leisure the documents that interest him.

When the Chancellor is in one of his summer residences, at

Johannisberg, Königswart, or Plass, the ambassadors are invited to stay and in this way the diplomatic work can be carried on in a pleasantly relaxed atmosphere. 'I do not think,' says Caraman, 'that it is possible to conduct business in a more agreeable manner.' (to Richelieu, Aug. 3, 1816. *Fonds Richelieu, Sorbonne*)

In some cases, fairly rare ones, the conversation has been deemed so important that Metternich has taken care to draw up an account and to have lithograph copies made of it for the use of his principal ambassadors. The publishers of the Chancellor's *Mémoires* printed an example of this, three conversations with General Belliard, envoy extraordinary of Louis-Philippe, in August 1830. It is clearly not an exact transcription and Metternich takes care to give himself a good part in it; nevertheless, there can be found in it, in an abbreviated form, that unbridled verbosity of the Chancellor and those 'unending digressions' which in the words of another ambassador, the duc de Laval, made conversation with him so painful. It was not unusual to have to endure an hour's lecture or more before being able to open one's mouth and come to the point.

Correspondence with ambassadors takes up the greater part of his daily work. With from two to four deliveries a month for the most important embassies, the relentless accumulation of this correspondence over forty years has created a mountain of archives, a great part of which will defy for ever any attempt at publication or detailed research.

The art of the diplomatic dispatch as practised by Metternich has probably never been surpassed. Not from the point of view of style which remains too often diffuse and colourless, but because under his system correspondence is intended not only to enlighten ambassadors, to supply them with arguments, to determine lines of action, but also to furnish them with an effective instrument. This is obtained by a process that might be called 'three-tiered correspondence'.

British diplomacy at that time knew something of the same sort, but that system was conceived as being a subordinate function of the Parliamentary system. There were three kinds of letter; official, numbered dispatches, which Parliament could insist on having communicated to it and might even lead to an official publication (Blue Book); confidential or secret dispatches, without consecutive numbers, from which the Minister could quote extracts if the need arose: and special correspondence between the chief Secretary of State and his agents abroad. Unlike the first two, which have to be consigned to the archives of the Foreign Office or of the embassies, these last remain in the possession of those to whom they are sent and can never be used publicly.

In the system used by the Ballhausplatz the division of letters into three categories—official, reserved, and secret—has nothing to do with the requirements of their *point of origin*, nor with any control of public opinion. It is entirely conceived as a function of the point of arrival, of the effect to be produced.

The uses of the *official* dispatch are always ostensible. The ambassador can read it or give a copy of it to the Foreign Minister and to his colleagues in the Diplomatic Corps. It is drawn up in such a way that its eventual publication could not be embarrassing. The *reserved* dispatch is considered to have been written exclusively for the ambassador's information; but it is drawn up in such a way that he could if necessary communicate it, as proof of the sincerity of opinions expressed in the official letter or as a mark of confidence designed to make a favourable impression on the person to whom it is addressed. Sometimes it may be communicated to one or several of the ambassadors of other Powers whose goodwill is desired. Is not the best way to make an idea prevail to plant it in several places at the same time? The echo of it which will resound from the different capitals will give it the value of a sort of unanimous consent.

Finally, the *secret* letter designed as a guide for the ambassador, will give him the innermost thoughts, the real idea behind the manoeuvre, and will at the same time provide him with instructions on the use to be made of the first two documents. To these three documents arising out of diplomatic correspondence and which will have gone through the departments, is sometimes added a fourth, the 'private' letter, from the Chancellor's own hand: on a more familiar note (My dear Paul . . . My dear Count . . .) it explains a detail, adds a confidential note, encourages, scolds, congratulates.

There is no lack of examples to illustrate this method. The difficulty is that they do not lend themselves to a brief summary: it would be necessary to explain all the circumstances. Here is one, condensed as well as may be. The occasion is a *démarche* made by the Czar Alexander I in 1822. The autocrat proposed the formation of a 'European' army with the object of intervening against the revolutions in Spain and Portugal. Under the date of May 7, Metternich replies to his ambassador Lebzeltern with a triple dispatch.

The official dispatch, which will be seen by the Czar's Ministers, is brief enough: England and France certainly cannot be counted on to help; and to what dangers would the King of Spain not be subjected? In any event before giving a reply the Emperor of Austria will wait to 'hear the views of other courts on the question as a whole, a question so serious that only the combined intelligence of the Powers can ensure a satisfactory result'.

The reserved dispatch is intended to be read to the Czar himself in the course of an interview which he will grant to the ambassador, but with no Ministers present. The opening paragraph straightway places the proposed step under the banner of the Holy Alliance, so dear to the heart of Alexander:

> In all confidence I feel I must put myself on the same footing as at Laybach and beg His Imperial Majesty of all the Russias to understand and interpret just as he did on that occasion those observations of my own conscience which it may be given to me to make about the affair as a whole.

After this exordium, Metternich develops at length the difficulties he sees in the realization of this undertaking, stressing in particular the danger of seeing England detach herself from the Alliance, and the risk of provoking disturbances in France.

The *secret* dispatch bluntly describes the Russian proposal as 'absolute nonsense'. The Chancellor explains it to himself as the intrigues of Pozzo di Borgo, Russian ambassador in Paris, and of Capo d'Istria, foreign Minister in Russia. Capo d'Istria had been hoping for some time to provoke a Russian intervention in favour of the Greek insurgents.

So far Metternich has managed to avert the danger by extolling the principles of the Alliance and by building up the moral pressure of all the other Powers. Capo d'Istria's little game amounts to this: on the one hand to detach Alexander from the idea of the Alliance, by providing him with a concrete example of the way in which all his generous impulses come up against the selfish and sinister opposition of Austria; on the other hand, a kind of blackmail against all the other Powers, showing them a picture of the Czar devoured by restless activity, and putting such fear into them that they will resign themselves to seeing this activity find an outlet in the East rather than risk the intervention of the Russian army in Western Europe.

As for Pozzo, who is probably behind this scheme, his object is to regain over his master, and over affairs in general, the influence he lost as a result of the fall of the Richelieu Ministry some months before. 'This ambassador wants some activity. The soil of France not being suitable, he has turned to Spain.'

This counter-offensive of Metternich's, together with other manoeuvres, which we cannot go into here, was to end in an unexpected success, for it prompted Alexander to dispense completely with Capo d'Istria's services.

In the same way even the communications of ambassadors must be capable, if the need arises, of serving Metternich's cause, when he has them read to the representatives of the other courts at Vienna. That is why they are also frequently divided into *official* and *secret*. Metternich is careful to explain to his correspondents what he expects from them in this connection. In July 1823, for example, he is trying to destroy the influence which he supposes Pozzo di Borgo to have over his master. This ambassador, too well disposed towards the French Minister, Chateaubriand, induces the Czar to believe that he is strongly supporting the point of view of the Alliance over the question of French intervention in Spain. And so Metternich invites his ambassador in Paris to send dispatches complaining of some pertinent fact which will give the lie to the attitude Pozzo pretends to hold: for example, Pozzo's refusal to persuade Chateaubriand that there should be periodic meetings between the ambassadors of the Alliance:

> Tell me that and more, and I shall know how to take advantage of these complaints, which will come quite naturally from your pen because they concern the failure to carry out a wish that has been expressed both by the Emperor our August Master and by His Imperial Majesty of all the Russias. I shall be able to put such a dispatch to the best possible use.

Communications which pass through the medium of an ambassador do not prevent Metternich from trying to establish wherever he can a direct contact with those who control the foreign policy of other countries. Here is what happens in the case of France: each time a new Minister takes up the portfolio of foreign affairs, Metternich loses no time in sending him a friendly letter of congratulation. Then, depending on whether circumstances require or allow it, there starts up a kind of dialogue, in which he tries to gain the confidence of the French statesman, to hint at good advice, and to get some insight into his private thoughts. We have published elsewhere examples of these exchanges of letters which are of a unique kind, half diplomatic, half private.

Metternich, driven by his zeal for effective action, always prefers to make contact at the point where policy is really decided. When General Dessolles, President of the Council in 1819, is Minister of Foreign Affairs, it is to Decazes that Metternich addresses himself. When the inept Damas is in office (1825–7) Metternich does not waste ink on him but goes straight to Villèle, President of the Council. When in 1829 the titular Minister, Portalis, emerges as nothing more than an uncertain instrument in the hands of his departmental chiefs, Metternich has no hesitation in addressing himself—he the Prince-Chancellor—to a modest 'employee', a certain Bourjot, head of the Foreign Affairs Department, who is responsible for relations with Austria. Conversely, when he finds, after 1830, that it is the King, and not his more or less ephemeral Ministers, who directs foreign policy, he starts a correspondence with him which lasts for some years and which reaches its climax in 1836. In that particular instance a direct correspondence would have been awkward for Louis-Philippe, and so Metternich uses his ambassador Apponyi as intermediary. The latter is instructed to read to the King the message which has been written to him with this object in view—the use he is to make of it having been revealed to him in a *secret* dispatch—and to render a faithful report of all the observations made by the King of the French. Metternich explains:

> I maintain with King Louis-Philippe a system of explanations, which I allow myself to describe as *direct*, not in order to discover what he wants, for I do not have to have it from his mouth to know that, but because I consider it useful to keep a channel open by which to inform him of the truth and to leave him in no doubt as to what we want, and equally as to what we do not want and will not permit. The more the King will do justice to the soundness of our thinking and to the frankness of our attitude, the more he is likely to feel obliged to moderate the outbursts of a detestable policy. (to Apponyi, May 13, 1834)

The most assiduous and shrewd correspondence does not take the place of those virtues which Metternich attributes to the spoken word, to his word. He always strives, it has been said, for a direct contact:

> Explanations between Ministers resemble, in more ways than one, reconciliation in the home. The tongue becomes looser, the heart opens, and the need to make oneself understood sometimes outweighs the dictates of a cold, hard calculation. (to Esterhazy, Aug. 14, 1830)

In such circumstances meetings between responsible Ministers appear to him to be the most effective method of settling important affairs of state. On one occasion he says:

> It has been shown that not one single genuine difference separates the courts of Berlin, Paris, and Vienna . . . in the Levant affair . . . that be so, let the three Cabinets work enthusiastically together to agree on the best choice of form. This will always be found . . . by observing the ordinary rules of healthy diplomacy. Little in writing, made up for by a correspondingly greater number of meetings, these discussions being concentrated under one roof, and the decisions reached and set down with the greatest care. That is the usual form and the one already used to good purpose on many occasions. (to Zichy, Feb. 25, 1826)

Practice establishes a scale in these international meetings. At the top *the congress*, solemn assembly attended by the sovereigns themselves, surrounded by a constellation of Ministers and dignitaries—such were the congresses of Aix-la-Chapelle, Troppau, Laybach, and above all Vienna. The springs that are the driving force behind these great machines are adjusted and wound up in the corridors, and the plenary sessions, the results of which are ratified by protocols, are only the outward show. Metternich only risks attending them after he has obtained the agreement of the parties in question by means of special conversations, continued afterwards by exchanges of notes.

It is clearly a very different conception from that which can be seen at work today in the assemblies of the United Nations. A very curious text enables us to guess at what Metternich would have made of that organization. These observations were inspired by the untimely claim of the King of Wurtemberg, who had protested, at the time of the Congress of Verona, against the kind of dictatorship exercised by the Great Powers alone:

> The government of Stuttgart appears singularly displeased with the form of these congresses. Would it replace this form by some constitution which would turn them into popular assemblies? Must European politics be subjected to a representative diplomatic system? Would the most complicated matter and the

most delicate problems perchance gain anything by being settled in meetings of forty or fifty Minister-delegates, independent of each other, voting by a show of hands, reaching, by means of a majority that would often be problematical and inadmissible, decisions on matters which an intimate meeting of three or four governments, experienced in prudence, hardly manage to settle satisfactorily? (*Mémoires*, IV, p. 31. See also on this question of congresses *Mémoires*, V, p. 407)

One step below the congress is the *conference*, a meeting of plenipotentiaries, who can only be the ambassadors in whichever capital is chosen, provided *ad hoc* with special powers. 'In principle it is always necessary to hold conferences in those places where the strongest action is to be taken.' (Oct. 13, 1830. *Mémoires*, V, p. 661) Hence the conference of the allied ambassadors which operated in Paris from 1816 to 1818. It enjoyed a wide degree of autonomy and the plenipotentiaries were not obliged to refer matters to their governments except in the event of disagreement between them or in matters of the first importance. Sometimes there will be two conferences, one on top of the other. Thus in 1824 the representatives of the Powers at Madrid meet regularly, but they take their orders from their ambassadors in Paris, which capital is considered as the sorting-house and meeting-ground for all the affairs of the Iberian peninsula.

Yet this system of conferences caused Metternich some disappointments:

The shape of the conferences is my own invention. I introduced it as early as 1813, and it remained in all its purity just so long as the old Alliance also remained pure. Once liberalism gained the upper hand in France and England, these assemblies degenerated. . . . For a conference between Powers to be of use, it is in the first place necessary that *the object of the meeting should be precisely defined and that it should be correct*. Next, it needs to be well organized, for without this, meetings quickly turn into real anarchy. That is what happened in London, where the element of vagueness in the minds of the British Cabinet was communicated to the conference as a whole. (to Apponyi, Jan. 25, 1852)

In another long letter (Dec. 8, 1832, *Mémoires*, V, pp. 415–18) he explains that where the London Conference went wrong was in arrogating to itself real powers, in cutting adrift from its principals, and in tending to become a kind of constituted authority whose decisions might contradict the intentions of the governments concerned.

These inconveniences make it preferable on more than one occasion to use the even simpler formula of the 'point of contact' or of the 'centre of information'. What Metternich means by this is explained in a dispatch of Sept. 30, 1819, to Lebzeltern on the occasion of the anxiety which had been roused by the internal state of France. This had given rise to a Russian proposal for the revival of the old conference of ambassadors in Paris:

> Let the four courts agree among themselves on the use of one of their capitals as a common point of contact, open to exchanges of opinion of every kind, and to the proposal and circulation of plans as might be called for by self-interest or by the unchanging and established principles of the Alliance.

This system will be strongly urged at the time of the trouble in Greece, but without success. It was, indeed, too evident that the motive behind the procedure was the concentration in Metternich's hands of the reins of every negotiation.

We should now proceed to look at those different processes in action, but would not that amount to going over the whole of European politics during the first half of the nineteenth century? Yet it is possible to point out some of the Chancellor's favourite manoeuvres.

Perhaps the one most frequently employed is what might be called 'the occupation of the arena'. If Metternich sees a question looming on the horizon, he immediately takes cognizance of it, and before anyone else can, throws out a proposal. In this way he is able to cut the ground from under the feet of those who might make suggestions dangerous to Austrian interests. A perfect example is to be found in the preparation for the Congress of

Aix-la-Chapelle in 1818. Metternich suspects Russian policy, directed by his intimate enemy Capo d'Istria, of wanting to take advantage of the meeting of sovereigns to restore to the Czar Alexander the rôle of principal mediator in European affairs. The game would consist of weakening the Quadruple Alliance of 1815, at the heart of which Russia is held in check by the Anglo-Austrian *entente*. In its place or, at least, on top of the old alliance would be set a 'Grand Alliance', which France and the Bourbon monarchies of Spain and Naples, all of them more or less clients of Russia, would be made to join. How is this danger to be avoided? As early as 1818 Metternich took the offensive. Affecting great concern that the deliberations of the approaching Congress should be effective over the widest possible field, and pretending to be anxious to avoid any risk of its raising hopes contrary to the settlement reached by the Congress of Vienna, he obtained from his allies a decision in principle to the following effect: (1) that only the representatives of France should be admitted; (2) that no questions other than the end of the occupation of France and the maintenance of the Quadruple Alliance should be raised. Thanks to this the Congress pursued its course without disagreeable incidents. And Metternich could write at the time it came to an end:

> I never saw a prettier little congress. It will not cause me any irritation. Everything is wonderfully well arranged. It will do us credit. Our affairs, the most hazardous and the least troublesome alike, pursued their course as though of their own accord.

Another favourite method of the prince's, related to the one that has just been mentioned, is that of the counter-barrage. In this case the initiative consists of proposing a measure that corresponds to the one he is trying to avoid, but which is calculated to draw its poison. An example: mention has already been made of the idea put forward in 1822 by the Czar of forming a European army to intervene against the Spanish revolution. This plan was likely to be brought forward again at the time of the Congress of Verona in the autumn of the same year. Metternich wished to avoid at all costs seeing Russian uniforms in Germany or Italy, and he was also afraid that too obtrusive an action by the Alliance would only feed liberal and nationalist passions in France itself. What, then, is to be done? To stand once again in the way of Alexander's wishes?

On the contrary. Metternich will set things going by making a proposal along the same lines, and thus he will be in a position to blunt the sharpness of the most dangerous thrusts. In his plan the military precautions to be taken by the Alliance will consist on the one hand of the concentration of a Russian army called a 'reserve army', which will remain inside Russia but on the frontier; and on the other hand of the reinforcement of Austrian troops in northern Italy. Announcing this decision to his ambassador in Paris, Metternich explains:

> This step is not alien to us. On the contrary, it was proposed by us to the Russian Cabinet on two grounds, its genuine usefulness and our desire to remain in control of a matter which otherwise the Emperor Alexander would have started on, although our opinion was not favourable to such an action. (to Vincent, Apr. 4, 1823)

A third variation of the procedure consists of proposing a plan which he knows to be impractical, but which corresponds to one that has been put forward by another government and which is not acceptable. In this way it can be arranged for everything to become swallowed up in a discussion which has deliberately been made involved and interminable. In 1817 the question of Barbary pirates in the Mediterranean was much in the minds of the great Powers. England submitted a plan for maritime police, hoping thereby to force into the open recognition of the 'right of visit', so odious to Austria and France. As for Russia, she sought to acquire a naval base in the Western Mediterranean, at the same time making a great display of her concern for the security of commerce. Then Metternich unfolds his plan: the resurrection of the Order of the Knights of Malta, who could be charged with the duty of policing the seas without rousing suspicions of hegemony. And there he is exploring tirelessly every avenue and supporting the plan with every kind of magnificent argument. In fact, as Gentz confesses, 'It was not with any great seriousness that he gave encouragement to such a fanciful idea. It is a weapon that he is in the habit of using against those who might by means of more genuine and dangerous plans cause troublesome complications.'

Numerous other procedures have been put into operation by the great conjurer of Vienna, but the description of them cannot easily be reduced to simple terms: to appreciate the skill a detailed knowledge of the circumstances is required. How, for example, is it possible to summarize in a few lines the long, diplomatic defensive war waged by Metternich from 1821 to 1828 to prevent a Russian attack on Turkey? 'To make this rupture look more absurd in respect of the motives that will have to be produced just the same, and by this means to make it more difficult—that is my whole secret', he wrote on April 24, 1822, to Esterhazy. In spite of this system which was diligently pursued, this bulwark of paper—dispatches and memoranda—was finally to collapse under the pressure of events, dragging down with it the system of the Alliance itself, 'the ark of the covenant'.

In the painful isolation in which Austria found herself during the years 1828 and 1829 Metternich managed to save her face and to make a virtue out of what he had suffered:

> To get close to what cannot be reached without disaster, is to expose oneself to great risks. To attempt to fuse two elements which by nature are incapable of it, is a fruitless endeavour. Let us remain what we are and we shall be stronger than he who aims at something he has no right to be. (to Lebzeltern, Mar. 3, 1825)

When he has exhausted every means of persuasion, Metternich comes to a stop—a favourite expression of his—and leaves it to time to work the improvements he desires:

> One of the conditions of success . . . is to make the best of the positions one has taken up. To try to reverse them is to make the wrong choice of method. Instead of making those go back who

have chosen a different route in order to achieve the same end, it is necessary to allow them to advance, taking care, just the same, to mark the spot where it has been arranged to meet them. (to Apponyi, Sept. 18, 1840)

The great game of diplomacy leads to more disappointments than successes, to more trouble than glory. 'One is less concerned with those who prevent the cannon going off than with those who fire it. The one is more necessary than the other, but the world runs after the noise.' (to the comtessse de Lieven, Dec. 6, 1818)

Metternich has been rather badly treated by the voice of history, whose verdict he confidently awaited. His patient spider's webs, a hundred times smashed and a hundred times renewed, will always evoke less admiration than a single battle of Austerlitz. However, in his realm, where the art of persuasion holds sway, where the only effective force is the power of words working in the service of the intelligence and the will, there remains one master whose company it will always be profitable to seek.

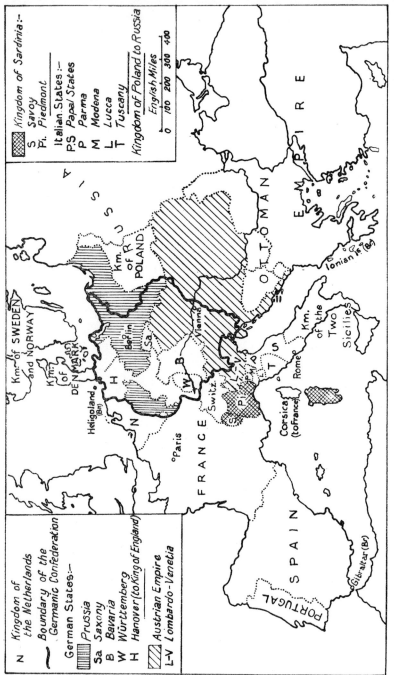

EUROPE AT THE CONGRESS OF VIENNA, 1815

Kingdom of Sardinia:—
S. Savoy
Pi. Piedmont

Italian States:—
P.S. Papal States
P. Parma
M. Modena
L. Lucca
T. Tuscany

Kingdom of Poland to Russia

English Miles
0   100   200   300   400

N   Kingdom of
     the Netherlands
─   Boundary of the
     Germanic Confederation
German States:—
     Prussia
Sa. Saxony
B   Bavaria
W   Württemberg
H   Hanover (to King of England)
     Austrian Empire
L-V Lombardo-Venetia

CHAPTER FOUR

Holy Alliance and Alliance

ISTORY CERTAINLY contains curious ironies! Is it not strange, for example, that Metternich's name should be associated from the start with an act—the Holy Alliance —the birth of which he would willingly have avoided, of which he never spoke with sincerity except to disparage it, and to which in his heart of hearts he refused to attach the slightest practical significance? It is no use adding that in establishing this link between Metternich and the Holy Alliance one is, of course, referring to the alliance of conservative Powers in Europe that was brought into being by the treaty of November 25, 1815, for it still happens that the best historians esteem the pact of September 26, 1815, to be an important element in what is called the 'Metternich system'. Therefore it is desirable to remove any doubts on that score at the outset.

I.

The account given by Metternich himself of the birth of the Holy Alliance makes it clear that the Emperor of Austria and his Minister were taken unawares by a proposal in which they saw no good, and they agreed to it only in order to avoid offending the Czar Alexander. Was this account, which appears to be dated 1829 'At the time of writing' . . . (1829 . . . *Mémoires*, I, p. 139), to some extent intended by the statesman to relieve him of any responsibility for an institution that was much discredited at the time? By no means. Castlereagh's account of the incident, given at the time, confirms the reticence of the Austrian Minister at every point, and even underlines it:

> He communicated to me in great confidence the difficulty in which the Emperor of Austria felt himself placed; that he felt great repugnance to be party to such an act and yet was more apprehensive of refusing himself to the Emperor's application; that it was quite clear that his mind was affected; that peace and goodwill was at present the idea that engrossed his thoughts . . . that he had found him of late friendly and reasonable on all points; and that he was unwilling to thwart him in a conception which, however wild, might save him and the rest of the world much trouble, so long as it would last. In short, seeing no retreat, after making some verbal alterations, the Emperor of Austria agreed to sign it. (letter dated Sept. 28, 1815, to Lord Liverpool, in *Wellington's Supplementary Dispatches*, XI, p. 175)

Later, when it came to submitting 'this piece of sublime mysticism and nonsense' to the Prince Regent for his signature, Castlereagh and Metternich examined every possible way of dodging the step, but the Emperor Francis did not dare to hold back. What is incontestable is that the pact of the Holy Alliance was signed in spite of Metternich. But might he not have taken advantage of it, once it had become fact, to set up his conservative system? Let us look at this and first of all at the text of the famous pact itself. Whichever way one looks at it, it is impossible to discover in it the slightest inclination to, or the slightest amount of moral support for, the system of restraint and preservation which became famous under his name. What is more, if there was any underlying political tendency, *it would be altogether in the direction of liberal principles.* Alexander, it should be remembered, was still in 1815 in that phase of his intellectual evolution in which it seemed desirable to him to encourage liberal ideas. So true is this that it needed all Metternich's skill to eliminate from the text, as first drafted by the Czar, several expressions which attached too much importance to the rights of the people in relation to those of the monarchs, and which for that reason had nettled his 'August Master'.[1] It is also known that the Czar did not hesitate to solicit the support of governments as far removed from absolutism as that of the Swiss Confederation (which accepted) and of the United States (which refused). Finally it will be observed that the fundamental idea of the Holy Alliance is not reconcilable with that of a European directory—which is on the contrary essential to the Metternich system—for the Holy Alliance is open to all Christian monarchs and all of them were to adhere to it effectively, each after his own fashion, except the Pope, who could not look with a favourable eye upon the vague and sentimental universality of such a pact.

To take the pact of September 26, 1815, in its most natural meaning and in the light of all that we know of its initiator's intentions,[2] we are obliged to agree with what Metternich wrote of it in his *Mémoires*: 'This document had no more sense or value than that of a philanthropic aspiration[3] disguised beneath the cloak of religion . . .'

> The Holy Alliance was not founded to restrain the rights of the people nor to encourage absolutism and tyranny in any form. It was simply the expression of the mystical sentiments of the Emperor Alexander and the application of Christian principles to politics. (*Mémoires*, pp. 210, 212)

But now the pact is signed. Has not Metternich, the great realist, found a way of exploiting it for his own ends? From the very first moment, according to Castlereagh, the Emperor of Austria and the King of Prussia saw in it a means of containing the territorial ambitions (the spirit of frontier jealousy) which had troubled them in the past, to contain, in other words, Russian expansionism. But the Quadruple Alliance, signed shortly afterwards, was to furnish a much more effective framework for

[1] These modifications can be found in Werner Näf *Zur geschichte der Heiligen Allianz* (Bern, 1928), pp. 34–37. See also C. K. Webster, *The Foreign Policy of Castlereagh*, I, p. 482 footnote.

[2] For the most authoritative explanation of these, see M. Maurice Bourquin's *Histoire de la Sainte-Alliance* (Geneva, 1954).

[3] In Metternich's vocabulary 'philanthropic aspiration', is often synonymous with 'liberal aspiration'.

the achievement of that. One suspects, but without definite proof, that Metternich suddenly discovered a new tenderness for the Holy Alliance when, at Troppau, he fought his great battle of diplomatic seduction in an attempt to gain the confidence of the Russian autocrat. Indeed, tactics were too naturally obvious which consisted of confusing the two names Holy Alliance and Alliance and of reinforcing the latter with the paternal sentiments which the Czar might feel towards the former. Much more sincere and precise is, in our opinion, the memorandum which we are about to quote. The occasion of it was the conferences which brought together the Foreign Minister of the King of France with the ambassadors of the three Continental Powers, the object of which was to establish a certain uniformity of opinion and action in Spanish affairs:

> I noticed in the memorandum of the conference of August 31 . . . that someone had put into the mouth of a head of Cabinet words entirely unsuited to a description of the representatives of the Allied Courts: the Foreign Minister of France addresses some remarks to them describing them as ambassadors and Ministers of the Holy Alliance.

> It was perhaps inadvertently that, in the drawing up of a Ministerial resolution, there should have been allowed to creep in such an out-of-place expression, the reproduction of which in communications between the Allied governments would cause considerable awkwardness. . . .

> The Alliance is one and indivisible by right; its component parts must not follow different lines of action. Whenever the representatives of the Courts come to Paris to consider matters of general European interest, they meet in the name of the Alliance founded in 1813 at Teplitz, confirmed at Chaumont in 1814, sanctioned again and published in Paris in 1815, reinforced by the addition of France at Aix-la-Chapelle in 1818, and subsequently put into practice at Laybach in 1821 and at Verona in 1822. To allow a subdivision of Ministers of the Holy Alliance to exist in such a state of affairs would be like giving sanction to a defection from, or a schism in, the grand alliance. . . .

I cannot refrain from mentioning one further consideration which strikes me as paramount and which arises from an observation which is itself rather strange. The act to which the expression Holy Alliance has been given is an abstract one in its moral aspect and particularly in its form. It was agreed between the monarchs and it belongs to their Cabinets neither in its origin nor in its drafting; thus *not once* has it been quoted by the Cabinets in any of their diplomatic exchanges.

It is the public alone, certainly not the Courts in any of their documents or their utterances, who have bestowed on the purely moral union which bears the name of the Holy Alliance positive conditions which are connected with the political alliance of the countries. Yet its name is generally accepted. It has been, so to speak, the motive behind a large number of attacks since 1815, directed by the revolutionaries against the monarchs and their governments, while at the same time the supporters of the monarchy and the guardians of positive rights have endeavoured to strengthen themselves by means of it. Properly established acts make up the code of our political religion: the Holy Alliance forms only the moral part of it. By this distinction I hope to make you acquainted with our way of thinking and to show you the serious reasons we have never to confuse issues which are quite separate. (*Arch. Vienna, Frankreich,* Oct. 8, 1824)

So much is clear, then. As Metternich says on more than one occasion: 'The Holy Alliance has never played a part in anything and it is precluded from doing so by the simple fact that what is in effect nothing can only produce nothing.' (*Arch. Vienna, Frankreich,* to Apponyi, Jan. 24, 1839. See also the private letter to Apponyi Jan. 26, 1839. *Mémoires,* VI, p. 188) In twelve years' time it will be no more than a 'meaningless shibboleth'. (Letter to Sir Travers Twiss)

Let us sum up what appears to be established. Metternich was totally alien to the conception of the Holy Alliance; he only accepted it reluctantly. Although, on certain occasions and for practical reasons, he could give the impression of attaching some importance to it, he never believed in its usefulness and took pains to draw a careful distinction between it and the Quadruple Alliance or the Alliance.

Why, then, does Metternich's name continue to be coupled with an institution which remained so foreign to him? The answer is that one hundred and forty years of public opinion wanted it that way and that this confusion is itself a fact which history should take into consideration. That may be, but what interest is there for historians today in a terminology the true meaning of which they have to explain each time they use it? Why insist on calling a dog a cat when one is obliged to add: of course, by *cat* I mean *dog*? I would therefore make so bold as to suggest that in future the name of Holy Alliance should be confined more strictly to the pact of September 26, 1815, and perhaps also to the mythical picture which the liberals painted of the conservative system of alliance with which the name of Metternich rightly remains linked. As to the system itself, each time it needs to be referred to objectively and as a reality it would be preferable to give it the same name that was used by its creator and guardian: namely the Alliance. It seems to us that in default of any other advantage this convention would save a little ink.

2.

What, then, is this Alliance, so precious that Metternich one day described it as 'the ark of the covenant'? It is here that the difficulty begins, for a glance at the texts is enough to reveal strange discrepancies. The best method in these conditions seems to be to follow a chronological order in studying the conceptions of the statesman.

We start—according to Metternich's own word—with a series of treaties; Teplitz (which is sometimes overlooked), Chaumont (1814), Vienna (March 1815), Paris (November 1815). Certainly the principal architect of these treaties was Castlereagh; at least, the Austrian representative accepted them and adopted the principles of them. It would be necessary to analyse their texts before it would be possible to single out passages which might establish a permanent system of conservative alliance in international law. The fear of unduly prolonging the present essay compels us to abandon the attempt. It is extremely difficult to summarize in a few unequivocal, infallible formulae the gist of the principles and undertakings laid down in these acts. One principle is certain: the union of the four victorious Powers with the object of consolidating the results obtained by the anti-Napoleonic coalition. Equally clear is the undertaking to make sure that France continues to respect the treaties of 1814 and 1815.

But elsewhere? Do the full guarantees, which were exchanged at Teplitz between the three Continental sovereigns for the safeguarding of their territories, extend to the arrangements drawn up at Vienna? Are they still in force? Do the 'dangers' against which the alliance is supposed to be a defence, does the 'great community of interests' which was to be the object of periodical meetings provided for in the treaty of November 20, 1815, include internal risings against established regimes? Yes, in the case of France. But elsewhere? 'Does the revolutionary spirit . . . suddenly become inoffensive when it appears in Germany, Spain or Italy?' (M. Bourquin, *Histoire de la Sainte-Alliance*) One can see where the logic of the system is leading. Was Metternich already conscious of the extensions to the system which were to come to light at Troppau and Laybach? We know of no text which would confirm it. Yet we have come across in a memoir of August 1816, from Friedrich von Gentz, Metternich's 'spare brain', this passage which gives food for thought:

> The coalition only survives because the governments of the great Powers see in it an instrument of high policy, a common expedient against the restlessness of the masses and the disorders of our time. If it did not have a much wider object than the reestablishment of order in France, dissolution would not be far off. (*Statni Ustredni Archiv. Fonds Plasy*)

If one could be certain that Gentz was in this case echoing the thoughts of his chief, the motive would be clear. But, once again, the proof is missing.

Let us at least see in what light Metternich considers the alliances of 1815 to 1818. One preliminary declaration: at this time Metternich never speaks of the Alliance but of the Quadruple Alliance. The latter appears at first to him as the guarantee of *internal* peace in France, for he is not afraid that the Bourbons can have the slightest desire to put the treaties of 1815 to the test again. 'The king, insecurely placed on a shaken throne, has to think about the conquest of his people before turning to the re-establishment of his influence abroad.' (to Lebzeltern, Aug. 1, 1816) He congratulates himself on having watched the Quadruple Alliance develop through the institution of the conference of ambassadors at Paris. 'I attach real importance to this conference which combines the dual advantage of keeping the four Cabinets accurately informed of what is going on and of sustaining at the same time that spirit of the Quadruple Alliance which it is so important to preserve if the peace of Europe is to be assured.' (to Vincent, Mar. 24, 1816) Against whom, against what? Against France or the revolutionary movement? Perhaps, but there is certainly something else:

> The principles consecrated by the acts of the Congress and by the treaties which resulted from it will in every case form your point of departure. You will always have to aim at bringing the Russian Government back to the observance of those principles and preventing its acting in isolation and straying from the spirit of the Quadruple Alliance and its commitments. It is by means of this act, by endeavouring to accustom the Emperor to a feeling of confidence, and by the fidelity with which we honour our own engagements, that we hope to stop the ambitious projects of this monarch or at least to check their growth. (Instructions to Lebzeltern, Aug. 1, 1816, on his departure for St. Petersburg)

Eight months later Metternich will put it even more bluntly to prince Paul Esterhazy, his ambassador at London: 'The Quadruple Alliance as it exists today acts as a brake on the actual or potential plans of the Emperor Alexander.' (Mar. 26, 1817) This Machiavellian application of the Alliance, in a spirit quite foreign to the fraternal one which it displayed to the world, in no way precluded its more general—and acceptable—use against the revolutionary danger:

> Each day brings me fresh conviction that the remedy for this evil which threatens the tranquillity of every State can only be found in perfect understanding between all the Powers. They should openly pool their resources and their energies to stifle everywhere that revolutionary spirit which was developed more powerfully and more dangerously during the three months of Napoleon's reign than it ever was during the first years of the French Revolution. . . . The conference of Ministers in Paris could become the centre of a system of surveillance over these revolutionary intrigues both at home and in other countries, a surveillance which would be instructed to consider and put forward repressive measures to be adopted against them. (to Vincent, June 22, 1817)

This wish was not to be realized. As Metternich says later, this was the fault of the Russian representative, Pozzo di Borgo, whose only concern at the time was to link France with his country's policy of European hegemony. From that moment on, in the opinion of the Austrian Minister, the Quadruple Alliance had strayed from the right path and its usefulness appeared to be much diminished.

The Congress of Aix-la-Chapelle was to give rise to a stream of discussion about the Quadruple Alliance. We will confine ourselves to setting down a few of the less well-known documents.

The first position Metternich took up is defined in a letter to the Austrian representative at Paris, General Vincent (April 5, 1818):

> The Emperor thinks that nothing could be more dangerous to the maintenance of repose than the renewal of these periodical interviews if they were ever to deviate from their original character and turn themselves into a congress. Convinced that the

repose of Europe is intimately bound up with, may perhaps even exclusively depend upon, the maintenance of the Quadruple Alliance in its original integrity and consequently in all its simplicity, His Majesty will always be ready to intervene in meetings provided for by Article six of the treaty of November 20 (1815). Similarly, he would feel obliged to oppose with all the strength of his reasoning any idea of a meeting which, instead of helping to maintain the established order, threatened to disturb it by raising doubts about the foundations of it and questioning what has already been decided.

What lies behind this phraseology? What possible explanation is there of the repugnance that is openly felt for congresses by the man who is supposed to have been the great promoter of them? The explanation is that at the time he saw in them an offensive weapon in the service of the Russian policy of domination. As for the 'maintenance of the Quadruple Alliance in its original integrity and consequently in all its simplicity', it is merely a question of preventing France from joining. Why? The Minister's fears find expression in some curious arithmetic (*Arch. Plasy.* c.30):

Mathematical difference between the questions:
Present state of the Alliance: 4
Future state of the meetings: 5
(1) Prince Metternich's proposal: $4+1=5$
(2) Russian proposal: $1+1+1+1+1=5$
Positive results of these proposals: given (1) $5 : 4+1$
           given (2) $5 : 2+3$

Let us translate these last two formulae into plain words. In the first instance, France would find herself isolated in the face of the four Powers. In the second instance, Russia would have the support of France against the other three partners.

The transaction that was finally decided upon is known: on the one hand the maintenance of the Quadruple Alliance, but in the form of a secret protocol making it clear that France alone was the target; on the other hand the admission of France to the conferences provided for in Article six of the treaty of November 20, 1815. How were these two combinations kept distinct in Metternich's mind?

> The Quadruple Alliance, far from running counter to the relations between the five Courts, acts as the basis of and motive for these relations. The fact has been given the force of law. The rights of the four governments are clearly defined in the transactions at Aix-la-Chapelle. Such rights as France can claim . . . are no less clearly defined . . . The sovereigns and the governments will no longer meet in a group of *four*, but there is nothing to prevent the four Courts reaching eventual agreement . . . over the scope of their alliance, which is itself only the palladium of the French Government's most precious guarantees and of the repose of Europe. (to Esterhazy, Oct. 10, 1818)

In spite of the satisfaction which Metternich affected, the solution was far from corresponding to his wishes. The Quadruple Alliance, once limited to the eventuality of an uprising in France, could no longer be used as a general instrument of control, and even in that limited rôle its effectiveness was going to be considerably reduced by the discontinuance of the conference of ambassadors in Paris:

> The Quadruple Alliance would thereafter be without a fixed meeting-point, and it would be hard to avoid the realization that a moral institution deprived of a central and visible representation must sooner or later fall into disuse. That is why every religion must have a cult. (to Esterhazy, May 26, 1819)

On the other hand, the common affairs of Europe were no longer dependent on four but on five Powers, and so Russia was going to regain a certain freedom of manoeuvre. Metternich was later to admit that this inclusion of France had, in fact, really destroyed the original Alliance:

> In place of the Quadruple Alliance, which no longer had any reason to exist once the practical end had been attained for which they had striven in common, there arose a *moral pentarchy*, of

which the Congress of Aix-la-Chapelle later determined the functions and also in principle limited the powers. (*Mémoires*, p. 215) [1]

Those provisions or restrictions arise from the terms of the protocol of November 15, 1818. The union of the five sovereigns, it is stated, 'can have no other object than the maintenance of general peace founded on sacred respect for the engagements set out in the treaties'. (Article 2)

> . . . that in the event of those meetings having as their object matters specially bound up with the interests of the other European States, they shall only be held in response to a formal invitation on the part of such States as are concerned in the aforesaid matters and on the express condition that such States be allowed to participate in them either directly or through their plenipotentiaries. (Article 4)

What, then, happened in practice to the action of the *pentarchy*? It is not easy to see, and the futility of an institution thus sugar-coated erupts in the declaration of November 15 which claims to be its manifesto: it would be hard to find a piece of phraseology more puffed out with empty-sounding words.

In the course of the ensuing months Metternich appears to be wanting to stress in any way he can the impotence of what remains of 'Alliance'. If Russia proposes an act of general guarantee bearing on the rights of property of each one of the contracting parties, the Austrian Cabinet rejects it as being superfluous and unacceptable to England. (to Neumann, Dec. 27, 1818, and *Mémoires*, III, p. 165) When St. Petersburg proposes, in the spring of 1819, the re-establishment of the Paris conference of Ministers, Metternich rejects the proposal, describing it as 'false in principle, and if that be not so, none the less false in its application, in view of the staff of the Minister (Pozzo di Borgo) chosen to attend the

---

[1] In September 1844 he will write: 'I perceived the danger of dissolving the present alliance in order to form a new one by admitting a heterogeneous body . . . My words did not meet with the support I should have liked. The union of the *five*, in the form of a *political unity*, was the outcome of the congress and the event justified my expectations.' (*Mèmoires*, VI, p. 559)

council of the representatives of the four Courts'. (to Esterhazy, June 8, 1819) At the beginning of 1820 Metternich refuses to act upon another proposal of the Russian Government: that of dispatching to the representatives of the four at Paris common instructions to be acted upon in the event of the death of Louis XVIII. He invokes as motive the reluctance of England and proclaims as a sacred principle the rule of unanimity which he himself was to throw overboard a few months later:

> The very first principle which His Imperial Majesty regards, and will always regard, as the most essential mainstay of the repose of Europe is absolute solidarity between the four Courts in all questions of general interest. In such matters, the Emperor will never speak and act entirely on his own. In such cases he does not accept the voice of the majority; it is to *unanimity* that he invariably responds. H.I.M. is so emphatic in this opinion, he regards it as so sacred, that he would always prefer to take his chance with events than endorse an isolated opinion, however useful and necessary it might appear to him to be. (to Lebzeltern, Feb. 23, 1820)

Finally, he offers the same resistance in the first months of 1820, when Russia raises the idea of action by the Alliance against the Spanish revolution. The basis of Metternich's thought at this time is perhaps revealed to us in a dispatch to his friend le comte Zichy (then Austrian ambassador at Berlin) (Apr. 12, 1820):

> The Quadruple Alliance, that basis of common safety, only exists now in a negative manner. As such, the Alliance is of the greatest service in acting as a regular moral meeting-point for the four Courts. Its very existence is enough to prevent new diplomatic combinations, that scourge, so to speak, reserved for feeble and restless minds . . . On the other hand, I am quite convinced that nothing can put life into the Quadruple Alliance. Russia perhaps wishes to have a try, and she will probably do so in good faith, for the principle of this Alliance is in accordance with the Emperor's thoughts, but there certainly exists no way of making Great Britain *move over anything*. The greater the

dangers to the general repose, the more immobile the British Government becomes.

The principle and the reputation of the Quadruple Alliance must therefore be nourished and cared for, like those fine reputations which live on after the activity of the individuals has ceased. It must be treated as though it could do all those things which, in fact, it can no longer do. But to rely on its support and to base calculations of safety on its material actions would be ruinous. (*Arch. Vienna, Preussen*)

If that was Metternich's idea at the time of the effectiveness of the Alliance, it is not surprising that he showed little enthusiasm in invoking support for it when the Neapolitan revolution broke out in July 1820:

If we had been able, at the beginning of the Neapolitan Revolution, to dispose of an army of twenty-five thousand in our Italian provinces, in addition to sufficient troops to face Piedmont and to ensure order in our own provinces, we would have marched on Naples in the first phase of the rising. Since that could not be, we were obliged to make a deliberate calculation and base our line of action on something else.

In other words on collaboration with Russia within the framework of the Alliance:

Nevertheless, our appeal to the Quadruple Alliance had to be half-hearted. We knew what to expect from that alliance. The positions of governments had changed and consequently their powers and hopes had necessarily changed, too. (to Esterhazy, Apr. 9, 1821)

Contrary to what is often imagined, it has been decisively shown that the Congress of Troppau was accepted by Metternich only as a last resort and after he had exhausted all other possibilities, and it would be quite useless to go back over that ground again. On the whole Russia successfully turned Metternich's own tactics against him: namely, using the Alliance to meddle with his neighbour's policy, to control it, to put a brake on it, in the name of fraternal assistance.

A confidential dispatch to General Vincent explains how the Austrian Minister was reckoning to manoeuvre at the Congress:

> It is desirable to move with the utmost speed . . . but in preparing the ground from which to advance beyond the Neapolitan affair . . . it is a question of finding the best way to secure a *rapprochement*, to concentrate in one centre those activities which are the highest expression of their free will, and finally to place the two Imperial Courts of Europe on the same footing, and that the most exalted. The present inclinations of the Emperor seem to to be favourable to such an outcome. (to Esterhazy, Dec. 24, 1822)

Is it necessary to recall here how the programme came to be corrupted in the end? In that winter of 1820–21, the twin Congresses of Troppau and Laybach probably represent the peak of Metternich's career, his greatest personal success. The Alliance which a little time before he had declared to be dying, ineffective, emerged profoundly transformed in its aim and in its methods, in its essence as in its forms.

(1) The first aim of the Quadruple Alliance had been to guarantee the execution of the treaties of 1814 and 1815: of secondary importance and applying only to France, it arrogated to itself the right of surveillance over the internal policy of a State. The new alliance of Troppau has as its objective the support of all 'legitimate' governments against revolutionary movements.

(2) The Quadruple Alliance made a law not to engage itself in the affairs of other States except at their invitation and with the participation of the representatives of those States. (Protocol of Nov. 15, 1818) The protocol of November 19, 1820, on the other hand, asserts a general right of intervention and goes so far as to draw up a catalogue of measures which may be taken.

(3) Finally, the new Alliance now binds only the three monarchies 'whose sceptre has not yet either been broken or dishonoured'. England openly repudiated the doctrine of intervention and although France finally associated herself, to a certain extent, with Austrian policy in respect of Naples, she did not dare

subscribe to the declarations of principles which preceded and followed this action.

> The first condition needed for active relations is only to be found today in the combination of the three great Continental Courts. They are independent in their actions and by this very fact they are obliged to unite and take action whenever necessity requires it. Our desire is certainly that governments enjoying representative systems should stand alongside us, but to wish to extend this desire to community of action would be asking an impossible condition of them. (to Esterhazy, Dec. 24, 1822)

Henceforward it will no longer be, in Metternich's political vocabulary, a question of the Quadruple Alliance, but simply of the Alliance by itself. Once this conception has reached the point where it conforms to his wishes, he showers on it expressions of almost fanatical devotion:

> I do not hesitate to ascribe to the Alliance in the political sphere an activity which is comparable to that exercised in the moral order by the doctrine of Providence. It is not necessary to see Providence to recognize and to feel the force of her laws, and this feeling is enough to reduce the evil that bad men do and to strengthen the resistance of good men to their attacks. And so, just as you have seen the ungodly and the lunatics persisting throughout the ages in denying the existence of Providence, so you have seen madmen and rogues in politics persisting at every opportunity in doubting and denying the Alliance, or in demonstrating that it does not exist. (to Lebzeltern, Mar. 31, 1822)

> That power can be neither replaced nor supplemented by another. Imagine one monarchy controlling the combined resources of the Alliance; not only would such tremendous power not take the place of the Alliance but it would gain nothing by attempting to do so, because it would be contrary to the *moral* power of the Alliance. It would be contrary for the very reason that the Alliance is clearly composed of heterogeneous parts and because, although it works towards a single, positive end, it embodies guarantees for the most widely varying interests. (to Lebzeltern Jan. 10, 1822)

Hardly had the great work taken shape when the whole question was raised again in the most unexpected fashion by the Greek insurrection, 'a firebrand thrown by the radicals between the great Powers and specially between Austria and Russia'. (Circular of Aug. 31, 1821. *Arch. Vienna, Circularien*) Indeed, the Alliance 'became problematical the day one of the Allied Courts (Russia) shouldered the burden of the war alone or . . . it was no longer considered formidable by the revolutionaries once the troops of several Powers were on the move eastwards together'. (to Lebzeltern, June, 6, 1822)

We know how Metternich faced this crisis. Once again the Alliance acted as a brake on the bellicose impulses of Russia, and all the more effectively because as it happened it was possible to present the great nationalist movement as a mere incident in the universal scourge of revolution. The Czar, having himself accepted that interpretation at the Congress of Laybach, could not without going back on his own decision support in the Near East what he had just opposed in Italy. The ideological argument might not have been enough in itself. Austria, on her own, or even bolstered up by Prussia, could not assume the rôle of arbiter without giving too much away. And so Metternich, by a new pirouette, suddenly found himself once more back at Aix-la-Chapelle, on which ground he could meet France and above all England. Now it is no longer a question of *three* monarchs, but of *five* allies, the union of whom is loudly declared to be indispensable. Alexander, mystified, intimidated, is obliged to retreat. In May 1822 he gives up the idea of armed intervention and turns to that of negotiation conducted in harmony with his good allies. Metternich is triumphant:

> The wrong line followed by the Russian Cabinet has had the advantage of uniting on common ground the Courts of Austria, Great Britain, France, and Prussia. . . . The Emperor of Russia has today only one line of conduct to follow, he must withdraw into the ranks of his allies to paint over his failure to act as an independent and powerful monarch in the real or supposed interests of his empire.

The game is won. I knew what I was doing in setting the Alliance and its correct principles against the guilty conduct of a few men. Once I was established on a basis as broad as it was solid, the impetus of events worked my way. (to Esterhazy. Another dispatch of the same date)

This result, as we know, was shortlived. The train of events was to lead, some years later, to the dreaded catastrophe.

But the respite at least allowed Metternich time to set in motion, in another direction, his beloved Alliance, painted to suit the occasion in the colours of Troppau. Yet everything is interrelated, and if Metternich's attitude toward the Spanish question is to be understood, it is necessary to take account of the Neapolitan affair and the need to furnish the Czar with some satisfaction which will allow him to save, in the West, the august face which he has been made to lose in the East. These two motives induced the Chancellor to modify the attitude he had adopted in 1820 in respect of the Spanish revolution. Then, it will be remembered, he had preached abstention. Now, in 1822, he is equally afraid of foreign intervention in the peninsula, but being unable to avoid it he will try to orientate events in the most favourable direction. And the Alliance will be the pivot of his manoeuvre. 'My first concern in the middle of this outburst must be directed to saving the principle, and that principle is the Alliance.' (to Esterhazy, Mar. 20, 1823) In the case of Italy the Alliance had acted as the engine, in the case of Greece as the brake. Now it will serve both as engine, to rouse conservative Europe to action, and as brake, to control the operations of France. (see G. de Bertier, 'Metternich and the French Intervention in Spain', in the *Bulletin de la Société d'Histoire moderne*, 1958, No. 2, p. 19)

There can be no question of recording here, even in abbreviated form, the meanderings of the Congress of Verona and of the diplomatic duel which followed it between Metternich and Chateaubriand, the former seeking to maintain France in the rôle of the secular arm of the Alliance, the latter willingly accepting the support of the Alliance against England, but making use at the same time of every possible evasion to free himself from Allied control. Metternich summarizes his own attitude in these words:

> Our concern is limited to speaking the language of the Alliance in these two towns (Paris and London). We tell the French Ministers: go forward on the principle which forms the basis of the Alliance, but *go forward* and you will find us, and the Allies, ready to give you every kind of support. We have told the British Government: You are afraid of action against Spain, we desire it against the Spanish revolution. The Allies have made pledges to France which must set her mind at rest about the course her own preservation prompts her to follow. If France goes forward on the lines of the principles of the Alliance she will have every right to its support. The Allies will see that she gets it. If on the other hand she were to adopt the wrong principle, the same right would not exist for her ... (to Lebzeltern, Mar. 30, 1823)

From another point of view the Congress of Verona marks an important date in the history of the Alliance. Ever since Troppau, England had isolated herself from it, but so long as her foreign policy remained in Castlereagh's hands Metternich had been able to flatter himself with the hope of finding him at his side if need arose, as had indeed been the case in the early stages of the Eastern question. The death of Castlereagh (August 1822) made the divorce irremediable:

> ... The old Quadruple Alliance has reached the end of its existence with the settlement of the last problem in France that was common to all four Courts, and if since 1815 we have not seen Great Britain go forward on lines openly opposed to those of the Alliance, the discretion she has shown has been due to the influence of one man alone. That man has disappeared and with him have vanished in England the last traces of the Alliance and even of its traditions. France joined the Allies in 1818, but she could never, either for herself or for the other Powers, appear in the rôle of mediator in the actual workings of the Alliance. That pact was incompatible with the revolutionary regime by which she was governed. (to Lebzeltern, Mar. 5, 1824)

Two months later Metternich was announcing that he regarded France as 'definitely situated outside the Alliance'. (to Vincent, May 12, 1824) As for England, no *rapprochement* will be conceivable so long as her policy is directed by Canning on lines opposed to those of the Alliance. A suggestion put forward by the comte de Münster, a Hanoverian Minister of King George IV, gives us the opportunity for a fine review of the principles of the Alliance:

> The moral essence of the Alliance reposes on two principles alone: *the preservation of anything legally in existence* and *comity between the leading Powers based on that principle* . . .

> On close examination that principle is the one that underlies the life of every State; it satisfies the first need of society, namely security of property. It exists everywhere and whatever form a government may take the principle loses nothing of its correctness or of the need to be applied . . . To attack the principle of the Alliance is to attack society . . . M. le comte de Münster asks me whether in the present state of affairs it would not be more useful to strengthen the bond between Austria and England than to drive them farther apart. My reply to this question will be as short as it will be precise.

> Austria, considering the essential conditions of her existence, must never deviate from the principles which form, as we see it, the true and only basis of that which usage has ended up by calling *the Alliance*. Anything which in the present trend of public opinion tended to cement a special union between us and England would be bound to ruin us. (to Esterhazy, Aug. 7, 1825. *Mémoires*, IV, pp. 222–4)

Let us stop here a moment to underline the evolution that has apparently taken place in the Chancellor's thoughts. The previous year (*Mémoires*, IV, p. 255) he was not prepared to recognize any other foundation for the Alliance than the diplomatic acts of 1813 to 1818. Now the Alliance is tending to become disembodied and to take on the character of a 'true political religion'. 'The Alliance in its true acceptation is indestructible, it is political *morality* . . . The Alliance cannot perish; it would exist even *without allies.*'

(to Zichy, June 10, 1827) *Without allies!* An astonishing thought, but one which the combination of political circumstances in 1827 makes intelligible. There had disappeared with the Czar Alexander, who died in December 1825, the last traces of the spirit of the Holy Alliance and especially of that tradition of trust which bound the two emperors together in the struggle against revolution. The death-blow was struck by the famous protocol of April 4, 1826, signed between England and Russia, for the settlement of Eastern affairs. But Canning's intentions, according to Metternich, went far beyond that of settlement. 'He hoped to strike a fresh blow, direct and obvious, against the Alliance.' (to Apponyi, May 31, 1826) The result? 'Russia has separated herself in fact from the Alliance, and the trouble she takes to justify that action proves that she is aware of what she has done.' (to Apponyi, another letter of the same date as above)

Nevertheless the Alliance cannot disappear, since now, in Metternich's mind, it transcends the plane of political combinations:

> The Alliance which you have looked on as being dead since last year is alive and will continue to live. It is I who tell you this: not an Alliance in the distorted form which those who wanted it least attempted to give it, but just as it is, that is to say simple, pure and strong like anything that conforms to the truth; in a word just as I for my part have always conceived it and applied it. (to the comtesse de Lieven, Apr. 30, 1826. *Arch. Plasy*)

What remains of the Alliance as a political combination? The realism of the statesman triumphs occasionally over the stubbornness of the doctrinaire:

> The order of things that had been set up between the years 1815 and 1818 is finished, because it is worn out and scarcely applicable to the new conditions . . . The system of union known as Alliance had been for a long time nothing more than a sham, a kind of formula, now evoked and put into use according to the whim of individual needs, now delayed and reversed in its application as a result of quite different feelings and needs . . .

How, indeed, would it be possible to recognize in England's policy since the advent of Canning any trace of the Alliance? . . . France has never understood the Alliance at all and never really belonged to it. Only Austria and Prussia have remained fundamentally attached to it . . . and it is ourselves, above all, who have never deviated from its salutary rules. We have acted in this way because the principles of the Alliance are those of public right, because of the importance we attached to continuing to preserve a name when the thing itself had ceased to exist. (to Esterhazy, Mar. 26, 1827)

Henceforward his only concern will be to maintain free of all embarrassment the principle of the Alliance, 'that moral power which is in its essence so pure and so great'. (to Apponyi, June 11, 1827) And so he rejects the advances made by Russia and France to induce him to take part in the treaty of London of July 6, 1827. The misfortune of the Alliance proper not intervening in the Greek affair is much less than would be the misfortune of seeing the Alliance change its essence, abjure its faith and espouse the political heresies of its most determined enemy [*Canning*]. (to Zichy, June 14, 1827)

The three Powers are free to bind themselves by a treaty, but such an act cannot claim for itself the same character as the Alliance. Only Metternich by adhering to it would have the power to confer that on it. Moreover, if the others wish to adopt the form of the Ministerial conferences for their own sinister designs, those conferences which Metternich, with his meetings of sovereigns, had made the Alliance's great means of functioning, they will be acting like heretics who adopt the cult of the true religion while scorning its principles. (to Esterhazy, Feb. 4, 1828)

By his unswerving abstention the Chancellor flatters himself that he has preserved, for Austria and for Europe, one last chance of safety. That is the gist of the great report addressed to the Emperor on October 9, 1829, which can be read in the fourth volume of the *Mémoires*. (pp. 602–8). The Alliance founded in 1813 and 1814, 'the exclusive aim of which was the triumph of the conservative system', has been 'actually dissolved' by the protocol of St. Petersburg, April 4, 1826. Prussia herself was ready to join the Treaty of London and so Austria alone remained strictly faithful to the spirit of the Alliance, and sooner or later she will be recompensed for it, 'for any Power that is drawn to the original idea of this Alliance and to the system for which it served as a basis, is necessarily obliged to range itself alongside Austria. That is bound to happen sooner or later; it is only natural that it should.'

The re-establishment of peace between Russia and Turkey, by the treaty of Adrianople, the prospect of a final settlement of the Greek question, give rise at the beginning of 1830, to the hope of seeing also the end of the 'immoral' collaboration between Russia and England. Could not the Alliance be reborn then as it was before 1826?

> I never knew any other purpose in it than that of giving solidarity to the leading European Powers in the maintenance of common peace. The basis of the Alliance, its watchword, its daily concern was respect for the real independence of all States, the preservation of friendly relations between all governments, the appeal for frank explanations . . . whenever a serious difficulty made the maintenance of peace problematical, and finally emphatic respect for all rights, for anything which has a legal existence . . . *To re-establish* the Alliance does not seem to me to be the formula . . . I would consider it more useful to prefer the formula of a *resumption* of the former relations between the Allies. To re-establish is to do something new in an old form . . . to resume a policy that has been given up is easier and has the same result in the end. Let the three Courts that have the greatest freedom of action pick up the thread again where they let it drop. Let them stand once again on the same moral ground, and the fact of their doing so will be enough to ensure *political repose*. (to Ficquelmont, Feb. 11, 1830)

The revolution of 1830 soon gave a burning topicality to these wishes. Metternich sees in it an opportunity to revitalize the Alliance as it had manifested itself at Troppau, and in his desire to get a result, he does not hesitate to contradict himself once again:

> The Alliance of 1813, reinforced by later transactions . . . has not ceased to exist . . . The principle of preservation which is that of the Alliance can and must be admitted by every government, but it must be adapted to the different conditions which form the foundation of each State's political existence. (to Esterhazy, Oct. 21, 1830. *Mémoires*, V, p. 68. See the development of his projects in the memorandum of Oct. 6, 1830. *Mémoires*, V, pp. 51 et seq. In July 1831, he will repeat: '. . . in reality the old alliance no longer existed.' *Mémoires*, V, p. 195)

The Chancellor explained, some months later, how this attempt came to fail as a result of the refusal of the Russian Government to allow the creation of a central point 'of crystallization'. In other words of a Ministerial conference, sitting in Berlin, which would have given substance to the resuscitated Alliance. (*Mémoires*, V, p. 196)

After this setback, it will no longer be a question of the Alliance in Metternich's correspondence, except in an historical sense; and even when, in 1833, the group of three Powers at Troppau appears to reconstitute itself at Münchengrätz, it will no longer in fact, be a question of anything except the 'three Continental Courts'. To think of re-establishing the old Quadruple Alliance, Metternich says again in 1841, is 'fanciful' (*Mémoires*, VI, p. 577)

Yet the principle is not dead, and in April 1847 the old Chancellor will be found evoking 'those powers that are united by a common bond under the name of conservative alliance. This alliance *does not rest on a written pact* but is founded on the otherwise strong basis of a full community of interests between those who make the triumph of its principles their primary concern'. (to Apponyi, Apr. 12, 1847)

One first observation arises from all those texts that we have quoted: the extraordinary diversity, even the uncertainty, of

Metternich's thinking on what was nevertheless an essential theme of his policy. Is it not striking to see him contradicting himself at a few months' interval on the question of knowing whether the Quadruple Alliance had been maintained or abolished at the Congress of Aix-la-Chapelle, and, later, on that of the survival of the Alliance after 1826?

As for his conceptions on the very nature of the Alliance, one discovers at least four consecutive and at times even simultaneous forms:

(1) From 1815 to 1818: the Quadruple Alliance, natural consequence of the coalition against Napoleon, sanctioned by a series of treaties. Its essential objects are the safeguarding of the treaties of 1815 and the support of the monarchical order in France, and as a subsidiary service acting as a brake on Russian ambitions.

(2) The *Pentarchy*, which arose out of the Congress of Aix-la-Chapelle. The introduction of France into the allied councils, the reticence of England, the restless ambitions of Russia deprive it in his opinion of almost all its usefulness, if they do not make it dangerous, and Metternich then seems intent on limiting its interventions.

(3) The Alliance of Troppau-Laybach, which is limited to the three absolutist monarchies and is used as an instrument of policy or active intervention against revolutionary movements.

(4) The Alliance, a moral entity, which no longer is the result of any treaties, no longer represents a definite group of associated Powers, but is only an abstract principle of political wisdom with universal value.

The only common denominator which remains underlying all these transformations is the idea that the union of conservative governments is the only means of saving European society threatened by revolutionary principles. A discovery, it must be admitted, that is not exactly an original one.

The uncertainties and extraordinary variations in Metternich's thought—at least in his expression of them—on such a fundamental point as his political system have allowed us to discover, behind this façade of unchanging principles which it pleased him to assume, the fluctuating opportunism, even the weakness and inconsequence of a policy which has no other compass by which to steer than the interest of the moment. There is, indeed, a big gap between principle and method.

Part II

PEOPLES AND STATESMEN

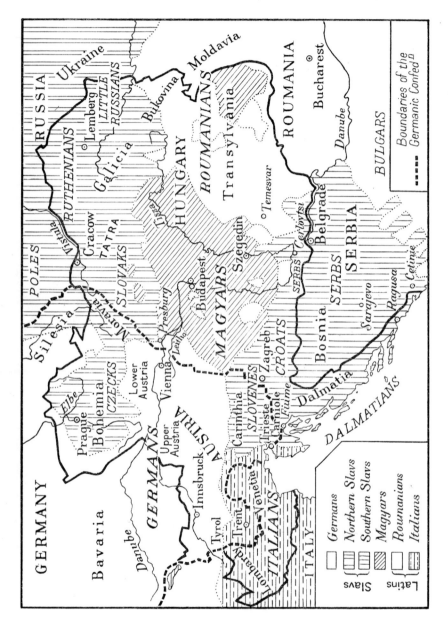

AUSTRIAN ESTATES IN THE MID NINETEENTH CENTURY

Map labels:

GERMANY

Bavaria

RUSSIA

Ukraine

POLES

Lemberg
LITTLE
RUSSIANS

Galicia

RUTHENIANS

Cracow

Vistula

TATRA

SLOVAKS

Moravia

Silesia

Elbe

Prague

Bohemia

CZECKS

Lower
Austria

Upper
Austria

GERMANS

Danube

Innsbruck

AUSTRIA

Tyrol

Trent

Venetia

Vienna

Presburg

Leitha

SLOVENES

Carinthia

Carniole

Trieste

Fiume

ITALIANS

Lombardy

ITALY

Budapest

HUNGARY

MAGYARS

Szegedin

Tisza

Zagreb

CROATS

Dalmatia

Bukovina

Moldavia

ROUMANIANS

Transylvania

Temesvar

Cernovtsi

Belgrade

SERBS

Bosnia

SERBS

SERBIA

Sarajevo

Ragusa

Cetine

DALMATIANS

ROUMANIA

Bucharest

Danube

BULGARS

Boundaries of the
Germanic Confedᵈ

Germans

Northern Slavs } Slavs

Southern Slavs

Magyars

Roumanians

Italians } Latins

CHAPTER FIVE

The Austrian Empire

THERE HAD never been, there never will be again, a body politic like the Austrian Empire which Metternich served. Although it was far removed, in extent and complexity, from its direct ancestor, the empire of Charles V, its appearance at the beginning of the nineteenth century was nevertheless rather disturbing. Bounded by a frontier which bestrode such obstacles as rivers and mountains as though by chance, what a conglomeration of mutilated natural regions, what a babel of languages and nationalities, what a chaos of institutions! Germans, Hungarians, Czechs, Slovenes, Serbs, Croats, Poles, Ruthenes, Roumanians, Italians, not to mention the ubiquitous Jews—such are the basic human ingredients.

Three main circumstances combine to complicate hopelessly their life together in the great house built by the Habsburgs. In the first place, although some of these elements form quite compact, homogeneous groups on the map—for example, the Italians in the plain of the Po—almost everywhere, and especially in the marginal areas, the dominant element is mixed with others and this creates minority problems. In the second place, the ethnical map does not correspond to those political entities which evolved with the years—kingdoms, principalities, archduchies, duchies, Croatian banats, and marches—and which had, by their accidental union, produced the Habsburg Empire. Thus it is that the kingdom of Hungary embraces Slav populations much against their will, and the kingdom of Bohemia embraces Germans side by side with Czechs. A final complication is that the German provinces, in addition to Bohemia and Moravia, but not the others, belong to the Germanic Confederation, successor to the Holy Roman Empire, and that the Emperor of Austria is the president of this union of thirty-eight independent States, of which Prussia sullenly disputes the hegemony.

All this explains why the Austrian Empire must have felt itself more threatened than any other by the movement of ideas which drew peoples—or at least their thinking *élite*—towards the liberal democratic regimes, and at the same time towards the affirmation of their original nationalities. If peaceful coexistence had been possible so far through common submission to a benevolent sovereign, what would happen the day each national element became free to advance its particular claims and to give itself representative institutions? The problem of minorities would raise its head, and the stirring of nationalistic emotions would give rise to internal strife. On the other hand, if Germany were to realize her unity on the basis of Germanic nationality, what would become of Austria? Her non-German provinces would not allow her to merge with the new formation, the Emperor would lose his traditional rôle, and his German subjects, finding themselves in a minority compared to the other elements, would be subject to the attraction of the great Germanic fatherland.

Metternich has neither been blinded by, nor has he remained indifferent to, these mortal dangers. But how can he stand up to them with such an ill-adapted, ineffective governmental machine? A confused mass of Ministries, councils, departments, chancelleries, with contradictory functions, in which responsibilities are diluted and energy is sapped. The French Ambassador writes in January 1817:

> This country keeps going by its own size, but the government has no energy and none is to be found anywhere . . . there is here neither will nor authority, everyone does more or less as he likes, and it is the subordinates who are the masters. Prince Metternich only exercises influence over affairs which fall absolutely within his province, but we look everywhere for the government, and none can tell us where it is. (*Fonds Richelieu,* Jan. 7, 1817)

As early as 1811, Metternich had proposed to Francis II the creation of a council of empire, designed to give substance to the unity of the different parties in the State, and also the creation of a proper council of Ministers. (*Mémoires*, II, pp. 442 et seq.) He returns to the attack in October 1817, with a lengthy report in which the fundamental problem is perfectly posed. (*Mémoires*, III, pp. 67 et seq.)

What was the fate of this project?

> . . . I handed it over to the Emperor at the beginning of 1817 and he put it *into his drawer*.

> When the Emperor had begun his convalescence, following his serious illness in 1827, he sent for me one day at eight o'clock in the morning.

> When I had seated myself by him he began by apologizing for having sent for me at such an early hour, then he said: 'I have a confession to make to you: I am returning to life after an illness from which I thought I should never recover. I tell you that while I was ill I felt guilty because I had not looked at your work. As soon as I am up and about again, I shall nominate a commission to study the question and you shall preside. Give me a list of the men you would like as colleagues.'

> On December 31, 1834, I visited the Emperor to wish him a happy New Year. 'Once again you see in me a repentant sinner,' he said. 'Your work has not been taken out of the drawer yet. I give you my word of honour that the year 1835 shall not pass until the body is set up.' Two months later the Emperor was dead. (*Mémoires*, VIII, pp. 528–9)

Unfortunately for Austria, Ferdinand I, who succeeded his father without any difficulty, was a half-wit, harmless but wholly incapable of ruling. Metternich, loyal servant that he was, never allowed himself to criticize either the unfortunate Emperor or the fatal decision of his father, who could probably have made him hand over his rights to Francis-Charles, a younger brother better equipped to wear the Crown. But Metternich did express an opinion about the consequences:

The Emperor's death affected my position profoundly . . . In our country, as in all monarchies, a Minister is powerful only so long as he feels sure of his sovereign's support. The archduke Louis who is the Emperor Ferdinand's representative in 'conferences of State', could not and cannot give me sufficient backing, simply because he is not the sovereign. Yet I have constant struggles with my adversaries. . . . Ever since the accession of the present Emperor I have felt paralysed. (to Hübner, Mar. 1, 1848. In Hübner, *Une Année de ma Vie*, p. 21)

My department and even I alone have represented Austrian power abroad while the vacuum was forming at home. Thus I became (and I found it morally repugnant) a phantasmagoria, an imaginary being, a spirit without a body, the representative of something that should have been in existence but in fact was not. (Mar. 20, 1848. *Mémoires*, VII, p. 615)

The consequences of this deadlock, for which Metternich, whatever he may say, certainly appears to have been largely responsible, are well known: the revolution of March 1848, which nearly caused the downfall of the Empire. The elderly statesman, removed from power, lavished advice on his successors, notably on prince Felix zu Schwarzenberg, who was destined to restore the situation by his incisive energy. It is not our concern to recall the way in which Metternich reacted to every phase of the crisis. But it is possible to find, in those of his papers concerning that period which have been published, a number of reflections and principles which throw light on his own conduct when he was at the head of affairs.

In the first place, there is the maintenance in the provinces of traditional institutions as the expression of the different nationalities:

Let us beware of destroying the provinces individually and doing away with the Emperor's position as sovereign of each one of those provinces. To do so would be to dissolve the bonds by which the dynasty is united with the personal element, and with it the best means at the Crown's disposal of preventing friction and strife between the different races which make up the monarchy. (in Hübner, *Une Année de ma Vie*, p. 17)

The Germanic element, which gave the Empire its reigning house, is certainly the true civilizing influence in this mass of peoples (to Apponyi, Apr. 12, 1841), but 'whenever it is necessary to reckon with differences that are really non-existent, the Imperial Government must guard against appearing to submit to the Germanic influence'. (to Buol, *Mémoires*, VIII, p. 415)

In fact, this eternal diversity could offer one great advantage in the struggle against revolution, Metternich explains it in 1830 to a Carlist *émigré*, the marquis de Villeneuve:

> Revolutions would not, in our case, mean a forest fire. If the Hungarian revolts . . . we should immediately set the Bohemian against him, for they hate each other; and after him the Pole, or the German, or the Italian. (Villeneuve, *Charles X en exil*, p. 16)

It was indeed by employing this method that Schwarzenberg was to overcome the revolution of 1848: *divide et impera*.

A second important principle is the maintenance of the monarchical regime:

> The only form of government which is suited to the concentration of peoples which makes up the empire as a whole, is the monarchical form, because the cohesion of the parties would be absolutely impossible under a republican form of government. . . This latter form is not applicable to the Austrian Empire. There is one reason for this, the non-existence of the Austrian people . . . Although a personal sovereign may rule over populations of different origin, it is impossible to imagine, on the other hand, a popular sovereignty superimposed on other sovereignties of the same kind and origin. (*Mémoires*, VIII, p. 539)

Finally, with regard to Germany:

> It is impossible for the Emperor of Austria to be placed with the German parties in his empire under the sovereignty of a German Parliament, and at the same time to protect his rights as King of Hungary. The German part of the Austrian Army cannot be handed over to suit the whim of the German Parliament while the section belonging to other parts of the Empire remains independent of that assembly. (*Mémoires*, VIII, p. 447)

Let us now leave the slightly austere domain of the constitutional problems of the Austrian Empire to consider, in company with Metternich, some human aspects.

And to give honour to whom honour is due, here, first of all, is Francis II. The official portraits show him as tall and thin, with a long, gaunt face and the cold expression of a dead fish—in short an appearance in perfect harmony with what is known of his narrow mind and obstinate character. To this he added, we are told, great affability. Metternich could have only praise for the prince who had showered him with benefits:

> Few sovereigns have brought more honour to their Crown than the Emperor Francis. His people recognized his worth as a man. He was their father, rather than their master, and he united in himself all the virtues of private life. Yet the brilliant qualities that distinguished him as a sovereign were not given by all his contemporaries the recognition they deserved. Pure in his morals, simple in his ways, opposed to any kind of ostentation (he even disdained that superiority of title which delights the crowd and which often makes princes appear different from what they are). In everything loving and seeking only the truth, firm in his principles, unfailingly honest, this prince among men nevertheless played what seemed to his contemporaries a subordinate part, whereas in fact the greatest successes owed everything to his resolution, his energy, and his good qualities. (*Mémoires*, I, p. 138)

Metternich is enraptured by his master's simplicity of taste:

> Nothing could be more curious than the way in which our Court lives when it moves to the country. I am sure no one would believe that the Emperor could be content with a way of living so simple that it would be far from satisfying to the needs of a rich landowner, or even of an ordinary individual with some private means. The standard of comfort and the kind of life that is led are more those of a gentleman who is almost in want. Anything remotely resembling luxury is banished from these households. One hardly feels oneself to be enjoying such comforts as small bourgeois means would allow . . . and it is precisely in this

extreme simplicity that the Emperor delights . . . There is enough of it to throw the most radical of radicals off the scent. (*Mémoires*, IV, p. 109)

The sovereign gives evidence of a touching affection for his Minister. In October 1823 they left together for a meeting with the Czar Alexander at Czernowitz, in Bukovina, but Metternich catches a cold and is obliged to take to his bed. On October 27 he writes to his wife:

> I cannot speak too highly of the Emperor's little kindnesses to me. He never let a day pass without coming to see me at Lemberg. He would sit for hours at a time by my bed or, on his return from Czernowitz, in my *salon*, not in order to talk business, but to amuse me with idle gossip. It was he who decided which doctor I should consult and sent for him, telling me that he would have left me his doctor if he had not been convinced that Doctor Massoir was better. (*Mémoires*, IV, p. 22)

> I find that it was he who made my lodging arrangements all the way along the route and he gave the strictest orders that I should be treated like himself. Although I have been aware for some time of the Emperor's genuine attachment for me, I confess that I had never thought him capable of such deliberate courtesies. (*Mémoires*, IV, p. 22)

Relations between the sovereign and his Minister are described in a letter from Metternich to the comtesse de Lieven:

> Another foolish idea is that of my compatriots who imagine that I do what I like and that that is why the Emperor is going to Italy. I hear this gossip repeated twenty times a year. The truth is this: *The Emperor always does what I want, but I never want him to do anything that he ought not to do.* He is convinced of it. He hardly asks any more of me, and I do the same on my side. We are both the easiest people in the world to approach and consequently easy to understand in our desires and our actions. It is the same in everything. (*Correspondence* . . ., p. 71)

Confidences let drop much later in Metternich's life show that he was not blind to the deficiencies of his 'August Master':

> I have never been a Richelieu. I never thought I had the makings of one, and I never felt tempted to become one. . . . Throughout the greater part of the long and glorious reign of Francis I, I was his first Minister, enjoying his trust and also, I think, his affection. I can say without boasting that he always adopted my ideas and followed my advice in matters relating to foreign affairs. On the home front things were different. It is true, that in this sphere, too, I had, in my capacity as Chancellor of State, the right to intervene, but I used it with moderation and only in moments of crisis, specially when the safeguarding of important principles was involved. . . .
>
> He attached too great importance, perhaps, to the secret societies which were undermining Italy and, to a lesser degree, Germany, and he thought the remedy for this evil lay in keeping a close watch on the so-called intelligent classes of society. This surveillance was carried out by the police, which thereby became one of the chief instruments of his government, by censorship of the Press, which was more irritating than efficacious, and finally by the moral closing of his frontiers against Germany and against foreign countries in general. But it is no use closing frontiers to ideas, they cross them just the same and turn up as contraband when they are not allowed to enter in the normal way. The effect was to produce in the educated classes a feeling of tacit annoyance with the government and of a vague desire for political reform. . . . And so this system, which had the merit of preserving the masses from the propagation of the revolutionary poison, had a bad effect on the upper classes. I called the Emperor's attention to it, but on this point he was adamant. Anything I could do to lessen the harmful effects of this policy, I did. (in Hübner, *Une Année de ma Vie*, pp. 18–19)

According to the British Ambassador, it often happened that the Minister would exaggerate his influence over the Emperor's mind and undertake rashly to give promises which he later found himself unable to keep. (Stewart to Castlereagh, Aug. 25, 1816. P.R.O., F.O. 7/128)

Metternich's gaze was principally directed outwards, and members of the Austrian Government do not appear often in his writings. His immediate predecessors, Thugut, Cobenzl, Stadion, are judged without indulgence (see *Mémoires*, I, pp. 27, 40, 79, 82), and the same is true of the Viennese as a whole:

No country is more barren of pleasant men than ours. The women are better, but they are too sharply divided into categories. There are hardly any who have both wit and charm. In our country intellectual women are usually far from being pleasant, and those who on first acquaintance appear pleasant, lack wit. Consequently there is not one here with whom I would enjoy spending an evening. (to the comtesse de Lieven, p. 184)

Lamentable illusions hang like a thick cloud over the poor city of Vienna. She believes that she holds the same position that Paris occupies in France; she thinks she can dictate to the Empire. It is a gross error. Vienna is merely the outer shell of a nut which constitutes the main body. She is only the leading town in the smallest province of the Empire and she only becomes the capital of it if the Emperor remains Emperor and lives there with the government of the Empire. For her to be the capital it is, therefore, necessary that there should be an Emperor and an Empire. (*Mémoires*, VIII, p. 166)

The newspapers which appear in Vienna are on the whole badly written. The reason for this lies in the traditional inability of the *strictly Austrian* population to write well. . . . The Viennese mind is full of *humor* and *whit* [*sic*]. It never misses an opportunity for a purple passage; the minute the Viennese take pen in hand they become long-winded. It is not the same in other parts of the Empire. I think the reason lies in the *patois* of lower Austria, which is pleasant but eminently incorrect. If the mind influences the tongue, the tongue in its turn exercises influence over the manifestation of the spirit. (to Sir Travers Twiss, Jan. 25, 1849)

Metternich is no kinder to the Hungarians:

Hungary is a veritable Bœotia in which members of the *petite bourgeoisie* and students set themselves up as States of the Realm and in which aulic counsellors, drawn up like circus horses, represent the government. But the situation is lacking in danger because their thoughts do not even rise *to that level.* (Nov. 7, 1825. *Mémoires*, IV, p. 204)

The Hungarian character is strongly attracted to Utopia. The spirit of the nation is easily carried away by first impressions; it is always ready to allow itself to be seduced by telling words, without worrying too much about their practical value. (*Mémoires*, VII, p. 59)

Yet the Chancellor always defended himself against the charge that he wished to interfere with the traditional privileges of Hungary:

From every point of view I recognize the preservation of the Hungarian constitution as so stern a duty for the servant of the State, and yet as so formal an act of justice, that I would have to deny my whole political life should I so much as feel inclined to listen to a proposal to the contrary. (Nov. 1825. *Mémoires*, IV, p. 254)

On the other hand, he does not believe in the possibility of an independent Hungary:

Short of getting involved in long-drawn-out struggles, Hungary is incapable of setting up an independent State separated from the other parts of the Austrian Empire. To achieve this she would first of all have to advance her frontiers to the east and south. Now, there is no way for the Magyars to do this except by brute force. But the other nationalities in the territory which is called Hungary, and which is not an exclusively Magyar country, are in this respect just as strong as they are. (June 26, 1849. *Mémoires*, VIII, p. 498)

As for the Slav nationalities within the Empire, Metternich treats them disdainfully:

Czech patriotism is an urge which gives rise to unimportant aberrations when things are moving along in their usual rut, but at times of general excitement it has as much influence on men as a salad of beans in an outbreak of cholera.(quoted by Bibl, p. 297)

Until almost the very end of his reign, Metternich does not appear to have had any doubts about the internal peace of the Austrian States, except those in Italy. The reasons for this confidence never varied:

> Our country, or rather our countries, are the most peaceful because they enjoy, without having suffered any previous revolutions, most of those benefits which undoubtedly arise from the ashes of empires overthrown by political strife. (to the comtesse de Lieven, pp. 180–1)

> Austria is sometimes accused of *standing still* . . . Nothing of the sort! We move with the times, but we are not in any danger of moving away from our principles. . . . If anyone takes an unbiased look at our Empire, he will everywhere find progress . . . Every justifiable demand put forward by the progressives has long ago been satisfied. Our Empire recognizes the absolute equality of men before the law. We have no privilege, no feudal levies. Taxes are equitable, justice is independent. All the component parts of the Empire have State assemblies and a municipal system more liberal than that enjoyed by countries under the modern representative system. In no empire is more respect shown to nationalities than in our own, and such respect is now looked on as a popular condition of our existence. Nowhere is there less governmental *absolutism* than in our country and it could not make its appearance without causing a reaction similar to that which was stirred up in our Empire by the reign of Joseph II. (*Mémoires*, VII, pp. 428–9)

Thanks to this internal stability, Austria can fulfil her destiny of providing Europe with a bastion against revolution:

> We present a solid mass, compact, not easily overturned or even shaken, and this alone must get in the liberals' way a good deal. From the first day of the French Revolution until now, Austria has always stood ready to thwart the organizers of destruction. In twenty campaigns our power could be seen on the battlefield fighting against revolution, and in the midst of political peace it was, again, on our frontiers that the revolutionary torches died out, unless our armies sallied forth to extinguish them on the spot where the fire had broken out. (to Esterhazy, Dec. 12, 1828)

This policy precludes any idea of conquest or aggrandizement:

Austria is a *saturated* power. She is big enough, she is rich enough, she has enough to do to preserve what she already possesses. The Emperor Francis often used to say: 'If anyone were to suggest that I should add so much as a village to our Austrian possessions, I would show him the door, for he would be either mad or endeavouring *to sap our strength*'. (to L.Veuillot, *Oeuvres complètes*, XXXII, p. 346)

That is why Metternich steadfastly refused to look for the slightest addition in that direction in which it could most easily have been made, namely in European Turkey. Some months before his death, he repeated his conviction on this point. (*Mémoires*, VIII, pp. 605–6)

It is useless to ask whether the policy advocated by Metternich might have spared Austria the disasters of 1859 and of 1866, the loss of her position in Italy and in Germany, and finally the utter collapse of 1918, but we can at least take note that the situation developed along the lines which the old Chancellor had foreseen: the realization of democratic and national aspirations, the expansionist thrust to the east, and European war.

CHAPTER SIX

Germany—Prussia

THROUGH FORCE of circumstance German problems figured prominently in Metternich's deliberations and therefore in his writings. Let us first of all see what he thinks of his compatriots in general:

> The German is phlegmatic, thoughtful, and loyal. He is given more to meditation than to action, specially when action is inseparable from the break-up of the family and the severing of personal ties. German patriotism is directed towards a variety of objects. Ever since the common fatherland came into being there have been quite distinct public trends. Provincial patriotism is the one to which the German is most accessible. (*Mémoires*, III, p. 186)

> The German mind is not easily stopped once it is on the move. Often receptive to folly, once it has absorbed such folly it ponders it and turns it into something sombre and serious. So we find in Germany today hundreds of men ready to sacrifice their wealth and their lives for the cause they are defending. (to Vincent, July 22, 1819)

> The German is cold and constant. He is not satisfied with empty words, but goes straight to the facts. He is not easily persuaded to move, but he goes on to the end. (to Thurn, May 6, 1819)

Finally, let us quote this rather striking prophecy:

> In Germany . . . the Jews accept what is virtually the principal rôle and are revolutionaries of the highest class. They have writers, philosophers, poets, orators, political journalists, bankers, and over their head as well as in their heart the full weight of their

ancient ignominy. One day they will give Germany something to fear, after which Germany may well do the same to them. (to L. Veuillot, *Oeuvres complètes*, XXXII, p. 357)

Compared with the form it is taking in France or Italy, the revolutionary threat in Germany offers some unusual features:

Revolution in its precise sense, indeed any revolution in any State, can only have two objects: the transmutation of every kind of private property or a change in the form of government. France has completed the first of these revolutions and there is no longer any danger of a repetition. . . . Germany runs much greater risks arising not only from the catastrophes that befell France in the aforementioned period but also from the sum total of the consequences that the revolution of 1789 had for that kingdom and for Europe as a whole. What the revolution destroyed in France still exists to a large extent in Germany, and consequently that which has been, so to speak, reduced to ashes in that country still exists as combustible material in Germany. (to Thurn, June 6, 1819)

Several other circumstances . . . tended to increase the danger (. . .). Ancient Germany, bound by a common nationality that was indestructible, was cut up into mutually independent sovereignties by the partitions of 1806. Thanks to the glorious events of 1814 which re-created a Germany, the Germans found themselves once again aware of their nationality. Once that happened a struggle broke out between the various German Courts and the people. The former were naturally able to put in the forefront of their anxieties and therefore of their calculations the need to safeguard their mutual independence (. . .).

Men of ideas among the German people for their part only aimed at developing as far as they could the principle of national unity. In the midst of this struggle . . . the universities, the only bodies in Germany to have escaped complete destruction and to have preserved their independence and their ancient form, wasted no time in raising themselves to a political and national level . . . (to Lebzeltern, Feb. 25, 1820)

In her leading universities the teaching posts were converted into platforms for radicals, lecturers not only dared to teach openly the most subversive maxims of any religion or social order, but set assassination up as a civic virtue and as a moral principle. Administration took on a revolutionary impetus; the middle class, so important in Germany by reason of its size and of the real aristocracy which it inherited from the ancient institutions of the Empire, the swarm of writers and students, all could be swept along with the torrent. . . . (to Lebzeltern, May 25, 1820)

Finally, the liberal movement is linked in Germany with a national movement towards political unity:

The principle of the fusion of all parts of Germany into one body politic is the real aim, and all at once, there is no denying it, it is the natural desire of the revolutionaries and of a whole crowd of progressive thinkers in Germany. Now, this principle cannot become operative until the political institutions which still separate the different parts of that vast country disappear. (to Lebzeltern, Sept. 30, 1819)

Yet this same division raises serious difficulties in another direction. That is why Metternich is firmly attached to the confederal form which makes it possible to preserve the old local institutions while giving to the whole the cohesion necessary to combat outbreaks of violence at home as well as dangers abroad:

So many princes of varying size set down in the centre of Europe haphazard and without any guarantees, indulging in isolated political opinions, could only give rise to a state of restlessness and turmoil for themselves and for their neighbours. If these same princes are united by a federal bond based on general and individual repose they will immediately be strong from their combined strength, and their confederation will therefore form a bulwark against the passions and opinions of aggressors. (to Lebzeltern, Feb. 23, 1820)

Three principal dangers were to threaten the stability of the Germanic Confederation created by the Congress of Vienna: the political ambitions of the princes ruling over the secondary

States, rivalry between Austria and Prussia for the leadership of the Confederation, and revolutionary movements of a liberal or national character.

The first of these was undoubtedly more embarrassing than deadly:

> The more aware these States and their princes become of the inferiority of their position in relation to powerful monarchies like Austria and Prussia, the more need they imagine there to be to fortify themselves by alliances and leagues . . . We must accept that there is only one alternative: either the States and the peoples of Germany will grow used to finding hope of peace and security in their natural ties with Austria and Prussia, or they will seek them in foreign connections. (to Zichy, July 17, 1816)

If, then, the federal institutions are to be made to work, the princes must learn to take account of the realities that underlie the surface of the written word:

> Although the members of the Confederation are unquestionably independent of each other and are only bound by certain mutual rights and duties, and although in any matter involving individual rights no compulsory resolution could be adopted without the free consent of the interested parties, yet the confederate princes of the lesser States would do well to remember that the political system, like the civil code, is in fact made up of inequalities. In both cases the difference in their social positions imposes on those in a secondary position the duty of not attaching too much importance to their equality of rights. To wish to make full use at all times of this equality of rights would be to introduce the spirit of democracy into the realm of the rights of people and this would cause as much inconvenience as in the domain of civil law. (to Trautmansdorff, Nov. 30, 1827)

The tension created in the heart of the Confederation by the inevitable rivalry between the two dominating Powers proved to be much more serious:

Two Germanies emerged from the Reformation. The old one remained under the protection of Austria; at the head of the other there stands a Power born of the Reformation. That Power is called Prussia and she does not deny her origin. A daughter of the Reformation, she is seeking to strengthen her influence in the conflicts of the present age by following the path of the Revolution . . . In 1813 Prussia threw aside the mask. She thought the time ripe for open conquest. Austria frustrated her plans, and as soon as peace was restored the Prussian Cabinet did its utmost, *per fas et nefas*, to stop the growth of the Confederation. I cannot offer you a simpler or more complete explanation of the *fata germanica* in their dealings with Prussianism which speaks only of Germany but never thinks of it. (*Mémoires*, VIII, pp. 519 and 314)

To combat this evil Metternich adopted the tactics, after 1815, of minimizing it and of seeking a working agreement between the two Powers on the very ground where there might have been conflict.

The domestic situation in Prussia and the personality of the men who governed the country must have weighed heavily in the political scales of Vienna. Let us see what picture Metternich has formed of the rival State:

The Prussian State, although united under one sceptre, is made up of several components which differ among themselves in respect of geographical position, climate, race and language. In this it bears a striking resemblance to the Austrian State, although the position of the latter is in every way more favourable. The divers elements which make up the Austrian monarchy are more solid. Geographically, the countries which compose it are better situated. Together they form a well-rounded whole. Of the two kingdoms Austria would take more kindly than Prussia to a purely representative system of government, if the differences in language and customs between her peoples were not so pronounced. How could such a system hope to succeed in Prussia when it is not possible for Austria to adopt it? (Nov. 14, 1818. *Mémoires*, III, p. 181)

From 1797 to 1840 there reigns in Prussia, Frederick William III, 'the most upright man in his kingdom' (to Apponyi, Sept. 17, 1829. In the *Mémoires*, VI, p. 470, there is to be found praise that is less guarded than in the unpublished extracts)

> He is certainly the wisest and most respected of princes. Always loyal and correct in his political dealings, he rightly enjoys general esteem . . . but there is no getting away from the fact that the King, for all those virtues and eminent qualities which distinguish him, is unfortunately a Protestant in the strongest sense of the word. Not only does he see himself as the head of the Protestant Church and as its guardian, but he is constantly at work trying to establish unity between the Lutherans and the Calvinists in his own States and in the rest of Germany. (to Lützow, Dec. 18, 1829)

> What is unusual about the King's way of thinking is on the one hand the perfect lucidity of his views as exemplified by his real love of justice, and on the other the ease with which he allows himself to be drawn into activities which he knows perfectly well to be wrong and even dangerous, at the same time comforting himself with the sad satisfaction of having predicted the evil which it was up to him to have prevented. (to Apponyi, Aug. 7, 1838)

> The King's most precious quality is his negative strength . . . Time and again in dealing with the most important business it would have been impossible for me to form a clear idea of what His Prussian Majesty would do, but I was always able to base my calculations on the absolutely certain knowledge of what he *would not do*. (to Zichy, Feb. 6, 1827)

The head of the Prussian Government from 1810 to 1822 is the Chancellor Hardenberg. He cuts little ice with Metternich:

> Prince von Hardenberg is physically and morally subject to weakness which borders on childishness. He desires what is right, he is even able to discern it, but as a result of this great weakness he is today, more than ever, under the influence of two elements which are always most dangerous for a statesman who exercises great authority. One is an extraordinary need to be

thought a liberal; the other is an unfortunate tendency to surround himself with strange people. Things have come to such a pass that it can safely be said that there is not a single man round him who either does not hold extreme democratic views, or who is not prepared to play an active part in the conspiracy against the Prussian throne itself. (Aug. 1, 1819. *Mémoires*, III, pp. 277–8)

But the foreign policy of the kingdom was directed from 1818 onwards by the Dane Bernstorff, who was himself replaced in 1832 by his colleague Ancillon, 'a man of eminently unsound intelligence' (to Vincent, June 24, 1823), and a descendant of a French Protestant family which had emigrated in the seventeenth century. Metternich has a paltry opinion of the ability of these two gentlemen, whom he considers to be 'very limited'.

Prussia's foreign policy appears to be encumbered with congenital weaknesses:

As bad luck would have it the moral attitude of the Court of Prussia presents a mixture of power and impotence. Prussia ranks as one of the great Powers without really having the necessary qualities; a kind of happy medium between the greater and the lesser Courts, she shares in the duties of the leading Powers, but her geographical boundaries, combined with a lack of certain essential internal resources, force her back into the second rank. (Oct. 22, 1833. *Mémoires*, V, p. 538)

That Power is the only one which is not, and it must be admitted can never be, satisfied with her position. The defects of the country's geographical outline are such that she cannot embark on a war with any of the great Powers without running the risk of finding herself cut in two at the first assault. Russian troops, once across the Vistula, would separate Brandenburg from old Prussia. If we advance from Bohemia we at once divide the possessions which Prussia has on the right bank of the Elbe from those which extend towards the Rhine and as far as your frontiers. And if a French army crossed the Rhine the result would be the same in the opposite direction. It is hardly surprising, therefore, that there exists a party, true to the policy of Frederick II, which is trying, so far as it can, to shuffle the cards in the hope of fresh territorial gains. But neither the king and his closest advisers nor Count Bernstorff will ever be a party to such projects. (reported by the French Ambassador, Jan. 25, 1830. *A.E. Corr. pol. Autriche* 412)

Metternich therefore feels sure of always dominating the foreign policy of Prussia:

> The mental superiority that we enjoy over the Prussian Government is so decisive that I have yet to see that Government fail to go back on what it has only too often advanced with great rapidity and frivolity, once it is sure that our point of view differs from its own. (to Vincent, June 24, 1823)

Did not this superb self-assurance blind Metternich a little? Did he not underestimate what schemes Prussian ambition might set in motion? While he was doing his utmost to block the way to innovations on the political level, the Prussian administration was silently perfecting what was to become the most effective instrument in the advance towards a Prussian Germany: the *Zollverein*, the customs union of ten German States under her direction. When Metternich raised the alarm in 1833 it was too late. (*Mémoires*, V, pp. 517–36)

The intrigues of liberal-minded revolutionaries, which constituted the third threat to the stability of the Germanic Confederation, were made easier after the peace of 1815 by some of the princes themselves. Bavaria, Wurtemberg, the Grand Duchy of Baden were given constitutions more or less inspired by the Charter of Louis XVIII. Even in Prussia a strong party, which made use of the names of Humboldt and Stein, urged the royal government to take the lead in pressing for a democratic and unified Germany.

Metternich writes in January 1818:

> We think we can see, and every day confirms us in this opinion, that the seat of German Jacobinism is in Prussia, and specially in Berlin. . . . It is only at Weimar, really, that the revolution is

openly organized, but the men who exploit these conditions are to be found in Berlin. It is still possible to deal with them, but it will not be so much longer. (to Zichy, Jan. 28, 1818)

It was, indeed, in the Grand Duchy of Weimar that the historic demonstration of the Wartburg had just taken place, one of the events which was going to unleash the forces of reaction. The episode occupies a place of honour in German history, and so we may be forgiven for presenting an account of it which we do not think has been published, the same one by which Metternich was given warning of it and on which he based his judgment. It is the report sent on October 27, 1817, by the comte de Bombelles, the Austrian Minister at Dresden and also the representative of the Emperor at the Court of the Grand-Duke of Weimar:

Your Highness will have seen from the papers that the Grand-Duke of Weimar had deemed it right to allow the students from the greater part of the Protestant universities to meet at Eisenach in order to celebrate on the 18th of this month at the famous Wartburg the double anniversary of the Battle of Leipzig and of the date of the Reformation. Several Ministers of His Most Serene Highness, among them M. Vogt, had made fairly strong representations to him about the danger of such a meeting. But the Grand-Duke, who is incapable of believing that any student might not possess all the virtues in the highest degree, was not satisfied with authorizing the holding of the meeting at the Wartburg; he allocated more funds to enable the students to find board and lodging. As early as the 17th a considerable number of students, not only from every Protestant university in Germany . . . but from Kiel and Königsberg as well, arrived at Eisenach. Quite apart from more than 800 students we counted 30 professors, including Martin of Jena, taking part in this Jacobin orgy. And on the morning of the 18th the crowd marched past two at a time and set off for the Wartburg in perfectly orderly fashion.

On arriving in the grounds of the castle where a number of tables had been set out for a meal, the students formed a circle and a young Westphalian began to speak. The new Demosthenes reminded his comrades of the incredible exertions of German youth in 1813 and 1814 to free the country from foreign yoke. He declared that the object of their action, the expulsion of the French, had, in fact, been achieved. But what, he added, had been the sequel to this tragedy? 'A meeting of despots, instead of granting the people the rewards of their labours, established a system of brigandage and injustice. Let us break the shackles that bind Germany and let us swear to die rather than to suffer tyranny!'

After this fine peroration the students produced a black plank of wood to which were attached every one of the acts of the Congress of Vienna, some of the works of Schmeltz, some passages from those of Kotzebue, and other books which have brought down upon themselves the indignation of this new type of legislator. A large fire was lit, the works were detached by means of manure forks and the Congress was the first to be thrown into the flames to cries of *Long live Liberty! Long live Jahn! Down with tyrants and their perfidious Ministers!*

One might think nothing could be more impudent than such a terrifyingly scandalous scene, but the next day proved this to be wrong, for the students having sent for the priest in charge of the Lutheran church at Eisenach, that ecclesiastic was feeble enough, either through persuasion or fear, to consent to their demand to be admitted to communion. All eight hundred of them duly made their communion and swore, on the bread that was set before them, hatred to all tyranny and a promise not to rest until they had acquired for Germany the liberty and independence which belong to her.

After this unworthy farce, which was equally offensive to religion and to the respect due to legitimate authority, the students left the Wartburg and made their way back to their universities. (The copy of this report was found in the mail sent from Berlin on Nov. 7, 1817)

Metternich's indignation may well be imagined. He was not going 'to be dictated to by a second-rate Jacobin'. But how could he put the petty German princes in their place if they could base their claims to independence and their half-hearted liberal proposals on the active sympathy of Czar Alexander I of Russia? The meeting of sovereigns at Aix-la-Chapelle, at the end of 1818, gave Metternich the chance to call the Czar's attention to the dangers of subversion in Germany. In the end a dramatic event ensured his moral support for the work of reaction: the assassination of August Kotzebue, the German man of letters who was in the service of Russia. (March 23, 1819. The reports by which Metternich learned of the drama have been printed in the *Mémoires*, III, pp. 232–5)

Metternich's conclusion is:

> The real misfortune which we deplore has for all that its useful side, for the sad end of the unfortunate Kotzebue furnishes us with an *argumentum ad hominem* which the Duke of Weimar, with all his liberalism, would not be able to resist. All my efforts are directed towards giving the affair the best possible sequel and to taking as much advantage of it as possible. I shall act vigorously to this end. (April 9, 1819. *Mémoires*, III, p. 235)

The threatened counter-offensive was going to be developed in three stages: interviews between the Austrian and Prussian leaders at Teplitz (end of July 1819), conferences at Carlsbad between the Ministers of the nine principal German States (August 6–31, 1819), and conferences at Vienna bringing together the representatives of all the German States. (November, 1819, to January, 1820).

Ten years of domestic tranquillity were going to justify, in the eyes of the Chancellor, the measures taken in 1819 and 1820. He declares with satisfaction at the beginning of 1824:

> The Restoration is progressing. Evil has suffered setbacks from which it will only recover with difficulty, and since the moral arena could not remain unoccupied for long, goodness is beginning to take possession of it. Germany, having almost reached the limits of revolution, has remained for three years a spectator of the great events. The proper and generous efforts of the Powers having been crowned with a success which the factions never considered likely . . . the innovators have lost as much in

audacity as the governments gained in strength and courage . . .
But this quite natural development of things is by no means the
only cause of the great moral change which has taken place in
Germany. In order to achieve their end the innovators undertook their work feeling that they needed to create some backing
for themselves from public opinion. To this end they promised
the people benefits not one of which could be realized . . .
What good has the representative system produced in the
countries into which it has been introduced? Taxes there have
increased to a terrifying extent. Those government acts which
are most obviously beneficial have been blocked, and partly
hindered or wholly paralysed . . . The peoples of southern Germany have outstripped the Courts in the expression of their
feelings. They have poured ridicule on the character of the
deputies. The pay the latter receive in the course of long and
uneventful sessions appears to those who have to find it as a useless
increase in taxation, and many a voice in the crowd has begun to
be raised in favour of a simple and less costly form of administration . . . (to Lebzeltern, Feb. 7, 1824)

The Revolution of 1830 in France had itself only minor repercussions in Germany.

The appearance on the scene in 1840 of King Frederick-
William IV opens the last chapter in the history of Metternich's
Germany. Metternich made more than one attempt to draw a
portrait of the new king:

Made up of an unusual combination of great qualities of mind
and heart dominated by an uncontrollable imagination, the
King of Prussia is sometimes right in what he wants, sometimes wrong. It is above all in his choice of means that he goes
wrong . . . The whole of his thinking is a peculiar mixture of
truth and error, of intentions that are generally well-meaning,
but which turn out to be impracticable. Where careful scrutiny
will reveal only insurmountable difficulties, the king with a
whimsicality all his own sees only a task calling for *genius*. The
religious spirit that animates him differs fundamentally from
his father's; the difference is as great as that between a fairy

story and an epic, and the progress made by the two sovereigns must, it follows, differ as well. The father was a Calvinist with a marked tendency towards Lutheranism, the son is an Evangelist with a tendency towards Catholicism. The first went from one mistake to another, the second goes from a fantasy to a truth, and the only things that strike him about this truth are its hierarchical forms and its vanities. There is one aspect of this maze of thought which does credit to the son, and that is the profound feeling he has for distributive justice. (to Lützow, Jan. 14, 1842. See also *Mémoires*, VII, pp. 330–1)

The King reckons too much on the power of his genius, and it is the kind of power which lets down those who think they can wield it on every occasion. (to Neumann, Jan. 14, 1842)

From the end of 1842 the reformist activity of Frederick-William begins to cause anxiety:

The eyes of Germany are turned today towards Prussia. The King marks each one of his days by an action which excites the thoughts of men not only within the boundaries of his kingdom but in the whole of Germany. Is this prince thereby following a system? If so, what is the system? I should find it hard to answer that . . .

Let us suppose for one moment that someone with the right to do so were to ask His Prussian Majesty to give an account of his views. It is a certainty that the King would reply that he was openly devoted to monarchical principles, that having found on his accession to the throne a Prussia incapable of definition, as much from the governmental point of view as from that of national or so-called national tendencies, he set about creating for his government foundations which took account of circumstances. He would say that he had no intention of weakening the sovereign authority by a form of popular representation after the fashion of modern constitutions, neither was he aiming at an administrative centralization which is the deliberate consequence of that legislative form; but that being sympathetic to legal liberties resting on *historical* foundations, he intends to secure such liberties for his country. That is, without any doubt, the reply that the King would give, and nobody is in a better position than I to encourage that conviction. But are the isolated will of one prince and the purity of his intentions enough of themselves to ensure the success of undertakings which make a direct appeal to the minds of men? That is the question I should feel bound to raise against the assurance with which King Frederick-William advances in the direction he has outlined. (Dec. 30, 1842. *Circulation*, 27)

The shipwreck which had been foreseen occurred at last, as we know, in March 1848, and sucked even Metternich down with it. An exile in London and later in Brussels, he followed events closely and showered advice on the Austrian and German leaders. And so there can be found in his writings an almost continuous commentary on the different phases of the history of the revolution of 1848 in Germany. (An important part of these documents has been published in Volume VIII of the *Mémoires*.)

In view of the complexity of this commentary which defies any attempt at summary, we shall avoid getting involved in it, and shall end this chapter by giving two excerpts, the first of which has the merit of never having been published before, and the second of putting forward in conclusion a prophecy which contemporary history has ratified only too well:

It is against the *Metternich system* that Germany rose, it is against this system that the thunderbolts of the *Teutonic Vatican* have been hurled; it is, in a word, this *absolutely personal* system that has been held up to public obloquy. Yet here is this system all of a sudden put forward as a thing, an interest and a power. Wherein lies the difference between me (for I can surely speak of myself in speaking of my system) and the followers of the religion of unity? Obviously it is to be found in the fact that what appears today as a great obstacle to reformers was seen, felt and judged by me in 1813 and 1814. What to their eyes looked like weakness looked to mine like strength. When some day the events of those two years are made known to the public, it will be my fate to be credited with a power of divination to which I lay no claim. It will be found that I knew that two plus two equals four, and what is known does not have to be guessed. I knew, and I did not have to guess, that between the idea of *unity* and *union* there lies more than a difference, there lies opposition. I knew that German unity could only be achieved with the help of complete confusion, whereas in *union* was to be found the guarantee that the national energy would be developed along peaceful and conservative lines. Looked at closely, the Metternich system has been *the cult of the thing*. It is its adversaries who have tried to replace the thing . . . by an abstract formula devoid in its application of any practical significance. . . . (to Sir Travers Twiss, Jan. 10, 1849)

In practice there is only one way for Germany to make her nationality secure, that is by forming a *confederation* of States. It matters little whether this confederation takes the form of a monarchy or a republic . . . Today Prussia sets up the federal State against a confederation of States . . . If Prussia's plan, so cleverly conceived, is successful (as it has a good chance of being) the consequences must *of necessity* be incalculable in respect of the dangers that it will create not only for Prussia but for the whole of European society. (to Kübeck, Dec. 31, 1849. *Mémoires*, VIII, pp. 502–3)

THE ITALIAN STATES, 1815

CHAPTER SEVEN

Italy

ITALY, PREY ever coveted by the barbarians from the north, had provided the Habsburgs in 1815 with succulent compensation for what they had agreed to give up in Germany and the Low Countries. From the remains of the Most Serene Republic of Venice, assassinated in 1797 by the hand of Bonaparte, and of the former duchy of Milan, time-honoured possession of the House of Austria, the kingdom of Lombardy-Venetia had been formed. A viceroy, prince of the Imperial family, helped by Austrian and Italian officials, governed these provinces, which were counted among the most highly populated and prosperous in Italy. There also were to be found, firmly established in the four main squares of the famous quadrilateral of Verona, Peschiera, Mantua, and Legnano, the strong powerful armies intended to maintain order in the whole of northern Italy.

Thus Austrian domination extended well beyond the frontiers of Lombardy-Venetia, over the neighbouring duchies of Parma and Modena, governed respectively by the archduchess Marie-Louise, eldest daughter of the Emperor, and by a grandson of the great Maria-Theresa. It extended also over the Grand-Duchy of Tuscany, where another Habsburg reigned, and over the Papal States, which had a common boundary with Venetia through their outlying provinces of the Legations and Romagna. The congenital weakness of its government subjected the Pope to a kind of protectorate in fact, exercised by the only great Catholic Power which was in a position to help it.

The little Duchy of Lucca hardly counted on the political chessboard, having been temporarily detached from Tuscany to serve as a dowry for a Spanish princess left over from the dealings at Vienna.

Only two Italian States were large enough to maintain a façade of independence. In the south there was the kingdom of the two Sicilies ruled over with a total and kindly inefficiency by old Ferdinand IV of Bourbon. The moral support, at least, of his cousins in France and Spain would have allowed him, had he so wished, to adopt a slightly more dignified attitude. In the north, the kingdom of Piedmont-Sardinia, which had absorbed the former republic of Genoa, overflowed the Alps to the north into Savoy and to the west into the *comté* of Nice. The economic activity of the kingdom, the ambition of its princes, of the ancient dynasty of Savoy, the proximity of France, which was a cause for anxiety, but which also acted as a useful counterbalance in resisting Austrian hegemony—everything guaranteed it a leading part in the resistance of Italian nationalism to the humiliating domination of Teutonic influence.

This was the map of Italy as Metternich saw it.

Is it not strange that he had to wait until 1816 before he saw Italy with his own eyes, the Italy, that is, of things and people? Even then he only saw northern Italy—Milan, Verona, Venice—and he was too taken up with business and too much troubled by his eyes to have a good look round. His real discovery of Italy dates from the following year, when he stayed a long time, from June to September. Combining business with pleasure, he escorted to Leghorn the archduchess who was destined to marry the Emperor of Brazil, and took the waters at Lucca. On this occasion, however, he went no farther than Florence. Not until two years later was he to see Rome and Naples, when he accompanied his 'August Master' on an official journey.

Like all Germans, Metternich fell deeply under the spell of that beautiful land. The vast collection of his *Mémoires* offers a splendid variety of letters, written home to his family and to his friend madame de Lieven in the course of his two visits. But to judge from the method of publication used—'pages piously collected by a son'—it is easy to believe that these documents are neither complete nor reproduced word for word. It would be a very good thing if a new edition were brought out based on the original documents. It would probably make it possible to give Metternich back the place he deserves among the illustrious bards of Italy.

Here are a few samples:

It would be difficult to give you an idea of the impression that Florence must make on any man who loves beautiful and grand things. Everything I have seen so far exceeds my expectations by a long way. Great Heavens! What men they were in those days! . . . The countryside is magnificent, but more, I think, from the point of view of cultivation than from layout. The town is situated on the reverse slope of the Apennines in a valley formed by the Arno. The soil is not very good and yet cultivation is turning Tuscany into one of the most productive countries in the world. It would be quite superfluous to try to count the number of habitations that can be seen from each prominence. . . . The climate is divine. It is very hot from eleven to five. The early morning, the evening, and the night-time are as it will probably be one day in Paradise. (*Mémoires*, III, pp. 25–26)

Rome has been for me like a person of whom I would like to have drawn my own picture not having met her: one always miscalculates on such occasions. I found her quite different from what I had supposed. I thought Rome would be old and sombre: she is ancient and superb, resplendent and new. (*Mémoires*, III, p. 194)

The situation of Naples is at once more beautiful and more ample than I had imagined. Everything there is on a vast and graceful scale. The mountains are high and rugged like the Alps. Vesuvius is a prodigious bulk, certainly bigger than the Schnee-berg. . . . What has far exceeded my expectations is the cultivation and charm of the countryside. The country between Terra-cure and Naples is much like Upper Styria specially round Cilli and Laybach. Add to these pictures valleys as broad as those through which the Rhine flows, inconceivably rich and thick vegetation, Vesuvius always in sight, and fresh glimpses every minute of the sea and of the most picturesque islands in the world, and you will have some idea of my visit to this country. I have seen many things in this world, but nothing at once more beautiful and more satisfying to the soul and the senses. (*Mémoires*, III, p. 204)

On the other hand Metternich, again like his compatriots, forms only a low estimate of Italians in general, and his opinion of them did not improve over the years:

The Italian makes a lot of noise, but he does not take action. The proof of this is to be found in the history of the last thirty years, during which there has never been in Italy a revolutionary movement in the proper sense of the word, in spite of all sorts of intrigues. The truth is that in the case of the Italians hatred never manifests itself against a thing but always against a person. And that is why in Italy detestation is felt between one province and another, and between one town, family, or individual and another. If disorder broke out in Florence the inhabitant of Pisa or Pistoia would take sides with the opposition because he hates Florence. And so it happens that Naples is resentful of Rome, Rome of Bologna, Leghorn of Ancona, and Milan of Venice. (May 7, 1819. *Mémoires*, III, p. 255)

The Italian on the whole is afraid of the organized gang. He does not like to be unprotected or to commit himself unless he can calculate with some degree of certainty the chances of buying success at small cost and at small personal risk to himself. (to Zichy, July 28, 1820)

Italy is full of idlers and proletarians who lavish words in cafés and in the other public places which usually pass for home with them. . . . The people of Italy are for the most part quiet, they are content to live peaceably on the certain products of a benevolent sky and soil. They fear movement and specially any which threatens to compromise their material well-being. Hating each other, their only real patriotism hardly extends beyond the province or the town where they first saw light of day. Italy presented as a whole is no more than a poetic image created by strangers, embellished and exploited according to their illusions or their secret designs. (to Esterhazy, Apr. 12, 1831)

To this series of overall judgments may be added some local impressions:

The Lombards:

There is in your character a kind of susceptibility which makes it practically impossible to direct your public thoughts. . . . The Lombards have never been more Austrian than when they were under the kingdom of Italy, and they have never been more opposed to Austria than under our government. (remarks made in November 1832 to the Milanese Paolo di Capitani, published by Franco Arese, *Un Colloquio inedito by de M*)

It is a pity not to be able to quote at greater length from this document, which is of outstanding interest in showing Metternich's ideas about Italy:

The Romagnols:

Nowhere does this double defect of weakness and cowardice exist to a greater extent than in the population of the Romagna. The merits of which the Romagnols boast are not of the same kind as those of the inhabitants of Bologna, of that singular collection of loafers of every class, of comedians and retired singers, lawyers without briefs and egotists interested and exclusively occupied in making money. . . . The true Romagnols, that is to say the country people, are perfectly tranquil, they have steadily refused to support the excitements and factions of the towns, and far from ever having taken part in a revolt, they have always shown themselves ready to support the restoration of public order. (to Neumann, May 10, 1832)

The Neapolitans:

A semi-barbaric people, totally ignorant, unreservedly superstitious, ardent and passionate like the Africans, a people who can neither read nor write and whose last word is the dagger, they make good material for the application of constitutional principles. (July 17, 1820. *Mémoires*, III, p. 360)

The Piedmontese:

The system of the see-saw, gymnastics, and juggling, this describes the Piedmontese. It is skill and agility of a low order applied to everything, great and small. In Turin that is called brains. I only see in it ambition and weakness. (Oct. 23, 1847. *Mémoires*, VII, p. 437)

Only the Tuscans appear to find favour:

One remarkable thing in this country is the type of culture that exists among ordinary people. There is not a peasant who does not speak his language with all the care and elegance of an academician from La Crusca. It is strange to talk with these good people. It is the language of the *salons*; no jargon, none of those shouts or raising of the voice which are heard elsewhere in Italy. A wine-grower who looked half negro served as my *cicerone*. He described and explained eveything to me as an antiquary might have done. (June 28, 1817. *Mémoires*, III, p. 29)

Bearing in mind the character which he attributes to the Italians, Metternich will not allow them the chance to govern themselves:

No country is less well fitted than Italy to be handed over to popular government, for the primary condition of the existence of this kind of government is one the Italians do not possess. They do not have in their make-up either the necessary serious-ness or bearing. In a word they are not a *people*. This truth was realized by a man whose personal opinion and whose aptitude for judging men could not be doubted. Napoleon told me more than once: 'The representative system is not made for Italians and they will never understand it.' So I have not given it to them. They need titles, ribbons and silent senators. They would only have to be allowed to open their mouths for the machine to stop working instantly. Anyone who knows Italy and her inhabitants cannot be deceived by the claims advanced by the factions. They want disorder which would allow them to give vent to personal hatred, to plunge their hands into the public funds, and to set themselves up as arbiters of salaries and pen-sions. The regime which still corresponds most closely today to the opinions and desires of the Italians would be general administrative disorder, a regime to which their beautiful country was subjected during the Middle Ages. (to Apponyi, Jan. 8, 1833)

As for Italian unity, it is an expression having no moral or material basis:

A portion of the earth which has been enriched by nature's most precious gifts, in which a willingness to do productive work is enough to ensure a fortune, a country where wealth is distributed among a number of towns which have the right to compete with each other without ever being inclined to make any sacrifice on behalf of their rivals, is in no way suited to political unity, especially when geographical conditions raise obstacles against a fusion of parties which would only lose by it. That is the real position in the peninsula and the truth with regard to the claim for an imaginary unity and indivisibility.

Never will the Italian peninsula be politically *one*, nor even *united*, and if by chance it were to be otherwise, such a situation would have no more importance, and would last no longer, than if it had been an accident. (Aug. 12, 1848. *Mémoires*, VIII, p. 475)

Austrian policy in Italy is clearly defined:

The Emperor is recognized as king of the Lombardo-Venetian kingdom beyond the Alps which forms a part of his empire. At the time of the major adjustment of territory in 1814, the late Emperor Francis did not even wish to allow the word *Italian kingdom*, the existence of which would have represented a permanent threat to the other sovereignties in the Peninsula. (Apr. 12, 1847. *Mémoires*, VII, p. 393)

Italy is a geographical expression. The Italian peninsula is made up of States that are sovereign and independent of each other. The existence and territorial outline of the States are based on principles of general public right and corroborated by the least controversial of political transactions. The Emperor, for his part, has decided to respect these transactions and to contribute, so far as lies in his power, to their maintenance. (Aug. 6, 1847. *Mémoires*, VII, p. 415)

We treat the maintenance of public order in Italy as a matter of life and death for ourselves. (to Neumann, Dec. 1832)

The Austrian programme for Italy is constantly being compromised by two principal factors: the activities of the secret societies and French ambitions:

> There is a swarm of secret societies. Detailed enquiries by the Austrian police in 1823–1824 revealed the existence of a good fifty secret bodies, either indigenous or imported from France and Spain: the Barabisti in Sicily: the Consistoriali in Ferrari: the Illuminati in Tuscany: Bersaglieri, Sabattini, Sanfedisti, Templari in Rome: Calderari and Decisi in Naples: Defensori della Patria, Ermolaïsti, Figlii di Marte, Figlii della Speranza, Fratelli del dovere, Fratelli artisti in the Romagna: Nastro Verde in Parma: Filedonica in Bologna etc. (*Kabinettsarchiv. Vertrauliche Akten* 144)

In the years before 1830 the Carbonari, who originated in Naples, were specially dangerous. Later it is Mazzini's *Giovine Italia*, supported and stimulated by the numerous Italian exiles who had settled in Switzerland, England, and France.

On the failure of a Mazzinist *coup de main* against Savoy in February 1834, Metternich makes an appreciation of the character and work of the great Italian revolutionary:

> Many people, and even those who were conversant with the plotting of Young Italy, maintained at the time that the sect was dead and could never recover from the blow it had received. But anyone who had studied carefully the character of Mazzini must have told himself that this modern Catilina would not give up the struggle, but would on the contrary lose no time in mending the broken threads and reassuring and comforting his numerous partisans. Also he would soon set to work to find a more practical substitute for the plan that had failed. From his earliest age Mazzini has had to contend with difficulties which he was never able to surmount.

> In the first place he found it impossible to unite Young Italy with the other sects which nibble away at the Peninsula, in particular the old and reformed *Carbonari*, which had a different emphasis. Secondly, in spite of the unbroken relations which this bold conspirator maintained with French propagandists, it is well

known that the head of the committee did not approve of Mazzini's plans, accused him of impetuosity and impatience, and did not put much faith in the strength which Young Italy claimed to possess. Several Italian secret societies and the propaganda of Paris abandoned Mazzini to his own devices at the time of the expedition to Savoy, and this conspirator harbours feelings against them which must have come to the surface in the new moves he is contemplating. (Circular of June 27, 1834. *Interiora. Circ. 26*)

Among Italian conspirator-patriots a special place is reserved for Silvio Pellico, whose famous book has brought tears to the eyes of generations of sensitive souls and has forced on world opinion the image of the Austrian as the jailer and executioner of Italy. It is only fair to give the accused a hearing. In 1846 a French historian, Jacques Crétineau-Joly, had undertaken, at the request of Pope Gregory XVI, a history of the Italian secret societies. The author believed with good reason that he would find information of the greatest value in Vienna, so along he went to seek permission from Metternich to consult the Chancellery's archives. After some delay authority was granted and he was also given permission to satisfy his expressed desire to visit the Spielberg prison, where Pellico and his companions had served their sentence of *carcere duro*:

> I was on the point of leaving for the famous State prison, Crétineau-Joly relates, when an official from the Imperial Chancellery handed me a parcel containing some books and some papers of different colours. I opened the parcel and the first volume which caught my eye was *Mie Prigioni* by my friend Silvio Pellico.
>
> It was a magnificent publication and magnificently bound in red morocco. At the beginning of this work, in which Metternich plays the rather unattractive part of the jailer and executioner, I read the following dedication written in Silvio's own hand: 'To His Highness the prince de Metternich, Imperial Chancellor, in homage with the respectful gratitude of the author: Silvio Pellico.'

Beside this strange expression of an even stranger gratitude, were the *Mémoires d'Andryane*, and a mass of letters written in their own hand, all addressed from the Spielberg or from the Piombi in Venice to M. de Metternich by the most distinguished prisoners of State, all overflowing with paeans of gratitude and love in his honour!

Maroncelli, the martyr, called him *adored father*; Silvio Pellico a *second Titus*; Confalonieri showered on him all the flattery in his Italian repertory; and the small fry of the Carbonari movement figuratively grovelled before his image.

Back in Vienna, I went to return to the prince de Metternich his books and his letters. 'Mon Prince,' I said, 'the lesson has been learned, and I thank you for it. But allow me to ask you why you refused publication of those letters which would provide such a splendid contrast to those stories which your Highness has perhaps less cause to complain of than the Imperial Government?' 'Ah! Why! Why!' he repeated as he paced up and down in his study. 'Well, good heavens, for the simplest of reasons. Because those letters have always seemed to me to be confidential, and their reproduction would not have provided a cure for the evil. The Press would have found some devilish way of turning them against us. . . . Silvio Pellico, Maroncelli, Andryane played their part as party men, outlaws, and victims: I wanted the Imperial Government not to lose dignity. And, besides, you have seen the kind of life to which our political prisoners are subjected. Let me tell you that when the Spielberg had the honour of housing the *élite* of the Carbonari movement, I went out of my way, so to speak, to provide them all as far as I could with a tolerable existence both spiritually and materially. They were men of imagination and the lack of books, paper and light made any intellectual work impossible. They had delicate constitutions and the wholesome but coarse food of the prison revolted them. They were men of society and cell life was torture to them. After receiving orders from the Emperor I ordered them to be given books, candles and other things; I gave word that they should be served with food more in keeping with their tastes and that they should be allowed to communicate with each other. Only on the question of uniform was I unable to bring myself to give way.

This drove Count Confalonieri to despair. The soul of this gentleman conspirator rose in anger at the feel of that egalitarian livery, and rebelled against the application to himself of his own doctrines of social equality. (U. Magnard: Jacques Crétineau-Joly, *Sa vie Politique, religieuse et littéraire*, Paris, 1875, pp. 354–7)

Three years later, in Brussels, Metternich made very similar remarks to Louis Veuillot:

'That man,' he said, speaking of Silvio Pellico, 'really abused the intellectual superiority given to him by God and the pardon granted him by the Emperor. I bear him the greatest ill will for having known how to turn a libellous book into a book of prayer. . . . God knows better than I, better perhaps than Pellico himself . . . why he *wanted to lie*. But there are lies and treason in this beautiful book. Lies: facts are falsely invented or exaggerated. Treason: he had promised when he received his pardon to respect the Emperor's Government and not to injure it in any way.' (ibid., p. 358)

The activities of the secret societies would not have been so dangerous but for outside help: from certain Russian agents in the years immediately after 1815, and specially from France. It is true that under Louis XVIII and Charles X the Italian revolutionaries had nothing to hope for from the Government: but at the same time liberally minded bodies—Carbonari, Freemasons, etc.— could supply them with money and arms, not to mention moral encouragement. The royal government itself, as soon as it was in a position to exercise an independent policy again, was to try to re-establish France's traditional influence in the Italian peninsula. It was not lacking in trump cards: in Naples the goodwill of the Bourbon monarchies: in Rome the influence of a great Catholic Power: in Turin the temptation for the Piedmontese Government to enjoy the advantages of playing one powerful neighbour off against the other: in Italy as a whole, memories of the Napoleonic era, and the attraction of a constitutional regime.

When it comes to the Papal States, Metternich's policy is inspired by very special considerations:

The Church State, from the point of view of its temporal existence and its territorial confines, possesses two guarantees which no other State shares with it. One of them lies in the quality which its sovereign possesses as head of the Catholic Church, the other in its geographical position. The whole of Catholicism must want its centre of unity to have temporal sovereignty, for it is only if the Papacy is independent that it can measure up to its important mission.

The desire of Catholicism as a whole must also be the desire of the great Catholic Powers, from the religious as well as from the political point of view. Since the position of head of the Church must, if it is to fulfil the terms of its office, be independent and since this independence can only be obtained in conditions of personal sovereignty, it follows that the Pope can be placed neither under royal nor national sovereignty. He who can be head of Catholicism can never be the subject of a prince or the first official in a republic. It is the Bishop of Rome who is head of the Catholic Church, and that being so, he must be sovereign of Rome. (Aug. 6, 1847. *Mémoires*, VII, pp. 417–18)

The Holy See must not, however, expect special treatment from the Emperor in political matters:

The Pope having accepted those conditions laid down by the Congress that are favourable to it can hardly refuse the others. In the matter of temporal property, His Holiness can only be considered and treated as a temporal Power. That is a principle on which you cannot insist too strongly at the Court of Rome which never feels inclined to recognize it when it runs counter to its interests. (to Lebzeltern, Aug. 21, 1815)

Pontifical administration is a constant subject of complaint.

The worst of all the systems is not despotism so much as a cowardly and weak government, and cowardice and weakness are precisely those fundamental characteristics which shape the course of Roman administration. (to Neumann, May 10, 1832)

The elderly Cardinals are more stupid than it is possible to imagine. (to Esterhazy, Aug. 12, 1820)

In the Sacred College only one statesman: Consalvi. But

... he is obstructed daily in his actions and in his system by the parties who are most opposed to his opinions and interests, namely by several influential cardinals who cling to the old forms of Roman government and who would like to have seen them revert completely to the era of the Restoration. They have, in consequence, openly declared their opposition to the administrative system introduced at that time by the Cardinal Secretary of State.

In spite of that we like to flatter ourselves that he will continue to exert a necessary and preponderant influence in the political affairs of the Court for as long as the reigning Pope lives, and we must even positively desire it, seeing that of all the statesmen in the country, the number of which is perhaps more limited in Rome than anywhere else, he is beyond question the one who offers us the best guarantee, thanks to his enlightened and unprejudiced mind, his experience of business, and the numerous and important relations he has established with us, which must have convinced him of the justice of our intentions and of the honesty of our views. (Instructions for Apponyi, Sept. 16, 1820)

When Consalvi disappears from the scene in 1824, Metternich grants him this funeral oration:

I had a high opinion of him and he had a lively affection for me. He had a remarkable intelligence and a rare equability of temper: passionate and lively like an Italian, he was as deliberate as a German. (*Mémoires*, IV, p. 91)

As for the Pontifical sovereign, Metternich only met him personally much later on, at the time of his journey to Rome in 1819:

He received me as if I had been an old friend. . . . He came to meet me. He had a stool set down beside him, and we talked together for an hour. . . . He talks very well, quite effortlessly and with much gaiety. In one hour of conversation on every topic under the sun, we must have spent a quarter of the time having a good laugh. Certainly no first meeting between Pope and Minister has ever been more courteous. (*Mémoires*, III, p. 196)

Having seen him for the first time he adds: 'I am once again convinced that there has never been a more simple and enlightened man in his position.'

The question of a successor to Pius VII preoccupied Metternich as early as 1817, and the reason for this was his determination to avoid, by means of an agreement with France, the election of a 'fanatical Pope', in other words, a *zelante*. An idea of his fears and hopes on this subject is given in a letter to the duc de Richelieu:

> If there was no Austrian, Russian or English interest to be disputed in the overthrow of Napoleon, there should not be Bourbon or Austrian rivalry in the next election. What we must look for is the man *the world* needs, not the man of this or that Power. I openly admit that what I am afraid of is Spanish intrigue and influence. Any Pope who sets out to base his government of the Church and of his country on the example of Ferdinand VII may cause the downfall of Europe. All that is needed is for him to adhere firmly to the principle that the past is not finished with because it should never have existed, to attack the principle of the sale of national goods, to praise the resistance of our bishops . . . to find it necessary to turn the laymen out of their jobs in the Papal State and to replace them by *Monsignori*. In short, a Pope has only to provide an example and a rallying-point for extremists in all countries to pave the way for and start a conflagration the effects and repercussions of which would be incalculable. (Apr. 17, 1817. *Fonds Richelieu*)

The conclave of 1829 gives Metternich another opportunity to explain his point of view on the choice of a Pope:

> In a word, what we want more than anything is a *good Pope*. Whatever his nationality or the party by which he is backed, provided the choice made by the Cardinals satisfies this important, primary condition, any other consideration can only be, in our opinion, of secondary importance and all the more so because we are persuaded that any *good Pope*, any really enlightened Pope, will at the same time be an 'Austrian Pope', since he could never fail to be aware that in Austria he has a

neighbour who is as loyal as she is powerful and who is the most zealous guardian of the interests of the Church and of social order. (to Lützow, Mar. 4, 1829)

Metternich, for his part, spared no effort to bring about reforms that were indispensable to the administration of the States of the Church. Unfortunately, he came up against obstacles which he saw only too clearly:

> The permanence of these improvements is exposed to two main dangers: the first arises from the elective form of the government which prevents a Pontifical sovereign from dictating laws which would have effect for longer than his reign. The second danger lies in the insubordination of the government officials who wish to be independent in the sphere which is entrusted to them, and who, in the administration of their departments, deviate in practice from the laws and regulations that are in force. . . .

> It is virtually impossible to supply an adequate remedy for such a state of affairs. Austria neither wishes, nor is able, to govern the Papal States. The immense services she has rendered to the Holy Father and the interest she has in destroying subversive elements in a neighbouring country give her no other right, no other means of influence, than that of *advice*, and even in giving this we must exercise a great deal of care and delicacy if we are not to antagonize a meticulous and sensitive government. (Sept. 20, 1834. In N.A.D.A.: quoted works)

The election of Pius IX in June 1846 was at first welcomed by Metternich as a happy event and he lost no time in offering advice to the new head of the Church. (*Mémoires*, VII, pp. 247–51 et seq.) But it was not long before he was singing a different tune:

> The Pope is shown more clearly every day to be lacking in any practical intelligence. Born and bred in a *liberal* family, he was grounded in a bad school: a good priest, but one who has never turned his mind to affairs of government. Warm-hearted, with little imagination, he has, since his election to the Papacy, allowed himself to become entangled in a net from which he is no longer able to escape and if events pursue their natural

course he will get himself turned out of Rome. (Oct. 7, 1847. *Mémoires*, VII, pp. 342–3)

It was not long before the prophecy was realized. In January 1848 things began to happen: riots in Milan, revolt in Sicily, the setting up of constitutional regimes in Naples and Tuscany . . . the recoil of the Paris revolution of February 1848 is about to complete the ruin of the *pax Austriaca* which had been stubbornly maintained by Metternich in Italy since 1815. [One can read, if necessary, in the *Mémoires* (VII, pp. 564 et seq.) a long dispatch dated February 17, 1848, in which Metternich analyses the general causes of the Italian revolutions of 1848.]

CHAPTER EIGHT

Great Britain

MORE THAN fifty years separate the two occasions on which Metternich stayed in England, for we cannot count the hurried journey of 1814 which was no more than a flying visit between Paris and London entirely devoted to official duties. It was in 1794 on his way from the Low Countries that young Clemens first made contact with British society and with the country in which he had the opportunity to remain at his leisure for several months. He was never to forget the noble sight of the Grand Fleet sailing from Portsmouth on convoy duty to the Indies; more than 400 sail all told manoeuvring in the narrows of the Isle of Wight. He was also introduced to the machinery of Parliamentary government by attending the debates, and he met a number of personalities, among them Pitt, Fox, Burke, Sheridan, Grey, and above all the Prince of Wales, the future King George IV:

> The Prince of Wales was one of the most handsome men I ever saw, and to an agreeable exterior he added the most charming manners. He had a great deal of good sense and he needed it to avoid becoming lost in the bad society which he frequented and in which he moved easily, yet without ever permitting the slightest want of respect in others. He took a great liking to me and was, I think, grateful for my forbearance in company I did not enjoy. (*Mémoires*, I, p. 17)

A somewhat exaggerated manifestation of this affection occurred in 1821 when Metternich met the sovereign in his German kingdom of Hanover:

The welcome given to me by the King was that of a *dear friend*. I do not remember ever having been embraced with such tenderness, and never in my life have I been in the way of hearing such pretty things.

Having endured a veritable deluge of compliments and eulogy in the course of which the King was kind enough to compare me to all the great men of antiquity, the Middle Ages, and modern times, I finally succeeded in talking business, and on this level everything went just as well as I could have wished. I shall accomplish great and good things without claiming on that account to raise myself above a Minos, a Themistocles, a Cato, a Caesar, a Gustavus-Adolphus, a Marlborough, a Pitt, or a Wellington, etc., for all these names His Majesty called me, just as one recites a litany of saints. (Oct. 25, 1821. *Mémoires*, III, pp. 480–1)

Three years later Metternich drew this picture of the King:

King George IV possesses indispensable qualities which are unfortunately tainted by a few defects. He has a real knowledge of affairs and his political principles are quite irreproachable. Persuaded in his youth to follow the opposition Whigs, he turned with the age of reason to the opposite camp. The lessons he picked up from the shocks of the French Revolution served to strengthen him in those principles. There are perhaps few men in Europe who know better than he how to separate the fundamentals of any matter from its outward appearance and how to distinguish in a misleading speech between that part of it which can be attributed to illusion and that which is allied to the truth. This reliable discernment and this tendency to throw light on what is good has raised to the level of a religion in him the confidence which he has felt in Austrian policy since 1815. His friendship for the Emperor, our August Master, has grown to exaltation, and the diplomatic character which you will take with you when you are introduced to His Britannic Majesty will be enough to put you, from the outset, on easy terms with him, an advantage which no member of any other Court is likely to enjoy.

But the influence of the English Crown is unlike that at the disposal of other European monarchs. The mind of a king of England only makes itself felt and appreciated by means of a long series of Acts of Parliament, and it would be misjudging him to attribute to him the vacillations to which English policy is only too prone. . . .

In spite of possessing great and vital qualities, the King allows himself to be influenced in his personal relationships. Since he is constantly absorbed in affairs of the heart, the mind of the woman who is the object of his affections at the moment soon makes its mark on affairs of State, if only through her ability to prosper the cause of those engaged in them. The attachment which preceded the latest one had been suggested by the Tory party, just as the outstanding one of his youth, that with Mrs. Fitzherbert, belonged to the Whig party. (instructions for Apponyi, end of 1825)

In his diplomatic correspondence Metternich seldom expresses an opinion on the English character in general. Is it through lack of having anything bad to say about them, or is it really because he is aware of not knowing them well enough? The complaint he most often makes about them is their ignorance concerning anything that is not England and their 'philanthropic spirit which is so general in its application that it no longer applies itself to realities':

Nothing is more necessary to the British than to see things close up. Judging everything by their own formulas and seeing everything through specially coloured glasses they will not accept truths until they have, so to speak, handled them. Honest and frank in their admissions, they freely acknowledge their mistakes. (to Vincent, June 11, 1823)

Two other British shortcomings:

The political sense of the English does not excel in foresight. (to Trautmansdorff, Nov. 3, 1829)

Great Britain is the country of stereotyped impressions and these end up by acquiring substance. (to Apponyi, June 20, 1842)

When the elderly statesman, turned out of Vienna, disembarked in England in April 1848, that land of refuge appeared to him hospitable and pleasant beyond anything that he had expected. He was mobbed, fêted, and best of all granted the most delectable of pleasures, a hearing. The letters he wrote at that time breathe an air of juvenile enthusiasm, a refreshing curiosity which was really admirable in a man of that age. He is amazed at the growth of London, 'an area that is called a town, it is true, but which is really a kingdom'. He pays visits to warehouses, museums, and factories; he goes into ecstasies over the comfort of the English home and over the furniture. The manors are charming; so, too, is the life that is led in them. Even the climate pleases him, although 'the London sun resembles the Naples moon'.

The man of order purrs his pleasure at the mildly regular habits of that Victorian society:

> In this country everything is arranged like clockwork; this regularity even extends to gestures. Everything is done at a set time; one eats dishes according to a plan, one laughs at certain things and takes no notice of others, however interesting they may be. The result of this is a calmness such as the Continent has long ago forgotten, and for which in its own interest it ought to recapture a taste. (Oct. 11, 1848. *Mémoires*, VIII, p. 194)

The English, he decides, 'have an enormous amount of common sense', and he admires the ease with which the Chartist demonstrations are contained and dispersed by the spontaneous control exercised over the masses by the propertied class:

> The ideas of *liberty* and *order* are so inseparably linked with the English character that the humblest groom would laugh in the face of any so-called reformer who tried to preach liberty to him. But what is most characteristic of the English is their plain sense of the practical. It is evident wherever one looks. It is always the *thing* that the English consider. They remain indifferent to the *form* it takes, and this contempt of form often goes as far as caricature. That is why the houses offer every form of comfort

that circumstances permit. It matters little in England if art is sacrificed to utility. In this connection Italy provides a striking contrast with England. The Italian palaces are uninhabitable because the architects put absolute perfection of form first. The English, on the contrary, take not the slightest notice of it, and in order to satisfy the demands of comfort, they give way to fantasies which often become ridiculous to look at. (May 2, 1840. *Mémoires*, VIII, p. 227)

The position of the British monarchy from a domestic point of view is, in Metternich's opinion, 'utterly false', for it is based on the principle of the sovereignty of the people. Then why does this principle not give rise to the same disastrous consequences in England as it does on the Continent?

First, the English Revolution of 1688, from which it emerged, has nothing in common with the French Revolution of 1789 or with the liberal revolutions of the nineteenth century:

> That revolution, made inevitable by a sovereign who had got himself into the sorry position of having to give up his throne and his country because he tried to introduce changes incompatible with the natural order, was directed by a prince of the royal house acting in agreement with the leaders of Parliament, the only remnant of supreme authority left after the flight of the King. The progress of the revolution was as steady, as wise, and as lawful as any public transaction could be at a time when extraordinary events had eliminated one of the essential elements of government. Not a single law was broken, not a single constitutional form violated, not one individual right destroyed. There was only as much deviation from the line of succession as was necessary to make it conform to existing statutes. Finally, the public, invariably submissive to established authority, never took it into their heads to intervene in the discussions which proceeded as calmly as though they were being conducted by a legislator. It was not one of those upheavals brought about by violence and revolt . . . (to Esterhazy, July 16, 1821)

The relative stability of Britain is also attributable to the fact that England is, so to speak, vaccinated against revolutions by her familiarity with them and by the antitoxins which she has managed to develop:

> England has been through every kind of revolution. Her government, and the same is true of the enlightened majority of her people, not only understands the risks and the evil consequences of disorder, but has laws that are adapted, or adaptable, to every circumstance. In no other country do words, which are the first weapon of revolutionaries in all ages and in all places, have less influence than in a country where every false assertion in respect of public rights is estimated at its true value by reference to the past, where any false principle has already been used to destroy itself, and finally where nothing could be said that had not been said before or had not been thrashed out and had judgment passed upon it. (to Lebzeltern, May 25, 1820)

> In that country the Parliamentary regime has found, in the respect shown to tradition and patronage and in the balanced inter-play of parties, an acceptance which it can never hope to encounter elsewhere.

> England is not only the model for the political life which is called representative or constitutional; the very expression *Parliamentary government* belongs as of right to England. For centuries she has lived under it. In the eighteenth century France hailed it as the model for Europe, but without being able to appropriate it to herself. In that country *Parliamentary government* turned into a caricature; it has become theoretical Parliamentarianism, something that can have no application to real life.

> This nonsense has crossed the Channel and is poisoning political life in the home of *Parliamentary government*.

> In what way does the difference between the two countries show itself? In old England *only things have any value*, and men have no other value than as the simple representatives of things. In French Parliamentarianism people take the place of things, and these have no value except as labels. (*Mémoires*, VIII, pp. 585–6)

The way in which the parties are distinct and well defined is a characteristic and agreeable feature of English Parliamentary life:

In England the Government derives immense support from its well-tried institutions, the most concrete advantage of which lies in the effective separation of the parties and in their clear classification. There are advantages which only time can bring and which make the future secure, and it is in these respects that England differs so widely from France. Although it is easy in the first of these governments to define clearly Ministerialists, Whigs, and reformers, this is by no means so easy in the second case with the innumerable shades of opinion into which Royalists, Ministerialists and self-styled liberals are divided. (to Lebzeltern, Nov. 13, 1819)

Yet Metternich would like to see the designations Tory and Whig replaced by Conservative and Radical (to Hummelauer, Mar. 10, 1839) and he gives the history of their evolution:

The two parties which emerged from the political revolution of 1688 were both conservative. Their aim was identical, to base the prosperity of the United Kingdom on the constitution of 1688, but they differed in the manner of achieving it. For more than a century the two parties took it in turns to manage affairs of State. These were bound to prosper since they remained firmly established on the same foundations. The political thought of the Tory party having developed along more practical lines, their reign lasted longer than that of the Whigs, a party tainted with ideology.

The social revolution which in 1789 came to the surface in France, strengthened the position of the Tories. The universal peace and liberalism introduced into France by Louis XVIII lent power to the Whig party. The last Tory Cabinet was that of Lord Castlereagh. That which bore the name of Mr. Canning shattered both parties, and Sir Robert Peel definitely buried them.

What parties did these two Ministers create? None to which any serious name could be given. Parliament was divided into *conservatives* and *liberals*. Conservators of what? And to what extent reformers?

M.–H

When serious and therefore clearly defined parties disappear, proper names are used to rally serious-minded men and the still undecided masses. This is what happened in England. The name of Canning became a qualification for the conduct of foreign affairs, while that of Peel corresponded to the conditions of the domestic life of the country.

Finally a permanent and powerful aristocracy represents in Metternich's view the best trump card in the English hand. (See above, p. 34) That is probably why he was worried by the proposal to create a university in London. And that explains this strange warning which he imparted in 1825 to King George IV, through his ambassador:

> There is one matter in which I would ask you to engage the King's attention, before you leave, and that is the project to establish a university in London. I authorize you to tell His Majesty that I am certain in my own mind that I am right in saying that if the plan were ever approved it would be all up with England. I should be proved right within a few years. But since this matter is strictly one of internal administration it is only to His Majesty that Your Highness can speak of it. I would like the subject to be broached; it will give me an opportunity to pursue the question. (to Esterhazy, Sept. 8, 1825)

British power had been the essential factor in the long struggle against Napoleon, and without it Austria would never have recovered from the blows she had been dealt. However much Metternich must have been disappointed by British foreign policy after 1815, he could never quite withhold a feeling of gratitude which he did not allow to other Powers. 'One does not give advice to such a Court as the London one, but it is possible to communicate one's thoughts to it.' (to Trautmansdorff, Sept. 19, 1828) One advantage that British policy has over others is that it can be calculated, 'for it constantly represents real interests'. (to Zichy, Mar. 28, 1823) It rests on the very conditions of her existence, which are:

Commerce and the merchant service which is the instrument of commerce and of political domination. These primary conditions have for centuries formed the basis of English policy. They provided her with a point of departure and they will never vary because they are incapable of variation. (to Apponyi, Jan. 3, 1838)

Even so, this does not prevent Metternich finding plenty of features worth investigating in the conduct of foreign affairs as practised in London:

The trouble is that the English Ministers only attach real importance to matters that are strictly English in origin or which affect one of their country's direct interests, and the incidents in the foreign policy of other countries are either not thoroughly investigated by them or are handed over to Civil Servants who deal with them as they think best. (to Neumann, Apr. 24, 1843)

Result of this proud ignorance: 'Of all countries England has always been the one in which least is known about the foreigner.' (to Apponyi, Jan. 27, 1833) In particular the English are bad in their understanding and judgment of France:

The institutions which govern France are always judged in accordance with English practice, which is in no way applicable to France, and which is contrary to the spirit of the nation and to the fundamental conditions of a stable government. (to Esterhazy, Aug. 20, 1829)

The English are divided into two classes. There are those who do not tremble for the safety of the neighbouring throne because the House of Brunswick is not directly threatened. The rest look on the French as charlatans and as being so inferior as to require no interference in their activities. (to Esterhazy, Sept. 21, 1829)

Other criticisms are expressed from time to time, the principal cause being the prejudice shown by British policy in favour of liberal institutions. Herein lies the fundamental reason for the maledictions directed against the policy of Canning and Palmerston, which we shall refer to later. When he rises above personal attacks, Metternich gives expression to this complaint in less bitter terms:

> The English Cabinet is capable of uttering eminently progressive remarks without desiring to give effect to them at home. England freely exports certain principles but at home she pursues a wiser policy, just as she has goods '*for export* and for *home consumption*'. (Aug. 20, 1840. *Mémoires*, VI, p. 440)

> English policy is tainted with mistakes. Anglican Protestantism has distorted people's minds and has replaced clear thought by a spirit of bickering and controversy in matters in which controversy has no place. (June 11, 1844. *Mémoires*, VII, p. 25)

The Eastern crisis of 1840 cast a glaring light on another fault of British policy.

> Men like Ponsonby and Lyons and other English agents are bound to cause indescribable confusion. Active, undisciplined and too often given free rein by their governments, these men are so many firebrands. Being incapable of working for law and order, they become active elements in causing trouble each time they pursue a dream which has its origin in their own thoughts, whether these be political, legislative or even philanthropic. . . .

> Of one thing I am becoming more convinced every day; it is that in the Levant every Englishman who has a political or military function to perform, consults his own inclinaton far more than the wishes of his government. (to Esterhazy, Feb. 28, 1841)

This applies to Sir Stratford Canning, who has for too long caused trouble in Constantinople:

> The character and disposition of this individual make him ill suited to the post he occupies and the present English Cabinet was wrong to entrust it to him. He scarcely obeys any other instructions than those which he issues himself. He is abstract in his thinking; full of likes and dislikes of men and things, an ideologist as the word was applied to the philhellenes of old, and a Russophobe . . . He is incapable of carrying out the orders of his superiors, or if he does he cannot restrain his personal impulses. (to Neumann, Mar. 30, 1843)

In spite of the setbacks, in spite of Canning and Palmerston, Metternich always remains convinced of the natural and fundamental solidarity between Austria and England:

> I only know three kinds of position in which a Power can find itself *vis-à-vis* another. The first is that of general community of interests considered on a large scale. The second is that of general divergence of interests, and the third is that of independence, fairly extensive but still relative because in politics absolute independence does not exist for States any more than it does for individuals in society . . .

> Into which of these categories is it fitting to place the natural relations between Austria and England? My intelligence tells me that, as far as their temporary and permanent interests are concerned, they are placed in the first and third categories at the same time.

> They must be ranged in the first category because a permanent common interest binds these two great States, one essentially maritime and having no Continental possessions, the other Continental and without colonies and having therefore no political interests requiring sea-power to defend them. But both Powers participate equally in the third condition because the geographical position of their possessions precludes any rivalry between them. On the contrary it calls for mutual support . . . Although in many questions of a temporary nature the two Powers can do without that aid which may rightly appear to them to be superfluous, there can be no serious political issue on which they ought not to combine in the maintenance of their permanent interests. . . .

> The two Courts find themselves in a position, *vis-à-vis* each other, that is quite different from that which exists between Great Britain and any other first-class Power. France and England are fundamentally rival Powers, and they will remain so for as long as there is an England and a France. Spain, reduced to her present position, will continue to be a cause of contention between the two great maritime Powers and will be as putty in their hands. Prussia, who by her nature has only become a first-class Power fortuitously, will be now assisted, now baulked in

her outbursts by Great Britain. Finally, Russia occupies a quite exceptional position in relation to England. The two Powers will be united or in disagreement according to circumstances. Either condition will tend to become exaggerated. The fundamental element which will remain is a substratum of mutual distrust, tolerably well disguised beneath a benign exterior which apes confidence without being able to establish it. (to Neumann, Feb. 5, 1843)

Up to the time of Castlereagh's death in August 1822, Metternich did not find it too difficult to act in agreement with England as he wished. Yet he regretted 'the too-long-drawn-out immobility of the English government and its ability often to subordinate the most important interests to secondary and minor considerations'. (to Zichy, Apr. 12, 1820)

He deplores

the system of temporization and condescension which were natural to Lord Castlereagh and, I think, much more so to the comte de Liverpool. A front-rank Power like England could not make a bigger mistake than to procrastinate over the choice of her ground, to allow others to occupy ahead of her the only position suitable to her ... In every single one of these instances the Ministry has encouraged the establishment of, or the daily strengthening of, the power of its opponents, giving them courage until a point is reached where the Ministry is no longer able, for all its moral and material strength, to provide a remedy for something which might have been settled in the first place by a word or a gesture. (to Esterhazy, May 16, 1820)

In spite of everything, the tragic death of Castlereagh—Lord Londonderry—was a particularly severe blow for Metternich:

I regard the loss of that Minister as one of those catastrophes which sometimes strike empires as well as individuals, from which no amount of foresight can shield them and for which no amount of cool-headedness can compensate. The British Government's system cannot change, for it is the outcome of unmistakable necessity. Where is the man who could unite a knowledge of affairs with a knowledge of those people who make the greatest impact on events, to the same degree as the Marquess of Londonderry who had himself acquired this knowledge through so many years' hard work and experience? . . .

That Minister had acquired the freedom of Europe and if regret is keenly felt in his own country, it is shared in an equal degree by our people. (to Neumann, Aug. 26, 1822)

It is one of the worst catastrophes that could have befallen me. He was devoted to me heart and soul, not only from a personal attachment but also from conviction. Many matters which would have been easy with him are going to need fresh study and renewed effort with his successor, whoever he may be. I had been waiting for him here as though he were my second self. My work would have been reduced by half because I should have shared it with him. For the moment I am left on my own and am thrown back on my own resources. (Aug. 25, 1822. *Mémoires*, III, p. 557)

After the disappearance of this friend, there remained in England only one man on whom Metternich thinks he will be able to count: Wellington. It is to him that Metternich turns whenever he wishes to deliver a grave warning to the British Government, or simply to seek its help. But the opinion he forms of the Iron Duke does not err on the side of flattery.

The Duke is one of those people who may make a mistake about a situation, but never about a matter of principle. (to Esterhazy, Apr. 15, 1823)

The Duke has the misfortune, for himself and for the general good, to be devoid of any political talent. Good general and honest man that he is, and steadfast in matters of principle once he has recognized them as such, he is lacking in the sureness and delicacy of touch which is the first requirement of a useful statesman. (instructions to Apponyi, 1825)

Until 1827 the nominal head of the government is Lord Liverpool, but he hardly counts:

Lord Liverpool has adopted fixed principles of administration and he enjoys a Parliamentary reputation which is probably deserved. But he lacks the degree of detachment which constitutes the real statesman and he has in common with most English Ministers the defect of not appreciating the positions and needs of Continental Powers. This lack of knowledge never made itself felt so long as the Marquess of Londonderry was at the helm in British politics. It has become all the more marked now that Mr. Canning frequently indulges in conduct which I can only describe as fantasy . . . (instructions to Apponyi, 1825)

George Canning, he is the real power behind British policy after 1821. By turning it in quite a different direction from Austrian policy he inflicted on Metternich the mortification of seeing his favourite work, 'the ark of the covenant', the alliance of 1815, ruined, and of witnessing the scandal of a great conservative Power extending a helping hand to liberal movements. Some months after the disappearance of this adversary from the scene, Metternich summed up in these words the antagonism that had existed between them:

I told you years ago that the great political question of the day had resolved itself into a hand-to-hand struggle between the late Mr. Canning and myself. . . . There is no doubt at all that although the wild desire which the English Minister felt to make a success of his career involved him in the overthrow of the political structure which had been built up at such cost since the partially successful restoration in France, yet the realization that simply by taking a step back he would find himself once again on the same ground as myself, not only prevented Mr. Canning from ever taking a fresh line but made him decide to plunge himself and his country ever deeper into a maze from which there was no advantageous way of escape. (to Esterhazy, Dec. 31, 1827)

But it is necessary to trace this incident back to its source. Here, first of all, is how the man came to power:

Born into a fairly undistinguished social class, without any aristocratic patronage, Mr. Canning nevertheless embarked on his political career by attracting the attention of the Ministerial party. It was not long before he acquired the reputation of an orator and showed signs of giving the government useful support by his easy mastery of sarcasm and of an irony, at once subtle and biting, which made him formidable to his opponents. Once the Marquess of Londonderry began to decline and at the sad time of his death the government found itself with no mouthpiece. Canning was to go to India. It was the Duke of Wellington who put in a word for him to the King and who was responsible for his being called to the helm. He thought he could attach Canning to himself and to the views of the government from a sense of gratitude. He was wrong.

It is not easy to decide precisely into which political party Canning fits, and it is equally difficult to disentangle the threads of administrative and political principle which might be said to be his own. I do not think I am wrong in putting him in that category of men who woo fortune by striving for immediate success, knowing their own ability yet not possessing the detachment and sense of responsibility which alone makes it possible to base their policy on positive and clearly defined action. . . . Mr. Canning is clever, and he knows it. He hardly questions the success he was skilful enough to secure for himself, but this kind of game cannot be kept up for ever and less easily in England than in any other country. He has accordingly made more than one move recently to build up support for himself in the King's estimation. His efforts seem to have met with some success, the extent of which can be measured by words recently uttered by the King. 'I do not like Mr. Canning,' this prince recently told Prince Esterhazy, 'and I never shall, but he has become the necessary man.' (instructions to Apponyi, 1825)

After the control of British foreign policy had fallen into Canning's hands in August 1822, it was only too obvious that England would refuse to have a part in the action that was being taken by the Continental allies against the liberal revolutions in Italy and Spain. Castlereagh would have sought to play down this difference; but Canning paraded it and used it to win golden opinions from his countrymen.

By April 1823, Metternich is wise to him:

What reliance can be placed on a Minister who after twenty
years in the service of his government offers not the slightest
guarantee of his reliability to any party? The simplest way to
deal with such a situation is to bear in mind that the man in
question lacks the principal quality that makes the statesman:
Mr. Canning may have intelligence but he certainly has not got
reliability.

It is so long since I expected or feared anything from the government of that country that whenever my political calculations are
concerned with Great Britain they invariably only relate to a
negative attitude. The satisfactory affairs are those in which I do
not come across England, and it could not be otherwise. . . .
Europe has only one major problem. That problem is the disease
from which the British Isles were the first to suffer, a disease
which is mistaken by most of the inhabitants of that country for
good health, just as individuals often feel they are getting better
when in fact the change is only from an acute illness to a chronic
complaint. (to Esterhazy, Apr. 13, 1823)

Metternich decided on the attitude he would adopt towards
the English Minister and his party:

Up to the present I have stuck to my original plan . . . namely
that of not going to meet Mr. Canning half-way. My opinion
of him then has been confirmed by all that has happened since.
Generally speaking, intelligence and, even less, a desire to escape
from the dictates of experience are not enough to distinguish a
statesman. He is eloquent and ingratiating. He will give way
when he finds himself in an awkward situation. That is why he
yielded to the opposition and is now courting its favour. The
day that the cause which we consider the right one becomes
more firmly established, Mr. Canning, if he is still in the same
Ministerial position as he is now, will again be the first to bow to
it. Since my conduct towards him is governed by this conviction,
it follows quite naturally that I should consider myself to be
wasting time and energy if I spent them in discussion with him.
I much prefer to devote them to strengthening the cause of

reason . . . You have never seen me confuse English power with the aberrations of one or the other of her Ministers. That power could certainly never be exercised on the side of evil, but it may from time to time refuse to take the side of good. That being so, the secret must lie in maintaining a position of sufficient strength to enable us to reach, without undue harm, a point when English common sense will regain the dominion which temporary, unavoidable mistakes have obscured without being able to destroy. (to Esterhazy, Oct. 17, 1824)

Mr. Canning . . . is pursuing a fanciful policy. Assuming for the moment that I adopt his formula of keeping in step with public opinion, what else can I do but recognize that he is basing his conduct on a system that is essentially unstable and variable. The political line followed by the Continental Courts, on the other hand, rests on fixed principles. The only possible point of contact between the two systems is where they cross each other. That being so they must be kept apart and the greatest care must be taken to avoid a fusion which in any hypothesis could only redound to the advantage of him who lives by disorder. . . .

Frankly we consider England lost to the cause which forms the basis of our existence and . . . we shall continue to think so until the day her government alters course. That day will come, there is no doubt of it. . . . Bonaparte also came to an end, and you have seen me base all my calculations, at the very time when his power was at its height, on a time when he would fall . . . I will not do Mr. Canning the honour of comparing him to Napoleon, but he has given me grounds to regard him as a scourge, and the whole of history tells me that scourges also have their downfall. Mr. Canning will fall sooner than Bonaparte because of the difference in the basis of their conduct and in the motive power behind it. In the case of Mr. Canning it was quite negative, of necessity bound by events, and therefore presenting only a bizarre collection of impulses and fears. It is not by means of such elements that States allow themselves to be governed for long. Mr. Canning will be obliged to shift towards radicalism or to attempt a return towards monarchy. In either event he will be lost. (to Esterhazy, Feb. 10, 1825)

The most painful blow to Anglo-Austrian relations was struck by Canning in 1826 when he joined with Russia to give the Greek question a solution contrary to the principles proclaimed by Metternich. After reading through the instructions sent by the head of the Foreign Office to the British Ambassador at Constantinople, Metternich allows his indignation to overflow:

> For a long time I have not had the smallest opinion of the stability of Mr. Canning's mind, and I frankly admit that any opinion to the contrary would have been destroyed by reading this hotchpotch of absurdities. If only there were anything but absurdity in the policy which the British Government is pursuing in Levantine affairs! But what a constant violation of principles! What a crude game even down to the most elementary rules of behaviour! Whatever the outcome may be, it is certain that the man or the government who allow themselves to carry on in this way must one day pay for the vast errors and failings of the present time. (to Apponyi, Sept. 25, 1826)

> The gauntlet is down between Mr. Canning and myself. Every day brings proof of the extreme virulence of his hatred for ourselves, our actions and our principles. . . . He has reached the very limits of moral confusion. . . . The monstrous alliance which he formed last spring with Russia, an alliance without a foundation and consequently holding out no prospect of a favourable outcome . . . must call for more than one explanation. Liberalism bound to autocracy, an absolute need for peace harnessed to the clearest aptitude for war—so many extremes together would be enough to cause the cancellation of an achievement conceived with unimaginable levity, applied right up to the present with rare ineptitude, and worked on with the kind of haste that always characterizes misconceived plans. . . . (to the comte de Munster, Dec. 26, 1826)

The Chancellor's exasperation was raised to its highest level by the famous speech delivered in the House of Commons on December 12, 1826. With a great display of oratory Canning threatened to unleash against the other Powers the forces of liberalism, and he compared England to Aeolus, King of the

Winds, restraining or releasing tempests at will. He also boasted that his had been the hand that fashioned the independence of the Spanish American colonies. This speech appeared to Metternich 'to come close to delirium' and to reveal a character 'of true criminality':

> If the emblem of an empire ever assumed the significance of an oriflamme of death and destruction to the social order, how many and how serious would be the reproaches to which its government would be exposed! If that were the case we should never be able to understand how it would dare to turn the greatest of misfortunes into an object of pride and boasting.

> Applied to the present time, against whom is the threat directed? Against France? But in what respect has that Power yet deserved ill of the British Cabinet? Or is it against Spain? In that case why supply the government in Madrid with overwhelming weapons for its defence? Or could it be that England is aiming, by making her threats general, to set herself up as the enemy of all peoples, of all forms of government, and of all existing institutions? Truth to tell none of it makes any sense.

> The most inexcusable part of the speech appears to us to be that in which the British Minister boasts so outrageously of a thirst for revenge that the dismemberment of the ancient Spanish monarchy would appear to be no more than a punishment which he, Canning, had inflicted on the Mother Country for having allowed a Power, friendly to Spain and an ally, yet reputedly a rival of England, to save the country from the most frightful revolutionary oppression, against which the English Government had declared itself powerless to act. Unfortunately for the spokesman, everything in such an odious claim would be both morally and historically false. (to Bombelles, Jan. 8, 1827)

Again, he says that Canning has made himself the leader of monarchical liberalism. 'He behaves like the captain of a ship flying a recognized flag but leading the life of a buccaneer'. (to Apponyi, Jan. 29, 1827)

To advance by bounds, to attack things for no other reason than to get oneself talked about, to launch oneself passionately down unknown paths and to get out of breath in the process, that is not governing. (to Zichy, Jan. 31, 1827)

In April 1827, Lord Liverpool was put out of action by an apoplectic fit and Canning was called on to form a Ministry. A difficult task: the hard core of the Tory party still objected to his liberal tendencies and the old guard of the Whig party regarded him as a turncoat.

I feel sure that Mr. Canning, once abandoned by the Tory party, will have tried to come to terms with the Whigs. It is very natural that the latter should want nothing to do with the man who stole a march on them at an obviously awkward time . . . And so he found himself reduced to forming an administration the principal members of which could only be drawn from the restricted circle of his intimate friends and from a small group of individuals who were either more or less independent of the two great parties or who were too strongly attracted by the prospect of office not to sacrifice the opinions of the party to which they belonged. The result is that the government of England has fallen into the hands of a small body of men whom it would be fair to label *Canning and Co.*

The question is to find out if and for how long he will last. The fight is on between the new and the old England, between the surface and the depth, between the froth and the substance. The old England will not be overthrown so quickly, or at least not without resistance. In a word, will it or Mr. Canning perish in the struggle? (to Zichy, Apr. 30, 1827)

The answer to this question was to be given two months later by the untimely death of the great British statesman. Metternich does not miss the opportunity to pass judgment on this 'immense event':

Mr. Canning undertook a great deal but finished nothing! He knocked down and undermined a great deal but he built nothing. His Ministry which lasted three months will occupy a place in the annals of history similar to that of another famous Hundred Days. Both of these periods resemble an irruption, they present a picture of avalanches blotting out everything in their path that is not destroyed. But that which has only been covered will not take long to emerge again, and such will be the case not only with a great number of individuals but with several causes. . . .

The death of the Prime Minister will have repercussions in one direction in particular. There had attached themselves to his chariot a host of spirits which will vanish away, which will buzz about and fly off in all directions like the swarm that has lost its queen. Mr. Canning was an immense phantom; that was the effect he produced on the spirits. His policy, although lacking in substance, attracted every eye. His followers will fly off into space or else offer themselves to different parties. It is quite certain that they will fight against each other, and since it is England they will fight with the utmost determination. Recently I formed some really important ideas and gathered some strange information concerning the political and social position of the man who has died. But I was perhaps less struck by his sudden death than most people because I knew of the danger that threatened him. It was not only his body that was attacked, but even his mind. Too much activity on the part of the cogs had broken the machine. (to Werner, Aug. 17, 1827)

The name 'of the man whom Providence had launched upon England and on Europe as a malevolent meteor' was to reappear more than once in Metternich's correspondence as the symbol of all he detested. Let us quote, at least, this curious parallel between Canning and Chateaubriand:

The spirit of the age has become incarnate in Mr. Canning. Ever since the evil star of England guided him to the head of the administration, that man has never represented or protected a single interest that was really English. He has only protected and represented absurd systems. France, too, has had her Canning but his successes have not been, and could not be, the same, for his intellectual faculties, his personal position, and the situation of France were different.

The person to whom I refer is the vicomte de Chateaubriand. Both Ministers have destroyed the old party qualifications. Starting more or less from the same point in their political careers, that of extreme monarchism, drawn later, one by feelings of frustrated ambition, the other by inordinate vanity, down disastrous paths, both men acted as solvents on the royalist party and as supports to the revolutionary party. Neither the Tories in England nor the Royalists in France being any longer able to recognize themselves, a good number of them became lost in the void that had separated the rival camps. A crowd of revolutionaries reappeared in the *middle* where the Goderich Ministry had taken up its position, and it is in that position, where all is weakness and compromise, that the present administration made the mistake of accepting the heritage of the previous Ministry. The Ministries of La Ferronnays and Martignac took up a position in France similar to the Goderich Ministry in England. (to Esterhazy, Mar. 16, 1830)

'We flatter ourselves that we have rediscovered an England', wrote Metternich in October 1827. But it was not long before he was singing a different tune. The Government formed by Wellington in January 1828 was distinguished by its indecision and feebleness. Metternich likened it 'to a man whose constitution although robust has undergone a powerful shock from great debauchery'. (to Trautmansdorff, May 4, 1828)

The administration is . . . like the Duke of Wellington, a singular composition of noble and essential qualities, eccentricities and veritable deficiencies. The Duke must have imposed, has indeed imposed, on the Cabinet a course of action which baffles all calculation. Strong where by inference it might be expected to be feeble, and feeble where it would be so easy for it to be strong, it is impossible to base a plan on such a mixture of droll contradictions. . . . Lord Aberdeen is one of those men, and there are a good number of them, who present two different aspects according to whether they are expressing their thoughts verbally or in writing. I have had many opportunities of proving the truth of this. The extreme loyalty of his character and the frank-

ness of his opinions none the less make him a useful member of
the Cabinet. I fear the weakness of Mr. Peel in dealing with
political questions in the Lower House. My opinion of that
Minister has not varied since he joined the administration. I
believe him to possess more than one essential quality, but what
I think he specially lacks is real firmness of principle. Any
Minister who could yield to Mr. Canning's influence as he did,
and who could defend and frequently adopt the political views
of his colleague, would scarcely give valuable service to the
cause, if it should ever need to be defended with courage and
strength. The rest of the Cabinet is nothing and England's position is a decidedly difficult one. (to Esterhazy, Feb. 11, 1830)

The shock of the revolution of 1830, coinciding with the
accession of a new king, William IV, put an end to the long reign
of the Tories and brought to power a team of Whig reformists,
presided over by Lord Grey. He hastened to introduce an electoral reform which was to wrench exclusive control of Parliament
from the hands of the landed aristocracy. It was, in Metternich's
opinion, opening the door to the most terrible catastrophes:

A country so far gone as Great Britain along the path to destruction can neither stop herself from falling now nor be stopped
by others. . . . I have for a long time thought England to be in the
same position as that occupied by France during the years before
the convocation of the States-General. The introduction of the
Reform Bill and the dissolution of Parliament which was the
direct consequence of it began for England in the year 1789.
That is my conviction and the future will justify it only too
fully.

So far the King has given evidence of the kind of character
which far from suggesting to my mind a remedy must on the
contrary encourage an extension of the evil. That monarch is
endowed with a courage fitting to those who commit suicide.
Men of his kind, quite unaware of the effect which the measures
they adopt are bound to produce, can only improve on those
which are leading to their ruin. . . . We shall see this empire going
through every phase of a revolution. Unfortunately it contains

within its boundaries material on which this scourge can feed, for in England there is a throne to overturn, a powerful aristocracy to ruin, a rich clergy to dispossess, a heavy public debt to reduce, tithes and feudal dues to abolish. In a word nothing is lacking for doing what was done in France between 1789 and 1795. (to Esterhazy, May 17, 1831)

There appears in this Whig Ministry for the first time at the Foreign Office another man of Canning's stamp who will prove just as exasperating to the Austrian Chancellor. Lord Palmerston was to be in the nineteenth century the most perfect incarnation of British haughtiness in dealing with 'lesser breeds', that is to say with anyone who was not born under the Union Jack:

> Lord Palmerston thinks he is in control of affairs, but he is wrong. He brings them to a standstill by obstructing them. He thinks he is pushing an English line of policy, but really it is a revolutionary one. He thinks that he is France's ally, but he is only her plaything. He looks for adversaries in any affair in that quarter where his real friends and well-informed advisers are to be found. He thinks he is creating an independent Belgium, and he is turning it into a French province. He thinks he is building liberalism in Spain and Portugal, whereas he is only making revolution in those two countries, or paving the way for the triumph of a blind despotism. In a word, Lord Palmerston is wrong about everything. (to Neumann, Feb. 2, 1833)

> The political course which Lord Palmerston has followed unswervingly presents an unbroken sequence of mistakes based on gross misconceptions. That Minister evidently belongs to the class of men who consult their own inclinations above all, taking them as their point of departure in any matter, who never take properly into account the point they are making for, and who flatter themselves that they can decide on it as they go along. Endowed with a cunning mind and a mischief-making temperament, he attempts either to scatter his adversaries by employing great violence towards them or to win them over with blandishments, according to the degree of importance which he attaches to the matter. As we are not afraid of the effects of his violence

... and as we are not to be won over by blandishments, we are in the same position as members of an audience seated in the best boxes, and we judge calmly the play that is being shown, without getting excited over the rumble of the thunder or a scene that makes the most flattering appeal to the senses. (to Apponyi, Dec. 1, 1835)

We know how Metternich described the agreement between France and England which was one of the results of Palmerston's policy. His attitude in the first Turko-Egyptian crisis of 1833 inspires this diatribe:

Never, no never, has a Cabinet shown ineptitude equal to that of which the London Cabinet has just shown us the strange and singular spectacle. Sooner or later that Power will wake up. Events will unfold before its eyes and then what reproaches will weigh upon the Ministers who have been dragged down by their inconceivable blindness! (to Neumann, June 9, 1833)

The formation of the first Tory Ministry of Robert Peel at the end of 1834 only appears to Metternich as 'a check on the downward slope'. Indeed, five months later the Whigs, with Lord Melbourne, regained power; and with them Palmerston, who was to reign over the Foreign Office until August 1841. What will become of Great Britain, Metternich wonders?

This much is certain, that the passing of the Reform Bill has altered the proportions between the two main parties in that country, the internal tranquillity of which was so closely bound up with the maintenance of equilibrium between those same parties. The old English constitution, as it had been modified by the events of the seventeenth century, could only survive to the present day by clever acting which the ideologists on the Continent took for reality, by an imaginary equilibrium between powers which really only existed in name, and finally by the aristocratic composition of Parliament which the Reform Bill has disorganized. Now that the democratic element has gained the upper hand in the elective chamber, it is there that power resides. What we are seeing is a fight taking place ... between the aristocracy of the country and the democracy of the Chamber, that is to say between the dispossessed element and that which is established by law. . . .

England is advancing with giant strides towards the brink of revolution. The proof of this is that in order to escape the catastrophe which threatens her existence it would no longer be enough to stop on the slope down which she is being dragged, she would have to pass through a counter-revolution by going back on the Parliamentary reform which has already been introduced. This is impracticable and yet without it a radical cure is not possible. The cleverness of the innovators consisted in their choice of the object to which their reform has been directed from the start. Instead of attacking abuses, they undermined the political structure, and by changing the proportions of the electoral roll they secured for themselves the means of overthrowing the old England and her secular institutions. (to Esterhazy, May 25, 1835)

The truth is that the revolution of 1688 had the same effect on the English constitution as the Reformation of the fifteenth century had on the State religion. The two events only served to spread a layer of varnish over an object which was full of cracks and which had suffered the ravages of time. It was a way of making it look new, but the appearance was deceptive. The varnish wears off in time, the old ravages reappear, new ones are added to them and together they reduce the object to dust.

Two striking facts support my comparison . . . I hear talk of reform of the Anglican Church . . . and today there is a proposal for reform of the municipal laws. England separated herself from the Catholic Church before the Council of Trent. Now . . . this Council reformed abuses in the Roman Church which the so-called reformed Anglican Church has for nearly three centuries carefully preserved, and which Parliament finally attacked through a series of measures which tend towards the complete overthrow of the religious and political structure in the United Kingdom.

The same is true of the outstanding abuses which have survived in local government and which were remedied long ago in almost all those countries which are supposed to be much less civilized than Great Britain . . . In that country much has remained as it was, generally speaking, in Europe during the Middle Ages, whereas in some respects civilization in England has not only outstripped that of the Continent but has even exceeded the bounds of true civilization. That country's civilization is indeed at fault when steam-driven vehicles on railways pass through towns and villages in which municipal government has not progressed beyond the fifteenth century. . . .

So long as the old edifice was well looked after, so long as articles of comfort, pleasure and luxury were displayed to superficial observers and shops filled with vast treasure caught everyone's eye, England appeared indestructible; but when daring hands and evil minds attacked the structure itself, her secular institutions and the foundations on which her constitution rests, the outward thing was bound to be exposed . . .

England is lost, in so far as it is possible for States to get lost. A new edifice is going up in the place of the one that has crumbled. The site is the same but the building is quite different. Miserable shanties are often erected on sites that were occupied by magnificent palaces. England is wealthy but wealth disappears quickly at times of social unrest, and since English industry is kept alive by credit, of which every revolution is the enemy, terrible catastrophes threaten the primary element in English power . . .

In the midst of those who are ruining their country today Lord Palmerston has arisen. He appears to be endowed with the necessary talent to make English policy agree perfectly with the course taken, relative to the form of civil institutions, by the Ministry to which he belongs. A veritable evil genius, he is all the more daring because he has personal antecedents to disown and a negligible reputation to avenge. (to Esterhazy, June 28, 1835)

Yet Palmerston appears to have shown signs at that time of desiring a *rapprochement* with Austria. Metternich does not believe in his conversion:

A man of Lord Palmerston's qualities can neither change for the good nor return to truth. A change of policy like this can be attributed to a need to change direction forced on him by imperious circumstances, and not to a feeling of inner conviction or a sudden virtuous impulse. The principal Secretary of State is a man of vicious inclinations who delights in contradictions and who must therefore feel frustrated when he is unable to indulge them . . . (to Esterhazy, June 18, 1835)

The accession of Queen Victoria at the end of June 1837 brings a ray of hope:

At the present time there is one factor which is no doubt of the utmost value, and that is the attitude of the young Queen, which is one of calmness and at the same time of a general and rational benevolence. If one wished to use this fact as the basis of a horoscope and to give it any deeper significance than that of a hope, one would undoubtedly be guilty of levity. . . . The Queen is a child, for at 18 queens are no more than children. There are good children and vicious children. Innate tendencies can be modified by the attentions of education but they cannot be destroyed. Of all men's natural tendencies, the one that comes to light most frequently is a spirit of opposition on the part of the pupils towards their teachers. This possibility has constantly played a part in the calculations I have made in respect of the young Queen, and it explains perhaps why today I felt less surprised than many others as I watched the first acts in the reign of this princess. (to Esterhazy, Aug. 2, 1837)

But behind the young queen Metternich perceives the shadow of 'Uncle Leopold', the ambitious King of the Belgians:

I am in no doubt about the dominating influence which King Leopold exerts over his niece. From what I know of this prince, and I know him well, it would be impossible for me not to admit that the advice he will not fail to give her will be conceived in two opposite directions. The advice he will give her on questions of government and administration will be in keeping with healthy doctrines. His political counsel, on the other hand, will be detestable. King Leopold will support revolutionary principles in the Peninsula and will throw fuel on the fire provided it is a matter in which Russia gets involved. He will not be *anti-Austrian*, but neither will he be in favour of our political line. He will humour us because he respects us, but since our principles are not in harmony with his position and not with what he regards as the interests of the Coburg family, he will harm the cause which is ours just as though he hated us. (to Hummelauer, Oct. 10, 1837)

The ardour with which Leopold I on all sides advances the interests of his family, gives rise some months later, to this comment:

That family, which is a product of our times, reflects the spirit of it. At a time when so many thrones are tottering there has appeared an *association* which casts a speculative eye over the vacant seats. It is the Coburgs who form this association, and if the Ottoman throne has so far escaped its covetous glance, it can only be because the natural heir to the throne finds that he is beyond the reach of a kind of industry the exploitation of which was reserved for our age of unlimited progress. . . . (to Neumann, Sept. 2, 1843)

It was natural that Queen Victoria, who finds her happiness in union with a prince of the House of Coburg, should feel well disposed towards her husband's family, but the kind of cult and passionate support which she devotes to anything in any way connected with that House is really too much. Still worse is the blind deference with which the Ministers of the Queen obey her wishes, sometimes subordinating to them their country's solemn interests. (instructions to Dietrichstein, Dec. 8, 1844)

About the middle of 1841 the Whig government was losing its momentum. At the heart of the conflict which was disturbing political life at that time was the question of import duties; was it necessary to continue or abolish the protectionist tariffs which encouraged agriculture but discouraged industry? On this occasion Metternich extends his thoughts into the economic sphere, whither he seldom ventures:

The fight . . . is not confined to the political parties but also involves agricultural, industrial and commercial interests. So long as the struggle is confined to the political parties, it does no more than skim the surface of social life, but it threatens the complete upheaval of the country as soon as it steps down into the realm of vital interests, and that is what will happen with the dispute which has been started by some very unwise Ministers in England. The immediate cause of the unrest which this great country is experiencing in the midst of prosperity is probably the fact that the balance has been upset between the three interests which I have just named. Of these, two have their limitations. Climate on the one hand and the quality and quantity of the land on the other stand in the way of agricultural production. Commerce finds its limitations in marketing restrictions. With manufacturing it is different. There is no limit to its productivity and in my opinion the primary cause of the conflict which has just begun lies in the unexampled spurt forward which industry has taken in England. (to Esterhazy, June 15, 1841)

Metternich deplores the fact that the question should come before the electorate and does not know which party to wish well:

I feel quite unable to estimate the difference between a Whig and Tory Ministry at the moment, and that is due as much to the policy which either party would be likely to pursue as to the probable duration of the Ministry. . . .

It would be in my opinion a fruitless task to try to understand the difference between the opinions of a moderate Tory and a conservative-minded Whig. Anyone who undertook the task would end up by being convinced that although individual shades of opinion conform to two different categories, the difference can only be explained by certain social conditions which have their roots in a spirit of *camaraderie*, and by the power which deference to public opinion can exert all too easily over men at the expense of what is really desirable. (to Esterhazy, June 15, 1841)

As events turned out the electoral struggle was going to favour the Tories, and it is the leader of this party, Sir Robert Peel, who will form in 1841 a Ministry which will last five years. Metternich expresses his opinion of the Prime Minister's ability and that of his team:

Sir Robert Peel is an upright man, an administrator who is beyond question conscientious and knowledgeable, but he is not the type that makes a real statesman. In particular he lacks *political sense*, the possession of which enables men to see beyond their immediate horizon. The Duke of Wellington, who has more diplomatic attainments, is very open to err in this respect. Finally Lord Aberdeen is a good fellow, but his range is extraordinarily limited. Lord Lyndhurst is nothing, not even a moral person.

The other Ministers, among whom Sir G. Clive Graham seems to me the most impressive, are no more than supernumeraries. (to Neumann, Sept. 2, 1843)

A year later, Metternich will sketch a more subtle portrait of the Prime Minister:

Sir Robert Peel is certainly a distinguished administrator and endowed with faculties which make it easy to place him at the head of the complicated governmental machine in Great Britain. A Conservative according to the fundamental basis of the old edifice . . . and on the other hand a man of our time and one well versed in the requirements of the age, he is able to take them into account as far as possible without compromising the fundamental tendencies of his system. Sir Robert Peel has undoubted personal integrity, a mild and moderate disposition. He is also eloquent and experienced, and consequently he occupies in the mind of public opinion in England a high position which makes him specially suited to bring to a successful conclusion the difficult task with which he has been saddled.

He suffers, however, from one serious defect in connection with the duties that have devolved upon him, that of being too abstract both in thought and in work that relates to England's foreign relations. Sir Robert does not know Europe and is not concerned to know it. According to him all that is needed for the welfare of Great Britain are well-ordered finances, a smoothly running administration, and a commercial system which maintains the flow of the nation's products as far as possible. Anything foreign or outside the range of immediate interests has so little effect on the United Kingdom that it is hardly worth taking the trouble to keep an eye on her, let alone devote time and energy to her. Such is Sir Robert Peel's attitude of mind that in the administration over which he presides the conduct of foreign relations is left almost uncontrolled. . . . (instructions to Dietrichstein, Dec. 8, 1844)

Perhaps Metternich had thought he might regain some influence over the British Cabinet thanks to his earlier connection with Lord Aberdeen, but he soon had to acknowledge that the Tory Minister of Foreign Affairs was drifting, just as his predecessor had done, into a detestable state of partiality towards France:

It will be necessary to strike the English Cabinet off the list of those on whom it would be possible to rely in the future. A government of pseudo-Whigs was preferable to that of pseudo-Tories. It is sometimes possible to reach agreement with one's enemies, but this possibility does not exist with a Minister who believes that a few hours' talk between himself and whoever is in charge of French policy at the time is sufficient to remove the rivalry between France and Great Britain. . . . It is like a dream when one has the misfortune to hear a man placed at the helm of English power putting forward such theories and holding forth with perfect good faith and from the bottom of an honest heart! Is it not time to sound the alarm? (to Neumann, Oct. 1843)

The Whigs returned to power in July 1846, and with them the detested Palmerston, who will continue to rouse Metternich's temper. In one of his last dispatches to London the Chancellor voices his grievances:

Lord Palmerston has placed himself at the head of every upheaval on the Continent. He it is who, with the support of the dissidents, starts the conflagrations, keeps the firemen at arm's length, and then tries to persuade us that he is keeping the fire in check. . . .

It is something new to see a great Power take the lead in a radical revolution, follow a demented leader, and thereby prepare the way for catastrophes the effect of which on its own country would be incalculable. In the light of this situation the alarming enigma which bears the name of Palmerston melts away before my eyes. I have the measure of the man, but I am still seeking the measure of the government. Reduced to simplest terms, Lord Palmerston is a mixture of bitter sentiments, a propensity for bad jokes, and a quick grasp of affairs combined with an unparalleled levity of action. This man is full of contradictions arising from the talents of his mind on the one hand and the defects of his character on the other. The fate of society has certainly fallen into bad hands. (to Dietrichstein, Feb. 23, 1848)

Less than a year later Metternich, a refugee in England, will be entertaining his old adversary in Brighton. Of all the remarks made at that memorable and delicate interview, we shall hear no more than the amusing exchange provoked by Metternich's deafness. (see *Mémoires*, VIII, p. 206) But at least the enjoyment with which the old statesman related the incident is evidence that in the circumstances he knew how to keep faith with his claim to have always been the adversary of bad causes and not of men.

CHAPTER NINE

Russia

METTERNICH NEVER knew anything about the Russian people and in this he shared the ignorance of the whole of western society. That being so, is there any need to be surprised at the paucity of his ideas and judgment on the internal state of Russia? Yet he clearly saw the falseness of western ornamentation superimposed on a nation that was half Asiatic:

> Russia is undoubtedly a strong Power, even to the extent of making a really dangerous neighbour for any State. But neighbouring governments in Europe might not always find the real strength of that empire where they looked for it. Russia resembles a large and imposing ornament facing Europe. From our position we can see into the workings of many of her machines, and a good number of them are structurally unsound. (to Esterhazy, Jan. 5, 1829)

He also noted 'the constant desire of the Russians to give proof of an advanced civilization' and the result of these efforts is the object of his merciless scorn:

> The political education of Russian society has been accomplished in much the same way as that of many young persons in Paris. The young person enjoys the reputation of having a special *polish*. She sings (in actual fact badly), but she dances magnificently. She can say the Lord's Prayer but she does not know whether there is one God or three. She does not know whether the world has been in existence for a million or a hundred years but she can recite whole scenes from Racine. She is, in a word, charming and before long you will meet her in a b . . . [brothel]. (to

Lebzeltern, Jan. 22, 1825. In the work published by the grand-duke Nicholas, *Diplomatic reports of Lebzeltern*, p. 324)

What is Russian aristocracy? Russian society?

That quagmire of half-men, composed of the vilest substances but gilded on all sides, 36-carat ignorant and bloated like so many balloons, running after fashion and yet only making themselves ridiculous, that crowd of effeminates who introduce themselves into every *salon* in order to give vent to their non-existent wit and to teach others what they themselves neither know nor understand—there you have the majority of the so-called civilized class in Russia . . . The streets in that country are too cold and this has obliged the populace to withdraw into the *salons*. (to Lebzeltern, Feb. 2, 1826. ibid., p. 321)

The trouble is that Russia has no aristocracy. She is made up of Court and people. She may have to pay dearly for the veneer of civilization which covers the upper class, a civilization which has not penetrated a single one of her institutions and which has created two peoples out of one empire, the one entirely of the *salon*, the other bound to the soil. The army, which has become a sort of infernal machine half-way between these two extremes, completes the picture. (to Damas, Feb. 20, 1826)

In the Russian regime only one factor counted: the good pleasure of the Czar. And so it is above all to the personality of the Russian autocrat that Metternich directs his attention:

For a long time . . . I have been making a close study of the strange course taken by the Emperor Alexander's mind. Napoleon once asked me, during one of those long conversations which I had with him after the Erfurt conferences, whether I knew that prince well. I told him that, since I had only met him in Berlin in 1805, I could not form a complete opinion of him as a person, but that I had seen enough of him to have no doubts about the workings of his mind.

'Well,' Napoleon replied, 'you will probably be called upon one day to get to know him better. In that case, see if you do not make the same observation about him as I do. It would be difficult to have more intelligence than the Emperor Alexander has, but it seems to me that *there is a piece missing* and I cannot discover which.' Since then I have twenty times been in a position to observe the aptness not only of the observation, but of the very expression which Napoleon used. Today I am convinced of the truth of it, and if a doubt still lingers it is that of wondering whether in a particular circumstance, there is a piece missing or whether there is one too many. (to Esterhazy, Aug. 28, 1817)

His heart and his conscience were honest; his mind was false. Similar opposition between a man's good qualities and his defects is often encountered, but what was unusual in the Emperor's case was the perfect balance between his anomalies, so that good and evil often cancelled each other out in the most important matters and also in many purely personal situations. (to Lebzeltern, Feb. 3, 1826)

Some years after Alexander's death, Metternich brought all his observations together into a psychological portrait which summarizes also the history of his thinking:

Alexander's character showed a peculiar mixture of *masculine* virtues and *feminine* weaknesses.

The Emperor Alexander was certainly intelligent but it was an intelligence entirely lacking in depth for all its shrewdness and cunning. He was as easily led astray by excessive mistrust of erroneous theories as by a weakness for them. His judgment was constantly being influenced by some idea that had taken his fancy for a time; they came to him as if by sudden inspiration and he embraced them with extreme ardour. Before long they gained the upper hand over him and made the subjection of his will an easy matter for those from whom the ideas came.

Such ideas soon came to be regarded by him as systems. As he was changeable and his mind was extraordinarily volatile these systems did not clash, but followed one another in rapid succession. From having been entirely devoted to the particular system which happened to enjoy his favour at the time, he would pass by easy stages and without realizing it to a new system diametrically opposed to the old. Nothing remained in his memory of the conviction by which he had just been possessed except a number of obligations to individuals which he had incurred through it. This led to a heavy load of almost insoluble complications, which burdened his head as well as his heart. It also led him to form attachments for men who had nothing in common with him. Hence the difficulty for those observers who were unable to perceive the real causes of these phenomena, to understand his attitude. . . .

Prolonged study of the Czar's moral qualities and his political conduct led me to the discovery of what I have described above as the periodicity of his mind. Each cycle covered a period of about five years. That is as close as I can get to it.

The Emperor took hold of an idea and straightway gave it its head. It took about two years to germinate in his mind so that it gradually acquired for him the value of a system. Throughout the third year he remained faithful to the system he had adopted, grew fond of it, listened with genuine fervour to its promoters. He was incapable of assessing its value and the dire consequences that might ensue from it. Some time in the fourth year, as those consequences became apparent, his eyes began to be opened. The fifth year produced nothing more than a shapeless mixture of the old and nearly extinct system with his latest idea, which was often diametrically opposed to its predecessor. The following facts lend support to this theory:

My first dealings with the Emperor Alexander go back to the time of my embassy to Berlin (1805). At that time he was liberal in the broadest sense of the word. He was untiring in his opposition to Napoleon, whom he detested as much for his despotism as for his victories. In 1807 his outlook altered considerably . . . and in 1808 his personal feelings towards the Emperor of the French underwent a change for the better. The year 1812 introduced a new phase. Even if Napoleon had not declared war on Russia, Alexander's feelings towards him would have been no less cold. His old beliefs in philanthropy and liberalism had not only resumed their sway over his mind

but they took fire from the inflamed spirit of the time. In 1814
these beliefs reached their zenith. By 1815 they had already given
way to religious mysticism. In 1817 this new trend of thought
was severely modified. In 1818 when I saw the Czar at Aix-la-
Chapelle, he was the ardent champion of the principles of
monarchy and conservatism and the sworn enemy of any
revolutionary tendency. Moreover, he was already on the
point of reverting to his religious mysticism. From then until
1823 he did not change. In that year came the trouble over
Greece, which his own advisers had stirred up, and he was able
to see the overflowing of those revolutionary principles, the
seeds of which he had, in his blindness, scattered throughout his
own empire. The accumulation of these painful circumstances
threw him mentally and morally into obvious prostration. From
that moment it became obvious that he was beginning to grow
weary of life. His constitution, to all appearances so strong, began
to be affected. It was during his visit to Verona, towards the end
of 1822, that Alexander confided to the Emperor Francis his
presentiment that death was near. The disease grew worse and
in 1825 Alexander died from a thorough weariness of life.
(*Mémoires*, I, pp. 316–20)

In Alexander's lifetime, Russian foreign policy found itself
strangely influenced by the agents he employed:

One thing worthy of notice is the ease with which the Russian
Government allows itself to be drawn on to the slippery slope
which leads to adventurers . . . Thus we have seen the Capo
d'Istrias and are still seeing the Pozzos and so many others of the
same stamp take over the principal rôles . . . It is never the truly
Russian spirit which dominates that empire's policy; it never
intervenes except in a negative sense; the authors of policy are
constantly guided by personal opinions or by foreign interests.
(to Lebzeltern, Aug. 11, 1824)

Thus for Capo d' Istria the supreme objective is the deliverance
of Greece:

Any means which leads to the attainment of that end appears
good to him. The Emperor Alexander is, in his hands, no more

M.–I

than an instrument which he believes he can put to good use. One would be quite mistaken in believing that a single genuinely Russian thought ever enters his head. He is only Greek, a revolutionary independent in the broadest sense of the words. (to Esterhazy, Mar. 16, 1816)

It is he who, before the advent of Canning in England, stood out as the 'anti-Metternich' in European diplomacy, and against this *bête noire* the Chancellor displayed an exceptional amount of vicious energy. Here, from among twenty others, is one sample:

> I know that Minister thoroughly; I know his character and his principles. The first is frank and basically loyal. Although he has a liking for petty intrigue, this fact is directly due to his Greek characteristics. He comes from Corfu and he lacks sufficient depth to have been able to overcome a tendency which is common to all his compatriots.
>
> His principles are utterly democratic. He lives only for his principles and for the execution of them. A great propensity for false philosophy, confusion of thought, pursuit of his favourite studies, these are the outstanding shades of his democracy. He is at once a great ideologist, guardian of democracy, philanthropist, the Minister of an autocrat, reformer of Poland, protector of the enfranchisement of the Greeks and of the civilization of Bessarabia. That is more than enough to expose him to a great disturbance of the mind and above all to a ceaseless struggle of ideas. I admit that it would not take as much to drive me mad. A good servant of a good prince, he will never allow himself to go back on a line of policy that has been outlined by the Emperor to his Ministry. All that he allows himself to do is to modify His Imperial Majesty's will in the execution of it. (to Vincent, June 20, 1819)

As for the Corsican Pozzo di Borgo, Russian ambassador to Paris, from 1815 to 1834, Metternich rates him a second-class adventurer, entirely without scruples:

> The salient features in his character are boundless ambition, a vitality which is with difficulty confined to its proper limits, a

quite extraordinary desire to appear as arbiter in everything and finally the desire to secure a vast fortune. In earlier times he always had his eyes on the Foreign Ministry in France; today his ambition is limited to the desire to create for himself an independent existence there which he could fall back on the day the monarch who has borrowed Pozzo di Borgo for his own services becomes disgusted with him. For long the agent of England, pensioned by that country and made use of in political intrigues on the Continent, General Pozzo is today placed in a position of absolute disagreement with the British Cabinet. . . . After England it is Austria for whom he bears the most active, long-standing hatred, and I do not consider that in the whole of Europe I have personally a more pronounced enemy . . . General Pozzo belongs to that class of men whom it is impossible to retrieve; one can only observe them . . . His diplomatic existence during the last few years of the Emperor Alexander's life was dependent on the opinion that His Imperial Majesty had formed of the range of his mind and of his great store of ability, as well as on the boundless confidence which M. le comte de Nesselrode has in his faculties generally. (instructions to Apponyi, Jan. 27, 1826)

This latter figure, permanent Chancellor under Alexander as well as under Nicolas, is not feared by Metternich. 'Nesselrode, who is a child, is today at my feet,' he wrote to Zichy in January 1826. 'If he ever gives a wrong order, it will be entirely due to his extreme good-nature.' (to Lebzeltern, Jan. 28, 1822)

There are fish which thrive only in hard water, others which prefer the soft water of ponds and marshes . . . Nesselrode belongs by nature to the trout family, but unfortunately he lies wallowing in a marsh. Ever since I gave him a little spring water he has cheered up in the most astonishing fashion. He has revived and he longs for the harder, clearer water which is his real medium . . . Probably that state will not last long . . . but the poor little fellow has moments when he believes he has found it again, and if he were a fish his fins would be waving. (Jan. 4, 1821. *Mémoires*, III, pp. 447–8)

In the years that followed the fall of Napoleon, Metternich was obsessed by the fear of seeing Russia dominate the Continent of Europe by methods strangely reminiscent of those of today:

> If the Emperor Alexander really does not want war, and I am persuaded that he does not, it is because he has no need of it to increase and extend his influence. Why should Russia want war, when she can look forward to getting herself, before long, into a position from which she could lay down the law wherever she liked. The way in which the Emperor might achieve this is by following unswervingly the system he has adopted, by carefully rallying the smaller Powers round him, by setting himself up as their protector whenever they find themselves involved in discussion with one of the great Powers, by continuing to make his influence felt in all parts of Europe through the numerous agents he employs, by using any means to increase the number of his partisans, and finally by maintaining a standing army ready to move from one side of the world to the other. (to Esterhazy, Feb. 15, 1819)

> Invasion is second nature to the Russian Empire. The prince who was not faithful to that national sentiment would very quickly cease to be popular . . . When the Russian monarchs wish to do something and have the power to do it, they do not share the profits from it with any other Power. They agree to co-operate only when they believe they are quite unable to achieve alone what is in the true interests of Russia, or when they think they can share the expense among several and still keep all the advantages for themselves . . . We must not lose sight of the fact that what may be difficult for other States is much less so for Russia. Adventurous undertakings can easily endanger empires which have neighbours, but Russia always sees the dangers, which others incur by defeat, come to nothing at her frontiers. (to Esterhazy, Dec. 3, 1827)

The 'encroachment' which Metternich fears must normally make itself felt in the weakest area, namely European Turkey. Austria cannot allow that:

> The government at St. Petersburg has too often entertained ideas of encroachment against the Ottoman empire and conquest

has for too long formed an inherent part of its political system for us to suppose for a moment that it has abandoned all ideas on this subject. . . . Our conservative principles in respect of the Porte are acquiring new importance these days on account of the attitude of Russia and of the considerable expansion which these latest transactions have secured for her.

She already embraces the monarchy in the north, and it is of double interest for us to see to it that the southern tip of this crescent should not extend south of our frontiers. We are equally interested in seeing that Russia never has an outlet on the Adriatic coast, and that she does not increase her influence over the Greek populations scattered throughout the Ottoman Empire and along all the eastern and southern frontiers of Hungary.

Finally, we should regard as a *casus belli* any Russian territorial expansion in the Levant which would extend her contact with us. Nothing could adequately compensate, as far as we are concerned, for the inconvenience of a partition, because it would mean sacrificing one sure neighbour for nothing more than the acquisition of the arid, sparsely populated lands which lie along our frontiers. It would also mean giving Russia a dangerous accretion of territory, whereas those territories, if left in the hands of the Turks, offer us advantages in respect of our frontiers and of our political position. The preservation of Turkey stands, therefore, in the forefront of our interests. (to Lebzeltern, Aug. 1, 1816)

Metternich counts on England to stop Russia's victorious march:

Great Britain is of all the Powers the one that can exert the most influence over Russia, and the reason for this is so much a part of nature that it stands out clearly. Russia is a Power that is always *wanting something*, consequently she is always unsettled. Relations between the two empires must reflect the fact that her temperament is diametrically opposed to ours. On our part there is no irritation, for we are not in the wrong; it is different at Saint Petersburg where it is unusual for one to be right *and nothing more*. Our strong and heavy bulk finds itself hampering by its impetus the ever-aggressive progress of the northern colossus,

who for lack of anything better attacks some other neighbour...
It is perfectly natural that we should not be popular, for nobody
enjoys being baulked, but no one dares declare open war on us,
for that might appear too serious an undertaking. As for Prussia,
she is not considered. As for France, she is not trusted, and in
spite of a great number of points of contact and affinities between
the two governments, there will never be a proper alliance between them until the day when it is based upon a system of
conquests and the destruction of the intermediary States.
There remains England. Without having any firmly based
contacts that Power can do anything with Russia, for she can
inflict a good deal of harm without Russia being able to retali-
ate . . . If England does not want something to happen, Russia
will not do it, and so it is in London and not at St. Petersburg
that we observe and seek to find the issues of the near future.
(to Esterhazy, Dec. 18, 1828)

In these few words is to be found the key to all the vicissitudes
of the Eastern Question in the nineteenth century.

Metternich is far from exercising the same influence over the
brother of Alexander, who is also his successor. But he respected
him:

He has a good brain, he is good-hearted and upright, his character is pure and strong, he is a man of his word and scrupulously
honest. On the other hand, the Emperor does not know the
world to the extent that one might wish. He judges men too
rigorously by Russian standards, and sometimes he is incapable
of turning useful and desirable distinctions to good effect. He is
quick to speak and to act, and it is difficult to get him talking
again once he has stopped. (to Apponyi, Dec. 2, 1835)

But with Nicholas I European politics are at an end:

The new Emperor has managed to surround himself with a
system of fear, and the regime of fear suits Russia . . . The
Emperor necessarily finds himself in a position that will hardly
allow him to *consult* anything different from or anything more

than the awkwardness of his own position. His policy will be Russian pure and simple. That policy may be good or it may be bad for him and his empire, but it certainly will not be European. (to Esterhazy, Dec. 2, 1828)

The accession of the Czar had been marked by an attempt at a military *pronunciamento*, the work of officers belonging to secret liberal societies. This crisis provided Metternich with the opportunity for a striking prophecy:

An empire which lies on the outskirts of civilization, bearing no resemblance to other European States and differing from them in religion, way of life, the spirit of her people and in all the material conditions which make up the individual existence of States, has just made it clear, by this event, that the disease which is eating away at society as a whole, has struck at her. I confess that it would be rather tempting to expect foreign fruits, once they have been transplanted to a frozen soil, to be lost and ineffective, considering the discrepancy between their nature and that of the soil, which is supposed to nourish them. For such a hope to be justified one would need to feel certain that Russia and the evil which such a terrible explosion has brought to light would remain isolated. Such will not be the case for the disruptive element will not have made the discovery in vain that the Russian Empire is infected and that in the heart of her there is hidden away enough material to start a conflagration.

The energies of the malcontents will be concentrated in this direction, and the effects of general uprising in this vast empire offer too good an opportunity for the pursuit of their criminal intentions not to be striven for with the greatest intensity. We may ask ourselves what would happen to Europe if thirty million slaves and an army of 800,000 men were turned loose. The malcontents are ever asking themselves the same question, and where we and every intelligent man in Europe see a picture of death, they see life and triumph. (to Vincent, Jan. 27, 1826)

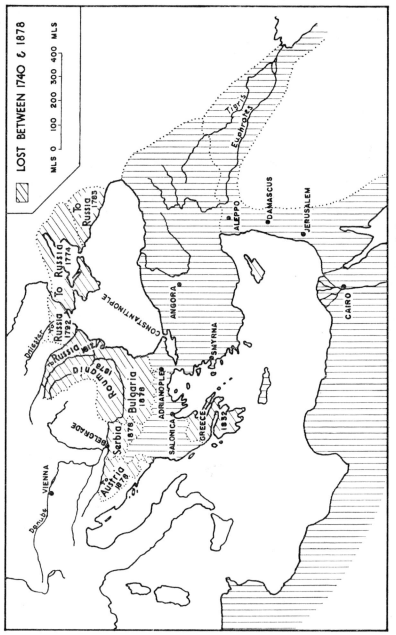

THE OTTOMAN EMPIRE UP TO 1878

Within the map:

LOST BETWEEN 1740 & 1878

MLS 0 100 200 300 400 MLS

To Russia 1783
To Russia 1774
To Russia 1792
To Russia 1812
To Russia 1878

Dniester

Roumania

Bulgaria 1878

Serbia 1878
To Austria 1878

BELGRADE

Danube

VIENNA

CONSTANTINOPLE

ADRIANOPLE

SALONICA

GREECE 1832

ANGORA

SMYRNA

ALEPPO

DAMASCUS

JERUSALEM

CAIRO

Tigris

Euphrates

CHAPTER TEN

The Near East—Spain—America

1. The Ottoman Empire

W E HAVE seen that the safeguarding of the Turkish Empire was one of the keystones of Austrian policy and the reason is this:

We look on the Ottoman Empire as the best of our neighbours: since she is scrupulously true to her word, we regard contact with her as equivalent to contact with a natural frontier which never claims our attention or dissipates our energies. We look on Turkey as the last bastion standing in the way of the expansion of another Power . . . (to Esterhazy, Dec. 2, 1828)

Unfortunately that empire, the maintenance of which appears so desirable, is stricken with a congenital weakness:

The conviction is easily reached in studying the history of the Ottoman Empire that it contains a fundamental and permanent cause of weakness. That empire still rules over vast territories yet it lacks strength and power. It has areas of great fertility yet it is without wealth. It is geographically well situated yet it has no commerce. There is contempt for life within its frontiers. Its armies know how to die but they can no longer fight. Decay is gradual. How does it come about that Moslem pride which would like to command no longer has the ability to do so? Why cannot love of power make use of all those elements which it possesses and which are capable of producing it? The answer cannot be provided by political considerations. The council-rooms and the big battalions count for little; the root of the evil goes deeper. There is a fundamental sterility and consequently a fundamental decay in the imperfections of Islam. Mohammed, who needed to win over proselytes, repudiated by way of inducement the sterner aspects of Christian morality. Through the medium of pleasure he handed man over to the dominion of the senses. Human intelligence in Turkey was destroyed by luxury. The whole social structure is designed to ensure physical enjoyment to the exclusion of the nobler emotions of the soul and the heart. The abuse of these pleasures, combined with shameful and depraved tastes, in time withers and consumes thought. Why is it that the only faculties that have been brilliantly and often dangerously developed at different times in the history of Mohammedan peoples are the warlike ones? The answer is that war, by severing them from the softness of their domestic lives, brought some vigour to their intelligence. The Turkish Empire is perishing not because it is Turkish, but because it is Mohammedan. Put an Arab empire in its place and nothing would change. The same causes of decay would continue to exist. (to Esterhazy, Mar. 1834)

What would happen if the Empire fell?

The day the Sultan's throne collapses, the empire itself will break up into several parts, some of which will pass into the hands of Christian Powers while others will endeavour to set themselves up as more or less independent States, offering the unedifying spectacle of Moslem anarchy such as characterized the regencies in Africa for centuries. A vast expanse of land will become the empire of the desert and remain under the rule of nomadic hordes . . . As for Europe, her fate when this heavy blow falls will be wars of political rivalry. (circular of Oct. 11, 1840. *Staatskanzlei. Circularien,* 27)

These disasters are not perhaps to be feared in the immediate future. Why not?

If the Turkish Empire is still in existence it is because there are millions of Turks who cannot mingle with the Christian population and because the Christians themselves are stupefied and thereby deprived of the qualities they need to enable them to become a nation. This sad combination of Christian and Moslem weaknesses is protected by a kind of Providence which by its nature is hardly less negative than the object of its protection. This Providence is the political rivalry that exists between the Courts of Europe and the jealous guard which they keep between them over the countries of the Levant. This rivalry alone sustains the throne which is occupied by a child of twenty already exhausted by the habits of the harem. (to Neumann, May 12, 1843)

It is still necessary to encourage domestic reform in order to postpone the moment of dissolution. But take care! Reforms *of a European nature* would do even more harm than good. This is what Metternich would like to tell the Sultan:

Establish your government in respect for your religious institutions which form the fundamental basis of your existence as a Power, and which form the first link between the Sultan and his Moslem subjects. Keep up with the times and take into account the needs to which they give rise. Put your administration in order, reform it, but do not go and overthrow it in order to replace it by forms which do not suit you and which, for that reason, expose the monarch to the reproach of knowing the value neither of what he is destroying nor of what he is trying to set in its place. Do not borrow from European civilization forms which do not fit in with your institutions, for western institutions rest on principles which differ from yours. The western basis is the Christian law; you who profess Islam cannot establish the Christian society. Remain Turks, but in doing so consult Moslem legislation and make speedy use of such facilities as it provides for tolerance. Grant your Christian subjects complete protection and do not allow the Pashas and subordinate agents to molest them. Do not get involved with their religious affairs; on the contrary, be the guardian sovereign of their privileges and keep the promises you have made them. Do not promulgate a law without having first made up your mind to see it carried out. Beware of place-seekers and advisers who have no business to be concerned in your affairs. Make a straight line towards what is good without taking any notice of what appears to you to be the public voice of the West, and you will have on your side the only voice which counts for anything provided you follow a just and enlightened course. (to Apponyi, May 26, 1841. See also *Mémoires*, VI, pp. 380–383)

Another cause of weakness in the Turkish Empire was that she extended her conquests into Europe instead of pursuing them into Asia:

> Never at home on civilized ground, it (Turkish power) should never have left its native soil. Its real frontiers lie in Asia, the only ones, that is, that have any lasting importance in relation to Russia's outlook on the Islamic empire . . . From this it follows that the reduction of their frontiers which would result from the expulsion of the Turks from Europe would be offset by the consolidation of their *real strength* against Russia. (to Zichy, Dec. 25, 1821)

Unfortunately, it is not easy to make the Turks understand reason or even to negotiate with them.

> There enters into Eastern politics a sort of shady reserve which the most persistent representations cannot make them give up. To keep silent on any matter is equivalent, in their eyes, to abandoning it, and not to repeat the same theme every time they open their mouths, however remote the realization of that theme may be, would seem to them like the loss of a right. Frequent dealings with the Court of Rome, which clings with equal tenacity to its system of reticence, have taught me to appreciate the truth of this and although such a rapprochement might appear too remote in its origin it is in practice none the less justified. (to Lebzeltern, Mar. 30, 1820)

2. Greece

The tragedy of the war of Greek independence which stirred the feelings of the West so deeply from 1821 to 1830 inspired in Metternich some atrocious observations worthy of those with which he himself reproached Napoleon. (*Mémoires*, III, pp. 472–95). This one, for example:

The complications which may ensue in the east defy all calculation. Perhaps it is of little importance. Over there, beyond our frontiers, three or four hundred thousand individuals hanged, impaled or with their throats cut, hardly count! (*Mémoires*, III, p. 495)

The malevolence which emerges from this verbal cruelty is probably explained by the fact that the Greek rising was going to ruin irretrievably the 1815 system of alliance. It is known that in its early stages Metternich pretended to treat the affair as if it were just a special manifestation of the European revolutionary spirit. Yet as time passes he will be obliged to make a more subtle appreciation of it, and the following account should be considered as reflecting much more accurately his real thoughts:

The Greek insurrection bears a much greater resemblance to the risings that occurred in Ireland at different times . . . than to events which racked Spain, Portugal and Italy, and which bear to a greater degree the stamp of the French Revolution and of the English one in the seventeenth century. The Greek insurrection would resemble even more closely the revolt of the American colonies, the object of which was to break with the mother country . . . What has probably been responsible for identifying the Greek insurrection with other revolutions we have witnessed, is the influence which the revolutionary parties have exercised over eastern disturbances . . . and again it should be noted that, whereas in the case of the Spanish and Italian revolutions the doctrines and incantations were directed against the foundations of the old social order, in the case of Greece they were only slipped in as subsidiary and played only a secondary part. (to Lebzeltern, Jan. 18, 1827)

Yet never will Metternich drop his initial malevolence towards the Greeks, 'a degraded nation', sad remnant of a people who were once glorious and from whom they have only inherited the vices. Even when an independent kingdom of Greece has been set up, under the aegis of the Great Powers, Metternich remains sceptical of its chances of survival. It is necessary to quote at this point a little-known text and one which deserves to be given in full, not only for the quality of its style, but also because there are in it examples of the application to a particular case of Metternich's general principles on the founding of States:

> Let us look for a moment at what it is we want. Lord Palmerston finds that things are going really badly in Greece, and so do I. He finds in King Otto a great inability to govern; so do I. A remedy must be found for the evil. I am in complete agreement. He does not see the remedy lying in Bavarian councillors; I concur. Lord Palmerston thinks the remedy should lie in a regime which would limit the absolutism of a prince who is not endowed with much genius; certainly, for I hate disorder and absolutism is an element of anarchy. He wants a constitutional regime; I am one of the most fervent guardians of constitutions. So far, so good! Let us proceed. Which constitutional regime is involved? That is the question that must be asked. I exclude the English, French, American, Spanish, Hungarian, and Bohemian constitutions, and even that of Lower Austria. What I would like to see would be a rational order of things, something *Greek*, something that was neither aristocratic in a country which has no aristocratic element, nor democratic where there are only recently emancipated slaves or *Klephts*, that is to say land pirates. I would like to see something which surrounded the throne with good counsel in the silence of the Cabinet, but which did not give vent to rubbish on a rostrum, something which acted as a support to the King, which was understood by the people and which did not understand political intrigue. And I would like to see something capable of building up the country as one builds a house, starting with the cellar and not with the roof as has been done by the Bavarian architects of pitiful memory.

> Never was country treated as Greece was, in respect of which the procedure has been as follows. Endowments:

> (1) A country lacking in proprietors and fixed property.
> (2) A public debt clearly written in a ledger, at a resounding 5 per cent.
> (3) As many journals as there are adventurers willing to write them.

(4) Many rival European political elements.

(5) A foreign king of a religion which is not the general one.

(6) A strong provision of capital to repay and individual hatreds to assuage.

Make out of this a prosperous country or even one that can function, my dear Beauvale, and you will be a great inventor! Capo d'Istria was an ideologist who tried to create a Greece with the Phanariots of *Pera*; he only succeeded in getting their throats cut. He had a hundred young Moraites educated at Geneva, Göttingen, Iona and Paris. These men who would have made bad professors made even worse citizens. He founded a museum of antiquities which was not filled, for the foreigner had been emptying Greece for the last two thousand years. He planted potatoes in ground which, however classical it may be, does not allow potatoes to sprout, let alone set. What he had forgotten was to distribute the land, to set down landowners on it, to start the cultivation of the vine, the olive tree and of silk, to *create a people*. For although one may extract professors and rhetoricians from the people, you cannot create a people out of learned men. Then came the Bavarians who wanted to make regulations for Peloponnesia on the circular model of Nüremberg and Munich.

There is not a single official missing in Greece from the most diffuse bureaucracy in the world! What would finish Greece off would be to give it a splendid modern constitution, lawyers, doctors, and pamphleteers as legislators, and a dozen Ministers, of Foreign Affairs, Finance, Justice, Public Works, Commerce, War, Admiralty and Education. As for amateurs there would be no lack of them. I myself know enough to upset half a dozen Ministries.

Well, my dear Beauvale, what do they think of the construction of Greece in your country? Does that correspond to it? If so, I am not in favour of it. Is it something practical, and therefore quite different? If so, I am in favour.

My kindest regards and humble apologies for these meditations. (letter to Lord Beauvale, Feb. 5, 1841. Communicated to Esterhazy, Feb. 15, 1841)

3. Spain

In Metternich's intellectual panoply there is a comparison of which he is particularly fond. It is one which likens the Spaniards to the Turks in the conduct of their politics:

> The administration is at once poor and rich: it is poor in revenue but rich in means of doing without it. In this respect it resembles those great houses of the nobility. For a time, the length of which it is often difficult to estimate, they lead an existence which astonishes observers who are accustomed to keep a strict account each day of what they spend, and who allow themselves no more than an income assured by a fixed revenue. The Spanish administration is sustained in a position which would be impossible in other countries by an army which is accustomed to not receiving its pay, by a swarm of Civil Servants almost certain of not being rewarded for their services, and by contractors who are in the habit of basing their fortune, not on fixed payments, but on embezzlements. The difference between Madrid and Constantinople is in this respect much less great than might be supposed. (to Vincent, Apr. 21, 1844)

Another of Metternich's pet theories is that the Spanish people are absolutely unsuited to a constitutional regime:

> The Spanish temperament admits of no compromise: a liberal Spain is a meaningless expression. Spain will always be either frankly monarchical or emphatically radical. (*Mémoires*, V, p. 467)

> Spain is a country which throughout the ages has found itself living in conditions which are uniquely suited to it. In no other Christian country was the throne more absolute and at the same time the people more free. The royal personage represented in the national sentiment the Divinity on earth. It was the representative of the supreme sovereign whom the Spaniards obeyed, not their fellow creatures. In the opinion of the enlightened and impartial observer, Eastern ideas and customs make their appearance in this kingdom and play an outstanding part in the

lives of its peoples. Without paying sufficient attention to the exceptional conditions, an attempt has been made to give Spain the benefits of civilization in the form of the modern representative system, which is the same as trying to turn Catalans into Frenchmen and Andalusians into Englishmen. The result was inevitable. It had the effect of dissolving Spanish society to its very roots. Unable to recognize itself, the country found itself delivered up to boundless anarchy. (to Neumann, July 19, 1842. See also *Mémoires*, VI, pp. 273 and 614; VII, p. 99)

Besides, the qualities needed for reform are lacking, namely:

an enthusiastic people, superstitious, loyal and ignorant; a king entirely lacking in any qualities; a government that can only be described as 'royal anarchy', politicians animated only by a sense of individual rivalry, whose hatred frequently rises to the level of fanaticism. (circular of Sept. 27, 1839) 'I have never met,' he said in 1820, 'a Spaniard who has not been either mad or less than mediocre.' (to Lebzeltern, May 24, 1820. Correspondence published by the Grand-Duke Nicholas, p. 225)

In conclusion, towards the end of his reign Metternich will be writing:

I have been following Spanish affairs closely for thirty-five years and the only conclusion I have reached in respect of them is that the action most in keeping with reason is the one that is the least likely to happen. (Apr. 24, 1843. *Mémoires*, VI, p. 681)

4. America

Connected with Spanish affairs is the question of her American colonies which had taken advantage of the revolution of 1820 to win their emancipation. In what way was that event of interest to Austria and the other European States?

In fixing their attention on the affairs of America, the European sovereigns have only two main interests to consult, two big questions to examine: the first is that of the preservation of the legitimate rights of reigning families; the second is that of maintaining, as far as possible, the monarchical principle against the advance of universal democracy. The rest hardly matters. (to Esterhazy, Feb. 13, 1823)

At the beginning of 1824, he will write:

The future may be strangely compromised, and indeed is bound to be, if the governments do not succeed in reaching agreement on the attitude they are to adopt towards affairs in the New World, that world which has already launched itself on a course such as is threatening every European government with dissolution and death . . . We desire that America should not, through the fault of the Powers, be put in a position to dictate to Europe. (to Wellington, Feb. 11, 1824)

But what can the Continental Powers do, separated as they are by the vast extent of the Atlantic Ocean? The fate of the old colonies was going to depend quite clearly on England and the United States. As early as 1822 President Monroe, in a message, had roused the gratitude of several of the new republics. The Chancellor is disgusted:

Reflecting on this message one cannot help being struck by the advances which revolutionary doctrines must imagine they have made for public men to believe that they are authorized to proclaim them as incontrovertible truths in more or less official declarations. If the system on which such messages are based were generally recognized in Europe, it is clear that from now on the most illegal and the most daring undertakings could only be judged by their material success, that every revolt would be sanctioned by that criterion alone, that results only would count, and finally that there would be no other law between men than that of force and no property except that dictated by the victorious usurpation of the moment and which the next moment might dissolve. (to Lebzeltern, June 5, 1822)

When, at the end of 1823, there was a question of submitting the question to a European Congress, Metternich rejected a proposal put forward by Canning that it would be necessary to invite the United States Government:

In our opinion the United States of America can never take part in a European congress, whatever the subjects under discussion might be:

(1) because the United States are not bound by any of the Acts which the European alliance has discussed and established since 1814, and to which nearly all questions for which the Powers might meet in congress would be referred.

(2) because the principal aim of these congresses, the maintenance of peace and legitimate order in Europe, is entirely foreign to the United States.

(3) because a great part of the principles recognized and sanctioned by the European Powers are not only foreign, but opposed, to the fundamental principles of the United States, opposed also to the customs, the civil and political regimes of their peoples. There may be friendly relations between the European Powers and the United States, there may be negotiations, treaties, alliances, and every kind of undertaking, but there is no common basis on which the United States could take her stand in a European congress.

No doubt the United States are more directly interested than Austria, Russia and Prussia in the future of the Spanish colonies, but the concern of these Powers is no less real or respectable. It might even be permissible to suggest that it is on a higher level. The interest of the United States of America is commercial, one of aggrandizement, of an extension of their power; it is a purely material interest. That of the European Powers, Continental and otherwise, is the interest of preservation, of stability, and of the material and spiritual well-being of the great European family. And if that family claims to be concerned with the future relations between Spain and her vast provinces in America, it is not from a desire to share the spoils or to obtain any political advantages, but in order to ensure that relations should not be too incompatible with the general peace and prosperity of Europe and that they should cause the least possible harm to the rights and interests of that sovereign family which has virtually created America and which has reigned over her for three centuries. (to Vincent, Nov. 26, 1823)

But all this discussion was going to prove of no avail. Some days later President Monroe issued his famous declaration burning the bridges: America for the Americans, was the substance of his proclamation:

> There has come to pass what sensible men and those best suited to judge questions of high politics had feared. It is the New World that has announced a break with the Old, a break that is neither optional, temporary, nor contingent, but a break in fact which separates the European States from the republic of North America, just as material incompatibility causes a break between bodies of a quite different nature. (to Lebzeltern, Jan. 19, 1824)

CHAPTER ELEVEN

France—Napoleon

Of all the countries of Europe the one I know best after my own is France. I have made a life study of it, and I draw on my own experiences whenever I need to make calculations concerning that State, concerning the activities of her rulers and the influence of passions which may dominate them. (to Zichy, May 28, 1823)

M ETTERNICH WAS, indeed, born at Coblenz, a son of the Rhenish Germany over which France had for so long exerted her political influence and to an even greater extent the influence of her civilization. Young Clemens's first contact with France was in 1779, and it is possible that this did not make too favourable an impression on his memory, for he was being taken by his father, who prided himself on keeping abreast of those enlightened times, to Strasburg in order to be vaccinated! A symbolic episode, none the less, for it was also at Strasburg, ten years later, that the young Metternich, then a student at the university, found himself immunized against the revolutionary germ thanks to the demonstrations which took place before his eyes. He saw the populace take the town hall by storm. His instructor in religious subjects was an ecclesiastic who, as constitutional bishop of Strasburg, was to burn publicly his insignia of office, and his tutor was a certain Frédéric Simon who was to become one of the organizers of the events of August 10, 1792:

> The doctrines of this Jacobin and the appeal to vulgar passions inspired in me a revulsion which age and experience have only increased. . . . The example of the mistakes to which dishonest thinking and an excess of passion can lead was not lost on me.

It influenced the direction of my thinking and it helped to preserve me from errors into which many people fell simply because
they did not have the unpleasant advantage of having witnessed
these atrocities. (*Mémoires*, I, p. 8)

Soon afterwards he will get to know another France: that of
Versailles and of the *ancien régime*, with its weakness and its charm.
At Mainz, where he is completing his studies; at Brussels, where
he is learning administration in his father's offices, or in the Low
Countries representing Austria, Metternich mixes with the first
wave of *émigrés*, whose characters have not been transformed by
the ordeal and whose purses have not yet been emptied by time:

> Intercourse with that *élite* society taught me to understand the
> faults committed by the *ancien régime* . . . in this way I got to
> know the French, to understand them and to be understood by
> them. (*Mémoires*, I, p. 11)

The French education of Metternich will be completed by his
two visits to Paris, first as Austrian ambassador, from June 1806
to June 1809; then from March to November 1810 as Minister of
Foreign Affairs charged with the duty of accompanying his
master's daughter, who was being handed over as a propitiatory
victim to the Corsican Minotaur. Paris seems to have made a
lasting impression on him:

> Paris is the town of the *world* just as London is the town of
> *commerce*. Neither resembles the other, for both have individual
> personalities. Vienna is like any other *inhabited town*. It boasts
> more streets than any other, but it is not any better than they
> for being bigger. The mind needs to be continually jolted if it is
> to extend beyond the commonplace. It is natural that a concourse
> of more than five hundred thousand individuals in one place,
> under a fine sky, in the heart of a fertile land, should tend to a
> development, an industrial and commercial activity, quite dif-
> ferent from those of other less populated centres. That is the
> secret of the perfection of Paris and London. Both of them are
> what ancient Rome and Heliopolis and, even more, antique
> Babylon used to be. (*Mémoires*, III, p. 135)

Modern Babylon will see Metternich on three more occasions: in the spring of 1814, for a longer spell in 1815, from July to November that is, in preparation for the Treaties of Paris, and finally for some weeks in the spring of 1825. Let us remember, too, that Metternich was throughout his life an assiduous reader of French newspapers and books. From all these contacts there arose and took shape an image of the national character that was hardly flattering and was sometimes well seasoned with contradictions:

The French character is singular and disconcerting. There are generally speaking two kinds of men in the world: those of the past and those of the future; in other words those of the day before and those of the day that lies ahead. The French are men of today, that is to say of the moment that does not exist. We go from the past to the future, from the day before to the day after. The day itself, the present moment, is no more than a bridge from the one to the other. Now the French leave the past, forget it, are contemptuous of it, and without giving the future a thought they insist on remaining on the bridge. (to L. Veuillot, *Oeuvres complètes*, XXXIV, p. 339)

The French mind is nimble, extremely volatile, and enterprising. A Frenchman translates his feelings into action without concerning himself about relevant details. He embarks on any enterprise that attracts him without going into the consequences of the adventure and he trusts to his skill and to good fortune to carry him through. (*Mémoires*, VIII, p. 600)

The main defect of Frenchmen is that they attach too little importance in that country to the forces of nature and because of that individuals attach too much importance to themselves. (to Apponyi, Mar. 20, 1839)

Any introduction to a centre of activity like Paris is bewildering during the early stages of a visit. Your Excellency will deduct from the intrinsic value of things the price of the clamour that surrounds them, and you will quite quickly reach a point where you will be convinced that the whole of this great phantasmagoria contains no more than a quite ordinary number of realities and a far greater collection of plain rumours, frivolity and, that peculiarly French trait, a tendency to boast. The French character, lacking weight and depth and being easily satisfied and impossible to pin down, gives rise to an impression that men and ideas multiply a hundredfold. It explains why the place in which the least actual business is in fact carried out is just the place where the affairs of the entire world appear to be concentrated. (to Apponyi, Feb. 20, 1826)

Underneath, Metternich detests the French because they are the incarnation of everything that he gave up his life to fight: liberalism, the representative system of government, nationalism, aggression, political and intellectual agitation. He has a grudge against France because she is 'the great factory of revolutions . . .' (to Vincent, Apr. 24, 1822) . . . 'the cavern whence blows the wind which breathes death to the social structure'. (*Mémoires*, VIII, p. 199)

> What good is it for Europe to have watched a system of material conquest collapse under its own weight, if its place is taken by a system of moral subversion much more dangerous, much more difficult to fight, and unquestionably more threatening to society as a whole than the transitory existence of a conqueror could ever be. (to Vincent, Dec. 28, 1819)

A free Press, as it exists in France, is in his view the Pandora's box from which the plague spreads throughout the world. He gets all the more irritated by it because he feels powerless:

> Since first the exchange of communications between distant States began there has been nothing comparable with the outpouring of the revolutionary journals of Paris. The evil that is caused daily in England is not to be compared with it, for the publications of the periodical Press there are more or less restricted to proper ground. But when we come to the evil which emanates from France, placed as she is in the centre of Europe and speaking a language that is generally taught and understood over a wide area, how much more real and dangerous are the inconveniences attached to the profusion of extreme revolu-

tionary texts that are circulated daily, read everywhere, and often painted in monarchistic colours!

France, internally quite peaceful these days, pours out moral poison over the surface of the Continent. Her daily publications have the effect of projectiles which do not worry those who find themselves beneath the parabola they describe, but which do not fail to have an effect when they reach their destination. (to the baron de Damas, Feb. 20, 1826)

As for the representative constitutional regime as it functioned in France from 1815 to 1848, the following chapters include a fair number of appraisals of it evoked by events. But some observations and judgments are of a more general character. Here, for example, is one dealing with domestic policy:

There are two reasons why the modern representative system was quite unsuited to France. One is that the spirit of France, if it is to be kept under control, must not be left to the influence of a Parliamentary rostrum. The other reason—and it is perhaps the more categorical—is that this system is based much more on theory than on practice, and the French mind is much more inclined to be practical than to feed on theories. (Apr. 30, 1836. *Mémoires*, VI, p. 144)

Then, as nowadays, the country suffered from Ministerial instability: then as now the result was the omnipotence of the bureaucracy.

In France the effects of the fall of a Ministry last no longer than the duration of the crisis which brought it about and only until the officials, who themselves have a short life ahead of them, take up their posts. Perhaps the most astonishing thing is the succession of men who believe, in spite of a host of examples to the contrary, that once they have succeeded in laying their hands on a portfolio they will be able to keep it. (to Apponyi, Sept. 17, 1836)

A phenomenon which I regard as unique in the annals of history is the increasing dearth in France of men singled out by public opinion as having taken over the helm naturally or as having the talent to govern. The Houses of Parliament, where from time immemorial future Ministers have been trained, can hardly stand as an example to France. In cases where the spirit of faction is split up into innumerable parts, statesmen do not come to light in the Parliamentary Assembly. . . . It is in the upholding of causes not in the clash of ambition or in personal greed that men make themselves felt and can establish their powers of intelligence. . . . The Restoration and the revolution of 1830 succeeded in wearing out statesmen not in creating new ones. It was quite another matter under the old monarchy and under the Empire, simply because under the monarchical regime the head of the State can try out men whom he thinks suited to high office and dismiss them if they do not come up to expectations. That is something the King of the French cannot do and that is why he lacks the instruments necessary to steer the vessel of State. Generally speaking it is not the place-seekers who are best equipped to fill the places. Still less fit to govern are those put forward by their parties, even if it is only a question of governing the party to which they belong.

It would be wrong to draw the conclusion that France did not hide away in her midst men capable of conducting affairs of State. What is lacking there is the environment in which one might get to know them, and at the same time what the King lacks is sufficient freedom of choice. (to Apponyi, Jan. 10, 1840)

France lives by her administration and her codes of law. Thus there are some organs of the great body politic called France which function, and which by so doing keep her alive, although by themselves they cannot guarantee her good health. (to Apponyi, Mar. 20, 1839)

What does the country get in exchange for such a series of shortlived Ministers? Complete disorder in the administration and a tyranny exercised by the lower grades of the Civil Service second only in ferocity to that of the revolutionary clubs. Foreign affairs which by their nature are so delicate are in the hands of a few clerks. . . . (to Apponyi, Sept. 17, 1836)

The result of this is a permanence in the foreign policy which is hardly to Metternich's taste:

The uniformity of the wording that is always noticeable in the diplomatic correspondence which originates in the department of Foreign Affairs is a curious thing and yet natural enough when one considers the departmental inertia in the midst of the turmoil occasioned by the replacement of the heads of the various Ministries.

Every directive issued from the centre is stamped with the same hateful prejudices against Austria and betrays a constant disposition to encourage and to spread the revolution. . . .

The fact that there is such a thing as a strong, powerful, and prosperous Austria represents a nightmare to that long succession of bureaucrats who are too low down to survey the whole truth and are yet high enough to distort it. The words of the king and of his Ministers are certainly not echoed in the French departmental offices, unless they be in direct accord with the thoughts that guide subordinate officials. I have a thousand times had proof of this truth. (to Apponyi. Dec. 1, 1834)

Throughout his correspondence Metternich inveighs against the foreign policy of France:

The accumulated proof of the outflow of political ineptitudes and false calculations which the French Government and its agents abroad are perpetrating exceeds all belief. I do not know a single French diplomat who could not be persuaded to admit the probability of something that is impossible, and what is more, I do not know one who, in choosing a subject suitable for reflection and to form the subject of a report, will not select from a number of improbable facts the one that comes closest to being impossible. . . . One thing exceeds the credulity of the French agents and that is the credulity of the Cabinet. (to Esterhazy, Dec. 16, 1829)

For a long time now—under the *ancient régime* as well as under the Restoration, and especially since 1830—governments in France have been making use, as far as revolutionary enterprises are concerned, of two weights and two measures. This unfortunate attitude, linked with an ambitious and ever-aggressive policy, has predominated in France at every stage of her history.

The French Government has at all times endeavoured to extend its influence, whether spiritual or material, even in defiance of the most widely accepted principles of human rights. In the course of the last three centuries no disturbance in the world has broken out to which France has not contributed directly or indirectly. Every single uprising, whether it be religious, spiritual or political, has been deemed worthy of this Power's support. That is why the French Government has been the constant supporter of religious reform in Germany simultaneously with the massacres of Saint Bartholomew's day, the Dragonnades, and the extreme measures later against the Calvinists within its frontiers. We find it again in Poland and Hungary lending support to the factions which divided those two States.

It was France who contributed substantially towards the emancipation of the English colonies in America, and it would be useless to recount here the repeated attempts that have been made by that Power in the course of the last forty-five years of revolution to spread disorder and disorganization, and to encourage upheaval in all corners of the world! This line of action, which has become second nature to France, is to be encountered again at the present time in anything connected with anti-social propaganda. (to Apponyi, Mar. 1834)

Metternich, like all his contemporaries, succumbed to Napoleon's fascination and to the end of his days he spoke with respect of the man who was his principal adversary in the early years of his career as a Minister. A recent publication relieves us of the necessity of quoting from the many interesting texts. (Metternich, *Napoleon. Sketches, followed by conversations and other details.* Paris, 1956, p. 160) But how could one keep from the reader the essential passages of that remarkable portrait of Napoleon, on which Metternich brought to bear all his great talent as an observer of human nature?

In the varying phases of my relations with Napoleon, my opinion of him has remained unaltered. I have seen and studied him in the moments of his greatest triumph: I have seen and followed him in the moments of his decline and although he may have tried to mislead me in regard to himself . . . he has in no way succeeded. . . .

Judgment is often influenced by first impressions. I had never set eyes on Napoleon until the audience he gave me at Saint-Cloud when I presented my credentials. I found him standing in the middle of one of the reception rooms with the Minister of Foreign Affairs and six other members of his court. He was in the uniform of the infantry of the Guard and was wearing his hat. This latter circumstance, improper in every respect since the audience was not a public one, struck me as uncalled for pretentiousness indicating the *parvenu*. I even felt like putting my own hat on. Instead I delivered a short speech which differed fundamentally in its conciseness from those which had become the habit at the new court of France.

His attitude appeared to me to indicate constraint and even embarrassment. His square, stocky figure with its unkempt appearance and yet at the same time an attempt to make himself imposing, had the effect of undermining in me the feeling of grandeur which is naturally associated with the man before whom the world trembles. This impression has never entirely left me. It was with me during every important interview I had with him throughout his career. It may even have helped me to see the man as he really was behind the disguises which he knew so well how to assume. In his tirades, in his outbursts of temper and his curt interruptions I came to recognize set scenes, prepared in advance and calculated to produce a certain effect on the person to whom he was speaking.

What struck me most forcibly in my early relations with Napoleon was the outstanding perspicuity and genuine simplicity of his mind and its processes. . . . Grasping the essential point, stripping it of useless accessories, developing his argument and only ceasing to elaborate when he had made his point perfectly clear and conclusive, always finding the right word or inventing one when the need arose, his conversation was ever full of interest. He did not make conversation; he talked. By the fluency of his thought and by his ease of delivery he would skilfully take charge, and one of his favourite gambits was to say to you: 'I see what you mean. You wish to make such and such a point: very well, let us tackle it straight away.'

Yet he did not fail to listen to the remarks and objections that were addressed to him. He accepted them, discussed or rejected them, maintaining all the time the atmosphere of a business discussion, and I never felt diffident about telling him what I thought to be the truth, even when it was not intended to please him.

As in his constructive thought everything was clear and precise, so in what called for action he knew neither difficulty nor hesitation. Conventions hardly troubled him at all. In discussion as in action, he went straight for his objective without stopping to consider points which he too often considered of secondary importance.

Where he could he chose the straightest line to the goal he had in mind and pursued it to the end so long as nothing obliged him to turn aside; but neither was he a slave to his plans and he would give them up or modify them the moment he happened to change his mind or when a new set of circumstances offered him the chance of achieving his end more effectively in another way.

He had little scientific knowledge, although his supporters took special pains to encourage the belief that he was an advanced mathematician. His knowledge of the mathematical sciences would not have raised him above the level of any officer destined, as he was, for the artillery: but his natural ability made up for his lack of knowledge. He became legislator and administrator, as he became a great military leader, simply through instinct: the strength of his character always inclined him towards positive action. He rejected vague ideas, had an equal abhorrence of the visionary's dream and the ideologist's abstractions and treated as mere parrot cries anything that failed to give him a clear outlet and tangible results. He really had no time for science, except those aspects of it which can be verified and controlled by the senses, and which are based on observation and experience. He had the greatest contempt for the false philosophy and the false philanthropy of the eighteenth century. Among the leading advocates of these doctrines Voltaire was the special object of his aversion and he never missed an opportunity to attack the generally accepted opinion of that gentleman's literary merit.

Napoleon was not irreligious in the ordinary sense of the word. He maintained that there was no such thing as a genuine atheist. He dismissed Deism as the outcome of rash speculation. A Christian and a Catholic, it was only to positive religion that he allowed the right to govern human society. He regarded Christianity as the foundation of all true civilization. He considered Catholicism to be the most favourable cult for the maintenance of peace and quiet in the moral world, and Protestantism as a source of strife and dissension. Personally indifferent to religious practices, he respected them too much to make light of those who followed them. It is possible that religion was less a matter of the heart to him than the result of an enlightened policy: but whatever the secret was he took care not to reveal it. His opinion of people was concentrated in a belief which, unfortunately for him, acquired in his mind the force of an axiom. He was convinced that every man called to public office or merely engaged in the active pursuit of life, was driven forward solely by the motive of self-interest. He did not deny the existence of virtue and honour, but he maintained that neither of those qualities had ever inspired anyone except those whom he described as dreamers, and whom, therefore, he dismissed as quite incapable of playing a useful part in the affairs of society. My own conviction rejected this argument and I often discussed the subject with him, trying to persuade him of its falseness, at least in the lengths to which he applied it. I never succeeded in making him yield on this point.

He had a special gift of being able to recognize those who would be useful to him. He was quick to discover those particular qualities of which he could make the best use. Without forgetting to look for the guarantee of their loyalty in calculated self-interest, he took care to secure them to his own interest, involving them in such a way as to block their way back to their old commitments. Above all he had studied the national characteristics of the French, and the story of his life proves that he learned the lesson well. In particular, he looked on Parisians as children and often compared Paris to grand opera. When I reproached him for the palpable falsehoods which abounded in most of his reports, he replied with a smile: 'It is not for you that I write them. Parisians will believe anything, and I could tell them a great deal more which they would not hesitate to accept.'

It frequently happened in the course of conversation that he would indulge in historical discussion. Such discussions usually showed up his imperfect acquaintance with the facts, but they also revealed an extraordinary sagacity in appreciating causes and foreseeing consequences. Thus he guessed better than he knew and while colouring people and events with his own imagination he explained them ingeniously. Since he made use of very few quotations, he must have taken the salient points of ancient and French history from a handful of books and above all from abridged versions. Yet he carried in his head a store of names and facts sufficient to impress those whose studies had been even less solid than his own. His heroes were Alexander, Caesar, and above all Charlemagne. His claim to be the lawful and actual successor to Charlemagne by right and title occupied him strangely. He would lose himself in interminable discussion with me trying to prove this paradox by the feeblest reasoning. Apparently it was my position as Austrian Ambassador which I had to thank for his obduracy on this point.

One of his keenest regrets was that he could not invoke the principle of legitimacy as the basis of his power. Few men have been so profoundly aware how precarious and fragile authority is which lacks this foundation and how much it exposes one to a flank attack. Yet he never lost an opportunity of earnestly protesting against those who imagined that he occupied the throne as a usurper. 'The throne of France,' he said to me once, 'was vacant. Louis XVI had not been able to maintain himself on it. If I had been in his place the Revolution would never have taken place, despite the great advance it made in men's minds in the preceding reign. Once the king had been overthrown the Republic took over the soil of France: I took the place of that. The old throne of France lies buried under the *débris* of it, and I had to found a new one. The Bourbons could not rule over this creation. My strength lies in my fortune. I am new, like the

Empire; there is, therefore, a perfect homogeneity between the Empire and myself.'

Yet I have often felt that in expressing himself thus Napoleon was merely indulging in wishful thinking or trying to mislead public opinion, and the direct approach he made to Louis XVIII in 1804 seems to confirm this suspicion. Speaking to me one day of this action he said: 'Monsieur's reply was dignified, it was steeped in fine tradition. There is something about *les légitimes* which goes beyond the mere spirit of the movement. If Monsieur had only consulted his own good sense he would have come to an agreement with me and I would have arranged a magnificent future for him.' He was also much struck by the idea of tracing the origin of supreme authority back to the Divinity. He said to me one day at Compiègne, soon after his marriage to the archiduchesse: 'I see that the Empress addresses letters to her father to His Sacred and Imperial Majesty. Is this title customary with you?' I told him it was from the tradition of the old German Empire which bore the title of Holy Empire, because it was also attached to the Apostolic Crown of Hungary. Napoleon replied in a solemn voice: 'The custom is beautiful and well applied. Power comes from God and that alone places it beyond the reach of ordinary men. Before long I shall adopt the same title.'

He laid great stress on the nobility of his birth and the antiquity of his family. More than once he went out of his way to show me that envy and calumny alone could have cast any doubt on the former. 'I find myself in an unusual position,' he told me. 'There are genealogists ready to trace my antecedents back to the Flood, and others who maintain that I am of common stock. The truth lies between the two. The Bonapartes are a good Corsican family, not exactly famous, because we hardly ever left our island, but a good deal better than many of those whipper-snappers who take it upon themselves to humiliate us.'

Napoleon regarded himself as someone isolated from the world, born to rule and to bend all minds to his will. He had no more regard for men than an overseer has for his workers. One of those to whom he appeared to be most devoted was Duroc. 'He loves me as a dog loves his master' were the words he used in describing him to me. Berthier's feeling for him he compared with that of a nanny. These comparisons were by no means contradictory to his theory of the motives by which men are actuated. They were the natural consequence of it. Where he came across sentiments which he could not explain by his theory of self-interest he attributed them to a kind of instinct.

There has been much talk of Napoleon's superstition and almost as much of his lack of personal bravery. Both these accusations are based on wrong ideas or misguided observation. Napoleon believed in fortune, and who had put it to the test more often than he? He liked to boast of his lucky star. He was delighted that the common people should not be averse from thinking of him as a privileged being, but he was perfectly honest with himself, and moreover he did not mind allowing fortune too large a share of credit for his rise. I often heard him remark: 'They call me lucky because I am clever. They are weak men who accuse the strong of being fortunate.'

Here I will mention a story which shows how much he relied on a vigorous spirit and how much he believed himself to be aloof from the accidents of daily life. One of the paradoxes which he liked to maintain on the questions of medicine and physiology (subjects for which he had a natural predilection) was his assertion that death was sometimes simply an absence of a vigorous will in individuals. One day at Saint-Cloud he had a dangerous fall (he had been thrown from a carriage and had narrowly escaped being impaled on a milestone). The next day when I enquired how he was he replied very seriously: 'I completed yesterday my experiments on will-power. When I was struck in the stomach I felt life was deserting me. I just had time to tell myself that I did not want to die, and here I am alive! Anyone else in my situation would be dead.' Those who would call him superstitious must at least agree that it was of quite a different kind from that which has been attributed to him.

It is the same with his bravery. He clung to life but, seeing that so vast a number of destinies were bound up with his, it was perhaps permissible for him to see in life something more than the puny existence of one individual. He did not, therefore, feel called upon to expose *'Caesar and his fortune'* to danger simply in order to prove his courage. Other great commanders have thought and acted as he did. If he lacked the dash that marks the daredevil, that was certainly no reason for accusing him of timidity as some of his enemies have not hesitated to do. The accounts of his campaigns are proof enough that the position he took up, whether it was dangerous or not, was always the right one for the head of a great army.

In private life he was easy-going, without ever having been of a pleasant disposition, and he frequently carried indulgence to the point of weakness. A good son and a good kinsman, showing those peculiarities which are found more especially in the family life of the Italian *bourgeoisie*, he put up with the excesses of some of his relations without showing sufficient strength of will to put a stop to them, even when it would have been clearly in his interest to do so. His sisters, in particular, obtained from him everything they wanted.

Neither of his wives ever had anything to complain of in Napoleon's personal conduct. Although this fact is well established, a remark by the archiduchesse Marie-Louise throws new light on it. 'I am sure,' she said to me some time after her marriage, 'that in Vienna they take great interest in me and that in the general opinion I am committed to a life of daily misery. So it is that the truth is not often probable. I have no fear of Napoleon, but I am beginning to think that he is afraid of me.'

Simple and even easy-going as he was in private life, he showed to little advantage in the world outside. It would be hard to imagine anything more awkward than Napoleon's manner in a *salon*. The trouble he took to correct the defects in his nature and in his upbringing only underlined his shortcomings. I believe he would have given a great deal to be able to add to his height and to bring a measure of nobility to his appearance which became more vulgar as he put on weight. He liked to walk on his toes. He had copied a way of moving his body from the Bourbons. His dress was carefully studied to provide a contrast with those round him, either by its extreme simplicity or its extreme magnificence.

There is no doubt that he sent for Talma to teach him what attitudes to adopt. He gave much patronage to this actor and his affection for him owed a great deal to the likeness that existed between them. He enjoyed very much seeing Talma on the stage; it might be said that in him he found himself again. Never did a gracious or neatly turned remark fall from his lips in addressing a woman, although the attempt to find one was often evident in his expression and in the tone of his voice. He only spoke to women of their clothing, of which he declared himself a scrupulous and severe judge, or of the size of their family, and one of his customary questions was whether they had suckled their babies, a remark which he usually addressed to them in language quite unsuited to the best society. Sometimes he took it into his head to inflict on them a kind of cross-examination on intimate, very personal relationships in society, which gave his conversation more an air of misplaced admonition—misplaced, that is, as to the choice of place and manner—than the characteristics of polite drawing-room talk. This lack of social sense exposed him more than once to rejoinders which he had not the skill to counter. His feelings against women taking part in politics or public administration amounted almost to hatred. . . .

The question has often been debated whether Napoleon was fundamentally good or bad. It has always seemed to me that these epithets, as they are generally understood, are not applicable to a character such as his. . . . There were two aspects of Napoleon. As a private individual he was easy-going and tractable, without being good or bad. In his capacity as a statesman he allowed no sentiment to enter in; his decisions were based neither on affection nor hatred. He removed or crushed his enemies without taking account of anything except the necessity or the desirability of getting rid of them. Once this object had been attained, he forgot them and did not persecute them. . . .

The opinion of the world is still divided, and perhaps always will be, on the question whether Napoleon really deserved to be called a great man. It would be impossible to dispute great qualities in one who, emerging from obscurity, was able within a few years to become stronger and more influential than any of his contemporaries. But strength, power, and superiority are more or less relative terms. To appreciate exactly what degree of genius it needed for a man to dominate the age in which he lived, it is necessary to have the measure of that age. It is at this point that opinions of Napoleon begin to make an important divergence. If the age of the French Revolution has been, as his admirers believe, the most brilliant and glorious epoch of modern history, then Napoleon who succeeded in taking first place in it and occupying it for fifteen years, has been without contradiction one of the greatest men who ever lived. If, on the other hand, he had only to rise meteor-like above the fog of a general disentegration, if he found round him only a society ruined by the excesses of a false civilization, if he only found himself up against opposition weakened by universal lassitude, by ineffective rivalries, ignoble passion, in a word by adversaries, at home as well as abroad, who were disunited and paralysed by that dissension, it is certain that the splendour of his success diminishes in proportion to the difficulty he experienced in achieving it. Since in our opinion such has been more or less the position, we are in no danger of forming an exaggerated opinion of Napoleon's greatness, although we acknowledge that there was something exceptional and imposing in his career.

The vast edifice he had built up was exclusively the work of his hand and he was himself the keystone of the arch, but this gigantic structure was lacking in essential foundations. The materials of which it was composed were no more than rubble from other edifices, some of it rotten, some lacking in consistency through and through. The keystone has been removed and the whole building has collapsed.

Such is, in a few words, the history of the French Empire. Conceived by him and created by him, it has only existed in him. With him it had to disappear. (*Mémoires*, I, pp. 277-92)

To complete this masterful effort, here is how Metternich saw himself in contrast to the great man:

I am convinced that Napoleon never knew me and understood me even less. The reason is quite simple. Napoleon, more than anybody else in the world, was contemptuous of the human race.

He had a marvellous gift for recognizing weaknesses in men; and all passions are weaknesses or give rise to them. He loved only men with strong passions and great *weaknesses*. By these defects he measured their virtues. He found in me a calmness which must have infuriated a man in the habit of speculating on passions. The result was that he had to deny the existence in me of reason or of any quality compatible with it. I have often smiled involuntarily in Napoleon's presence when I became aware that he was misjudging me. That is precisely why I knew him better than he knew me. It took only seven years of patient study to get to know a man who conceals nothing, specially from an observer who does not allow himself to be led astray by feelings of fear and admiration. (*Mémoires*, III, p. 554)

Metternich passes judgment on the Imperial regime as it appeared in 1809, at the end of his embassy in Paris:

France needed rest and she knew it. The feeling not only prevailed among the masses but was even shared by Napoleon's companions in arms. These men, who had risen for the most part from the ranks, had won the highest military honours. Weighed down with loot, made rich by the Emperor's deliberate generosity, they wished to enjoy the splendid position they had won for themselves. Napoleon had ensured a brilliant life for them. The *prince de Neufchâtel* (Berthier) had a yearly income of more than 1,200,000 francs. Marshal Davonst had amassed a fortune which brought in an income of nearly a million francs. . . .

Many people in civil life had, like the generals, reached high places. One source of wealth, which had been open to a whole class of adventurous spirits during the revolutionary wars, was exhausted. The war which Napoleon declared on fraudulent army contractors and the strict discipline he introduced into the handling of public funds caused a reaction among this class, which had been so numerous before the advent of the Emperor. It inspired in them a dislike of those warlike policies for which they and those with whom they dealt had hitherto shown the greatest sympathy. The nation, decimated by annual levies of troops, far from taking an interest in military operations carried on so far from France that it did not even know the names of the places where the latest victories had been won, went so far as to curse the conquests, the political importance of which they could not understand. In a word, France desired peace and it was a great mistake of the European Courts at that time that they failed to take account of this fact. . . .

The Emperor enjoyed a popularity in France such as is always bestowed on a sovereign who knows how to hold the reins of power with skill no less than with strength. His practical mind made him recognize the needs of a country where the social edifice had to be rebuilt. Outwardly a man of war, inwardly he was a legislator and a skilled administrator. Therefore the country was sorry to see him and his work constantly exposed to the dangers of war. . . . Had Napoleon confined his ambition to the preservation of what had been conquered under the Republic, his popularity would have increased, but his warlike temperament carried him much farther. He was born conqueror, legislator, and administrator and he thought that he could pursue all three paths at once. His undoubted genius furnished him with the means of doing it, but the feelings of a great majority of the nation would have been satisfied if he had confined himself to the responsibilities of government. (*Mémoires*, I, pp. 68–70)

After these observations comes a portrait of Talleyrand:

Monsieur de Talleyrand had an exceptional brain. I was near enough to him to study him closely and to realize that he was intended for destructive purposes rather than to preserve. Being a priest, he was yet compelled by his temperament to oppose religion: noble by birth, he argued in favour of the abolition of the nobility. Under the Republic he plotted against the Republic. Under the Empire he was constantly plotting against the Emperor: finally under the Bourbons he worked for the overthrow of the legitimate dynasty. *To prevent the accomplishment of anything definite*, that was the greatest talent of that statesman. Napoleon had the same opinion of him and he was right. In the course of a conversation, held after one of M. de Talleyrand's numerous resignations from the Ministry, the Emperor said to me: 'When I want to do something I do not make use of the *prince de Bénévent*: I turn to him when I want to do nothing without appearing to want to.' In private life M. de Talleyrand was a safe and pleasant person with whom to do business. (*Mémoires*, I, pp. 70–71)

A quarter of a century later Metternich will find himself at grips in the diplomatic field with his old adversary-cum-accomplice, now the mentor of King Louis-Philippe. From this arises a whole series of fresh appraisals. The opinions that these two princes of diplomacy formed of each other make reading too interesting for them to be in any danger of being overlooked:

> That Minister was turned out by the Corsican conqueror, but he is completely at home under a middle-of-the-road leader, for the middle of the road, that mixture of truth and falsehood, is the very essence of him. (to Esterhazy, July 17, 1834)

> His most notable talent is not his ability to simplify matters, but rather so to complicate them that he alone is able to find the way out of the maze. (to Esterhazy, Jan. 21, 1834)

> The prince de Talleyrand is at one and the same time the friend of political peace and the enemy of tranquillity. He lives on intrigues and on diplomatic complications. His counsels are always dangerous to follow, not because of their frequently impractical aspects, but because even when they are practical they still conceal some moral danger and the possibility of some material surrender of principle. (to Neumann. Dec. 11, 1832)

And this final characteristic which contains, perhaps contrary to its author's intention, the most surprising eulogy that ever came from the lips of the most enigmatic personality of his time:

> M. de Talleyrand is of all the diplomatists the one with whom I should have the least difficulty in reaching an understanding, and the one whom I should fear the least in those matters where we found it impossible to agree. I had so many dealings with him that it would be unpardonable in me not to know him, as he, for his part, must know me. M. de Talleyrand, as a man and as a thinker, faithfully represents *France* as she is, whereas the majority of those who are sent abroad often only represent parties and sometimes just themselves. (Dec. 4, 1834. *Mémoires*, V, p. 621)

CHAPTER TWELVE

From Louis XVIII
to Louis-Philippe

I F METTERNICH is to be believed, the Emperor Francis and himself never envisaged any other solution for France, once Napoleon had been eliminated, than the Restoration of the Bourbons. (*Mémoires*, I, pp. 182, 186) Whatever ideas Metternich may have entertained in 1814, once he had made up his mind, he was to find sufficient justification for adhering strictly to that decision:

> The return of the Bourbons to France was a work of justice and the immediate consequence of the successes achieved at the expense of the heir to the Revolution. Without the return to France of the legitimate dynasty, the allied Powers would by their glorious efforts have achieved much and nothing: *much*, because the overthrow of the French Empire was in itself a tremendous political event; *nothing*, because the first principle of all would not have been satisfied, namely that which is closely connected with stability and ownership, the primary interests of any society. (to Lebzeltern, June 5, 1820)

Unfortunately, from the beginning this Restoration had gone wrong:

> From the outset the Restoration was incapable of making an accurate appreciation of the forces at its disposal and of the weaknesses by which it was threatened. Finding itself between two elements in opposition, it more often than not chose the least appropriate and the least practical methods. Two main

considerations helped to give a wrong direction to Louis
XVIII's thinking. One was his ignorance of the real situation in
France in 1814, a situation which he neither understood, nor
could hope to, seeing that what he did know inevitably bore the
stamp of the *émigré* influence. The other was the policy he had
adopted of taking the opposite line to that of Napoleon, who
knew France well. Being thus unable to establish himself in a
France that did not really exist, and not wishing to establish
himself in France as she had been modified under the Empire,
there was no alternative but for the Restoration to take up a
position between the old regime and the last one, and the gap
which separates those two eras could only be occupied by
the Revolution. It was, in fact, the edifice of 1789 which Louis
XVIII shored up. In trying to organize France after the manner
of England, he handed her over to the hazards of a system of
opposition which failed to provide that counterbalance which
the foundation of the political structure in England had for so
long given to royal power, and the first elements of which
simply did not exist in France in 1814. (to Hügel, Sept. 4, 1837.
See also *Mémoires*, I, p. 209; V, pp. 82–83; VIII, p. 428)

It should not be thought on that account that Metternich desired the destruction of the regime set up by the Charter of 1814:

> Never has our government shown in its public or private actions
> a tendency to attack the foundations on which any legitimate
> government is based. King Louis XVIII granted his kingdom a
> fundamental law; the King may have been mistaken in some of
> his measures, but to try to shake the foundation on which he has
> set the social edifice of France would be to overturn the structure
> itself. (to Apponyi, Sept. 17, 1829)

Let us pick up again the chronological thread in order to discover what Metternich thought of the state of France and of the
personality of her leaders at different times during the Restoration. The main cause of his uneasiness in the early days of the
second Restoration is the opposition of the ultra-royalists supported by a part of the royal family. Responsibility for this

'deeply distressing' state of affairs 'is attributed very largely to the spirit of the emigration':

> Heaven has created a class of incorrigible men. The *émigrés* of every country and every age have this misfortune in common. Civil death has only to be protracted a little to produce in some respects the same effects as physical death. Any machine that is stopped becomes rusty and decomposes. It no longer fits in with the world which never stops and which can become *ancient* without becoming *old*. Men do not enjoy the same privilege and old men in a new world will always find it difficult to get along. (to Wellington, Mar. 17, 1816. *Supplementary Despatches*, XI, p. 338)

The year 1818 was to mark a fundamental change in Metternich's attitude towards the French Government. Doubts begin to be raised in his mind. Had it not been unwise of Richelieu, and especially of Decazes, to throw into the arms of the opposition those who were by nature the most loyal supporters of the throne? Would not the electoral law which they had passed in 1817 open the way to victory for the liberal left from the inside? And could they rely on those who had been kept in power or who had regained their position? What would happen if Louis XVIII, whose health was failing, should disappear from the scene?

Without going into the details of this eventuality, let us at least put on record the opinion Metternich had formed by the eve of the Congress of Aix-la-Chapelle in August 1818:

> Relations of mutual trust and friendship have always existed between the duc de Richelieu and myself. That Minister is very friendly disposed towards Austria, even though he is attached to Russia's interests by bonds of gratitude and of well-established custom. The reasons for this are a wide identity of interests and the memories of his youth. Besides, we regard him as pre-eminently French and if he had the necessary qualities for taking the helm in an administration as strong as the one for which he is responsible, we could not point, with things as they are, to a better Prime Minister in France. I think I can briefly outline

our attitude towards M. de Richelieu by telling you that we have the same degree of confidence in his character as we have doubts about his talent as a Minister.

Monsieur Decazes is the man of the moment by reason of the need which the King has always felt for favourites, and no less by reason of the real talent which we imagine him to possess. Satisfied in his relationships, overwhelmed with honours, he is certainly not conspiring against the King's person. But is Monsieur (de Richelieu) in the same position? Would he be prepared to sacrifice his fortune and his astonishing career to uphold the principle of legitimacy? . . . We very much doubt it. A man of revolution, he is and must be unscrupulous in his choice of the means by which to keep himself in power, and we perceive in this latitude of conscience very real dangers to the legitimate succession to the throne if the King were to die before a *rapprochement* took place between Monsieur and the all-powerful Minister. (to Vincent, Aug. 23, 1818)

Metternich earnestly desired this *rapprochement* and sought to bring it about by all the means in his power. In the course of the conversations he was to have with Richelieu at the Congress of Aix-la-Chapelle, he firmly insisted on the need for a turn to the right on the part of the French Government. We know what came of it. Richelieu, back in Paris, found himself incapable of overcoming the obstacle presented by Louis XVIII's senile attachment to his favourite, and he left the government. Decazes, in order to avoid the limelight, brought General Dessolles to the Presidency of the Council. He himself took the Ministry of the Interior and dominated the whole of French policy until his fall in February 1820.

The elections which took place in the early autumn of 1819 brought to light dramatically the dangers of the government's policy. Everywhere its candidates were defeated by liberals, who saw themselves as masters already, without a fight, of the legislative majority. Goaded by the knowledge that he would be the first to suffer from that eventuality, perhaps troubled also by the increasingly threatening attitude of the great Powers on the

Continent, Decazes decided to turn about and to seek safety in the very course of action which Richelieu a year before would have liked to pursue: *rapprochement* with the right and reform of the electoral system. As three of his colleagues refused to follow him, Decazes found himself obliged to take the Presidency of the new Government himself. Metternich took a stern view of this *volte-face*:

> Never was such a contradiction, so pronounced, so direct and so energetically upheld by the same men, offered to the public in any country at any time in history. We consider these events and every peculiar circumstance connected with them, to be the height of irresponsibility and weakness, and an epic example of it. . . . Certainly there does not seem anything unreasonable to me in the objective which the present administration has set itself . . . any more than it is unreasonable to wish to remedy serious mistakes . . . but the same men, the very same administration which committed the mistake, which upheld it with determination, and which owed its existence to this mistake and to its perpetuation, can these men and this administration hope to go back on a series of facts supported by a series of reasonings? (to Lebzeltern, Dec. 15, 1819)

We know that the fall of Decazes was hastened in a dramatic manner by the assassination of the duc de Berry, the nephew of Louis XVIII:

> The era of the great favouritism of M. Decazes struck the final blows against royal authority. It is regrettable that this Minister, endowed with great intellectual talents, strong in several aspects of his character, and brought up under the Empire, never discovered what it was that formed the foundation of that order of things: namely *power*. His versatility, his personal ambition, the confidence he had in the Emperor's men, all this contributed to his downfall and to his having brought royalty to the brink of the precipice [. . .]

> M. Decazes unquestionably kept one constant end in view: first to raise himself and second to keep himself up. But the means he employed to achieve this were calculated and put into effect from

one day to another. Unwisely rejected by the royalists, he thought he could get the men of the Empire period to hold his ladder for him. Rung by rung he drew himself up it, forgetting that the higher he climbed the farther he got from the ground of legitimate royalty which had ended up by no longer being his. (to Esterhazy, Mar. 18, 1820)

And so, once again, Richelieu is back. Metternich's satisfaction is genuine but qualified by distinct uneasiness:

No one does greater justice than I to the noble and disinterested attitude of M. le duc de Richelieu, to his austere probity, to his love of what is good, and finally to his moral qualities which entitle him to the widespread esteem that he enjoys. But we cannot escape the fact that it was under his Ministry that there first appeared the evils from which we are suffering today and which he himself has been called on to fight. Perhaps past experience will help the Ministry to steer clear of those reefs on which it foundered during its first administration. I very much hope so. . . . (to Esterhazy, Mar. 1, 1820)

Richelieu was nevertheless to succeed in restoring the internal situation, and to pass an electoral law which put an end to the continued advance of the liberals and gave the Chamber a right-wing majority again. All this pleased Metternich, of course, but in 1820 and in 1821 his attention was engaged elsewhere: the revolutions in Spain, Portugal, Naples, northern Italy, and Greece, brought into action the machinery of intervention of the Holy Alliance, together with the Congresses of Troppau and Laybach.

The attitude of the French Government remained equivocal in this crisis: wishing neither to become deeply involved in a repressive policy nor to encourage liberal movements abroad. 'Negative and suspicious moral attitude', 'lamentable weakness', 'a vacillating and tortuous line of action', with such expressions did Metternich characterize French policy at this time. And he summarizes his condemnation of it in these words: 'France involved in revolution and France devoid of any activity are two extremes, and extremes always make for trouble. We have reached the point where in matters that are worthy of consideration we find no French Government at all, or else we find one indulging in spontaneous impulses, subordinate influences, and even in calculations unworthy of a great State.' (to Vincent, Oct. 1, 1821)

This self-effacement was, incidentally, to prove fatal to the Ministry on the domestic level; reduced to a minority in the Chamber by a coalition of right-wing and left-wing opposition parties, Richelieu retired at the end of 1821, making way for a homogeneous Ministry.

The outstanding personalities of the new team were the comte de Villèle, the Minister of Finance, and the vicomte de Montmorency, Foreign Minister. This right-wing Ministry had been welcomed at Vienna with the greatest reserve. Who, pray, were these nonentities emerging on the level of international politics? Nevertheless, the resolutely conservative provisions of the new Ministry and its inclination to co-operate with Austria were before long to induce Metternich to adopt a more favourable attitude:

> Everything goes to prove that the new French Ministry is made up of strong elements, for the simple reason that they are pure elements. One of the proofs is the daily *rapprochement* between us. Earlier Ministries were never able to draw closer to us. The present one aims directly at this. (to Lebzeltern, July 15, 1822)

The Congress of Verona (October–November 1822) was to enable Metternich to secure a real ascendancy over the mind of the French Foreign Minister. Yet Montmorency, who had lain down the lines on which co-operation with the Allied Sovereigns was established, almost immediately handed over the Ministry to Chateaubriand. Clearly Metternich would not be pleased with this change.

Relations between Chateaubriand and himself were not going to be easy. Ever suspicious of the intentions of the French Government, Metternich will try to keep it strictly dependent on the

Alliance: Chateaubriand, anxious to flatter national pride, will aim at giving France an independent rôle. 'The whole tone adopted by that government towards the public is wrong and underhand', Metternich writes on February 24, 1823. Yet at that time it is Villèle rather than Chateaubriand who is held responsible for anything objectionable:

> The trouble with M. de Villèle is his utter lack of political experience—knowing only France and never having had his attention directed to the policies of the other Powers, he will go wrong whenever it is a question of co-ordinating the conduct of his Court with that of his allies. On the other hand, it must be feared that the man who would get on well with M. Decazes would often be ready to yield on a matter of principle. (to Lebzeltern, June 8, 1823)

The picture that he formed of Chateaubriand will continue to be tainted with dark colours. His opinion is recorded in a curious comparison which he draws between Chateaubriand and Canning, another of his *bêtes noires*:

> Neither Mr. Canning nor M. de Chateaubriand is a statesman. Neither possesses a single one of those qualities which might later turn him into one. Both have wit. Canning has a wrangling mind which might be suited to a lawyer defending, according to the demands of his pocket, both a good cause and a bad one. M. de Chateaubriand possesses those qualities which distinguish the man of letters but which by no means distinguish the man of learning. Mr. Canning is at the moment liberal and he is fighting against colleagues who are less so than he and a good number of whom are not liberal at all. M. de Chateaubriand, on the other hand, is closer in his outlook to the monarchical standpoint than is the President of the Council. There is to a greater extent than in the case of his English *confrère* a doctrinaire quality about his mind which makes him feebler than Mr. Canning and which will always prevent his being on his guard against the trick that Canning is playing on him. (to Lebzeltern, Mar. 6, 1824)

When Chateaubriand, after his downfall, was thrown into opposition against Villèle, Metternich gave vent to his irritation in terms that grew increasingly bitter:

> No one, it seems to me, has ever prostituted himself as *le vicomte* has done. More revolutionary than the genuine revolutionaries, more of a sophist than they and more extreme than the men of the Terror, he stands to be condemned by all those who have been so blinded by his smooth talk as to gain a false impression of his mind and his personality. Men of M. de Chateaubriand's kidney always start where I leave off. They take an open dislike to me when I ignore them, whereas my dislike of them invariably follows on their actions.

At the same time Metternich's impression of Villèle was taking an opposite direction:

> My opinion of Villèle is known to you. You know that I regard him as an administrator of rare talent. He is lacking in knowledge and consequently in political opinions. As a result of this deficiency he seeks the foundations of his country's policy in an imaginary independence. Yet M. de Villèle has taken the first steps along the path to a healthier policy since he took over the portfolio of foreign affairs. . . . Can it be that he has become convinced that an isolationist policy is not the one best suited to the needs of the moment, or has the foolishness of his adversary forced him back on to more rational ground? The future alone can show. (to Lebzeltern, Aug. 11, 1824)

The new reign which opened in France in September 1824 allows him a little hope:

> Louis XVIII is dead and that is an end of it. What would have been an important event a few years ago is at the present time an insignificant fact. Things are going better in the world for the moment, and so kings can die in peace. The old King was a weak master. If he had been a private individual he would probably have had a bigger share in the mistakes of his age. Charles X is quite different. He is kindhearted and upright. If only he possessed greater strength of character, he might stand

out above the ordinary monarchs. I am not a regicide, but I am certainly entitled to say that there are *ordinary* monarchs. In any event it is fortunate for Charles X that he was not in Louis XVIII's place, for reaction against his return to France would have destroyed him. (Sept. 23, 1824. *Mémoires*, IV, p. 111)

The year 1825 was to see even closer relations established between Vienna and Paris. Metternich's stay in the French capital during the month of March contributed to this. The general impression left on him by all the contacts he made in Paris is summed up in a long letter to the Austrian ambassador in Russia:

The opinion I have so far been able to form of the French Government can only be a favourable one. The Ministry has a better understanding now of the true political interests of the kingdom. The talks that I had with MM. de Villèle and de Damas were in this respect highly satisfactory. The Ministry's attitude towards domestic matters continues to cause them trouble and it could hardly be otherwise in a country where public morality is lost. I cannot tell you, M. le comte, the distressing effect France has on me. I did not find anything there of which I was not already aware or which I had not suspected, but there is always a difference between observations made at a distance and impressions gathered on the spot. The effects, no less sad for being inevitable, of a regime which is not attuned to the spirit of a nation were bound to make themselves felt as the new institutions developed. Intelligence is the commonest commodity in France. It abounds everywhere, but the same is not true of rationalism. If there is one country which needs to be led by a government with strong and vigorous authority that country is France. And yet it is precisely this authority, so badly needed, that is unable to establish itself in the present regime. Representative government is upheld by underhand means and intrigue degenerates into open corruption more quickly here than anywhere else. The political parties in France are fundamentally a poor lot. They are really only surfaces, for underneath there is nothing even remotely resembling a principle and everything becomes a gamble. The effect such a state of affairs must have on public morality is easily imagined: and so it no longer exists and France resembles in my opinion a vast arena in which the vilest passions are constantly at war with each other.

In the midst of this rabble of individuals, this demoralized mass who know no other god than money, no other cult than ambition, no other aim than self-interest, and who have no regard for the general welfare, in the midst of this chaos, I repeat, there stands out a group of upright and religious men. These men resemble the inhabitants of another world.

They are courageous and they combat evil, but their number must be diminishing daily, for here as in Germany discontent is paying particular attention to the corruption of youth. . . .

Ten years of Restoration have brought forth fruit which in its most important aspects is hardly worthy of the Restoration's sacred aim. This was bound to be the effect of a regime which has nothing social about it except its name. The Ministry is going through a critical time; either it will be turned out or it will greatly strengthen its position. In the final analysis that Ministry consists of only one person and he is undoubtedly a man of superior talents. (to Lebzeltern, Mar. 25, 1825)

The agreement between Vienna and Paris was not destined to survive the year 1826. When, in April of that year, Russia and England agreed to settle the Greek question in a way that was opposed to Metternich's wishes, the French Government chose to join them without allowing themselves to be deterred by the arguments of the Austrian Chancellor. As a result he conceived a violent feeling of resentment. After the hurried elections at the end of 1827, he utters this condemnation and a prophecy:

M. de Villèle is a *bold gambler* by nature, and it is not on this ground that I deem it fair to base the first of my main accusations against him. There is one fact which is much more damaging to the public interest, and that is the extreme flippancy with which he decides to embark on a venture. M. de Villèle would have made a very distinguished administrator, but he is a very dangerous Prime Minister for a country such as France. The day he gives up his position as Minister he will find that he is merely an individual, never again the guide and restraining influence behind a party. (to Apponyi, Dec. 31, 1827)

We know that in the end Charles X was obliged to accept Villèle's retirement. The Ministry that succeeded him has kept the name of the Minister of the Interior, Martignac, although he was not President of the Council. Metternich has nothing to say about this gentleman, but his opinion of the new government is merciless:

> The Cabinet . . . will not last. I have widespread personal experience of the members of it, and although some of them may have a number of intellectual distinctions, I do not know one who would be remarkable for real strength of character. (to Trautmansdorff, Jan. 15, 1828)

However, he accepts the comte de la Ferronnays, the Foreign Minister, as 'the French diplomat he would prefer to see, above all others, in charge of the foreign policy of France'. (to Apponyi, Jan. 24, 1828)

> There is not a perfect balance between the heart and the head of that Minister. The first always follows a perfectly straight line, while his head is inclined to bias. . . . Finally, M. de la Ferronnays is one of those men with whom it is impossible to hold a series of discussions on the same subject at short intervals. The warmth of his sentiments and the lack of healthy criticism in his reasoning unfortunately makes it impossible to be sure that something in his brain will not induce him to substitute a new error for one which his sincerity had persuaded him to eliminate. A woman of wit characterized the moral essence of that Minister perfectly when she described him as a 'liberal knight'. (to Apponyi, Dec. 12, 1828)

Metternich, with his 'fairly strong propensity for liberal ideas', particularly resented La Ferronnays' good feelings towards Russia, in which country he spent a long time as ambassador. 'His feelings are those of a blind supporter of the Emperor of

Russia's own cause', and so true is this that the French Cabinet can only be regarded as 'no more than the sleeping partner of the Cabinet at St. Petersburg'. (to Esterhazy, Mar. 7, 1828)

The formation of the Polignac Ministry was greeted by Metternich with a mixture of satisfaction and uneasiness. (*Mémoires*, IV, pp. 593–4) 'The kingdom needs a third restoration', he was writing a few days afterwards:

> The royal government in France will only be able to continue if there is a change in the electoral law or in the laws relating to the periodical Press. Of these two indispensable conditions it is probably easier to fulfil the first; as to the second, I confess I should be very hard put to it even to suggest a way of satisfying that. (to Esterhazy, Aug. 20, 1829)

He is as much surprised by Polignac's inactivity as by the appearance he gives of feeling secure:

> It is only in well-established States and in well-ordered conditions that a government can indulge in the practice, sometimes so useful, of remaining still until the storm has passed.

> When the ground shakes under governments it is no good their trying to stay still, nature will not allow it!

> Real action in France is in the hands of journalists and they could never run a State [. . .] In France the established order is really no more than a pure demagogy under a leader who holds the title of king. It is no longer a monarchy with a representative regime for the representative bodies are ruled with the same rod of iron as the government. If you admit that in the next session the Chambers will support the government, you will find them liable to the same condemnation.

> Things cannot go on like this. A great outburst will drive them either to revolution or to a new restoration which might prove to be the real one. I do not say the crisis will be confined exactly to next winter, but sooner or later it will come to pass because it would be impossible for it not to. (to Apponyi, Oct. 28, 1829)

The crisis, in fact, broke in March 1830, when the King decided to dissolve the Chamber of Deputies after it had delivered a hostile address. Metternich approves of the King's firm line, but he perceives a limit beyond which it could not be followed without danger:

> A government that has the will and the intention to act is very strong, and if moreover it takes its stand on its just rights it should succeed. . . . It is on the basis of the Charter that the government should take up its position, and on this ground I consider it to be unassailable. . . . (Apr. 14, 1830. *Mémoires*, V, p. 2)

Metternich in his early forecasts attached no more importance to the July monarchy than that of a prologue which would be followed by Republican chaos. 'The prologue of the new revolution has come to an end in Paris,' he writes on August 15, 1830. 'I do not say its first act, because the play is only just beginning.' Louis-Philippe himself inspires no confidence:

> In the character of this prince a boundless ambition is allied to a weakness for slavish popularity. He satisfies these two passions alternatively by means of lively intrigue. A prince who is absorbed in such influences and who finds himself at a time like this at the head of a nation herself devoid of any moral restraint, presents such an awkward combination that the dangers involved in it are incalculable. (to Esterhazy, Feb. 19, 1831)

> The real ringleader is La Fayette. He appeared on the scene with a reputation for being a simpleton with which the gentlemen at Court had burdened him, but I had always held a quite different opinion of the moral character of this deplorable person. What follows will throw light on the active rôle which he played and the influence he had for long been exerting on the catastrophes of the age. . . . He was unquestionably the greatest expert on the technique of revolutions that the present era has produced. (to Werner, Aug. 15, 1830)

Miracle of miracles, Louis-Philippe somehow manages to keep

going, and gradually Metternich, instead of condemning him out of hand, begins to estimate his chances of survival.

But he will never recognize in principle the regime which came out of the revolution. He will never believe that it can last. 'Every hour of its existence is a fight against death.' (to Apponyi, Aug. 25, 1832) The reign of Louis-Philippe can only be 'a more or less prolonged agony'. (to Apponyi, Feb. 10, 1832)

> *The royal throne surrounded by republican institutions* is a meaningless expression, a monster lacking vitality, an abstraction which no amount of work by its authors and partisans will ever furnish with substance. A perpetual struggle between those two warring elements must be the inevitable consequence of such a conception, but this conception has clothed the form in a solid fact. That throne, which is so badly constructed and which is merely *a wooden chair not even covered by a strip of velvet*, represents France in the political sense; it is with this throne and nothing else that we have to deal. That being so, let us cling to whatever royal qualities it still possesses (June 3, 1831. *Mémoires*, V, p. 169)

The expression *juste milieu* invented by the occupants of the regime fires his imagination. It is nothing more than 'the application of the doctrines of preservation to the conditions of destruction' (to Apponyi, Aug. 4, 1832); it is 'the spirit of the left trying to enlist the support of the spirit of the right' (to Apponyi, Jan. 25, 1832); it is 'a political Protestantism' (to Viale Prela, Sept. 4, 1846, p. 34), 'a cardboard machine' (*Mémoires*, VI, p. 160).

In 1833 Metternich discovered that the king of the barricades was at heart a conservative:

> Of all the men of the July revolution there is one who would not be able to find employment under a different regime from that created by brickbats, and that man is the King. Tight corners are very conducive to straightforward action. When men have no choice, when there is only one place for them, they cling to it tooth and nail and even lose their enthusiasm for Utopias. . . . One of the great curses of the last nineteen years has disappeared for him. The cast-off clothes of liberalism he only uses now as a

covering. There is no longer any liberalism to make, the material is discredited by those very people who on their own admission had decked themselves out in it during fifteen years of comedy. Ever since the King has become what he did not want others to be, anything which has helped to clear a space for him and to instal him in it no longer stands a chance of being considered by him. In that individual relationship lies the key to that striking difference between the moral and material situation of the King of the French and that of the other members of the government and of Frenchmen in general. (to Hübner, July 28, 1833)

Shortly afterwards there began a dialogue—it was spread over several years—between Metternich and Louis-Philippe through the medium of the ambassador, Apponyi. The Chancellor really seems to have thought, at least in the early stages, that he could convert the other to his views:

The only part of our relationship with the French Government which I do not regard as wasted is the time that I spend composing notes for the ostensible attention of the King of the French and reading reports of our conversations with this prince. The rest is nothing and in my opinion counts for nothing. (to Apponyi, Oct. 30, 1835)

In the final analysis these relations did not bear the fruit that Metternich had counted on, and one is indeed obliged to admit that it needed a certain touch of *naïveté* to believe that it was possible to match his cunning or to influence him. The judgments that are passed on Louis-Philippe after 1840 become more severe. This one, for example, inspired by the rejection of the demand for an endowment that had been made by the King on behalf of his second son, the duc de Nemours: 'One of the most memorable scandals of the age', writes Metternich.

Louis-Philippe, who is endowed with outstanding gifts of intelligence and leadership, unfortunately has a passion for money, and an inability, which is no less unfortunate, to distinguish what is despicable. In the impudent demand for the endowment of his second son he made an abstract principle out of the son's private fortune. I frankly admit that if I had been his Minister I would rather have resigned than be a party to making the request, and if I had been a deputy I should have voted against the endowment. Whatever happened to the good sense of the prince in this affair? (to Apponyi, Mar. 5, 1840)

The final opinion of Metternich on the eminently utilitarian character of Louis-Philippe is to be found in this letter of 1845

In any matter the King sees only *himself and his own*. Principles only affect him in so far as circumstances enable him to take advantage of them. His religion is based on the cult of what seems useful to him in the direction I have just indicated. In his calculations he confuses men with things, and makes use of both of them according to the advantage he can get from either of them. (to Apponyi, May 20, 1845)

We cannot follow, year in year out, the unfolding of the foreign and domestic policy of the July monarchy, but, once again, chronology offers us the most practical background against which to evoke a few well-known figures, to sketch some important situations, and to emphasize features of general interest.

First, to pick up the play again at its prologue where we left it, we have Casimir-Perier, a man of strong character who really founded the July monarchy:

That Minister is, in my opinion, the first man of character France has produced since Bonaparte. But there is certainly a difference between the two, and a difference also in their positions. Before he could reign Napoleon had to create a France capable of being governed. M. Perier is trying to govern France as she was made by the Revolution in 1830. Napoleon proved that his undertaking was possible. M. Perier's undertaking did not bear the same fruit. That need not prevent our marching in step with him as long as the earth does not open and swallow him up, and we much prefer him to any rival less gifted than himself. (to Apponyi, Oct. 28, 1831)

Unfortunately for France, cholera removed him prematurely, and his successors found themselves immediately at grips with opponents on either side: the legitimists who were drawn into an attempted rising by the duchess of Berry and the Republicans who covered Paris with barricades again:

> The royalty of the barricades has been attacked by means of fresh ones. The July barricades question the legitimacy of the June ones. The case is not one to be argued in a court of law but to be settled in the streets. Victory has gone to the July barricades, sure enough, but it remains to be seen whether it will be a lasting one for the government. (to Neumann, June 24, 1832)

Of the Ministers who succeeded Casimir-Perier the one to whom Metternich pays most attention is the duc de Broglie, the Foreign Minister, stepson of Madame de Staël, and like her inclined to be liberal-minded. After reading a special letter from the Minister to the ambassador, Sainte-Aulaire, Metternich comments:

> I confess that I had formed a more favourable impression of M. le duc de Broglie than the one I must hold to-day. . . . Although it may be natural for doctrinaires to make mistakes easily . . . that is not to say that one of them is bound to combine every fault in himself. Yet such is apparently the case with the Minister of Foreign Affairs, for unfortunately in his profession of faith he is wrong in absolutely every respect. . . . (to Hügel, July 16, 1833)

This is how Metternich sees the internal situation in 1834:

> Having taken possession of the throne, Louis-Philippe wishes to remain there. He exercises personal power as far as he can, and it is by his undoubted skill that he has managed to maintain his position. The Ministry is a mixture of revolutionaries, egotists, and depraved nonentities, such as the existing order of things in France is bound to bring to the direction of affairs. France is divided into three parts: the majority of the population who want to live quietly, the radicals, and the legitimists. The number and weight of the first part is fixed: the second, by reason of its

intense activity, merits serious consideration: the third fuses into the other two and only counts so far as it represents the principle of sound law as opposed to the material conditions under which France is labouring. (to Apponyi, Sept. 17, 1834)

Furthermore, Thiers was, at this moment, the man on whom Louis-Philippe counted to rid him of the duc de Broglie's inconvenient tutelage, and he formally asks Metternich to enter into personal relations with his Minister of the Interior. It is not without some disgust that Metternich agreed to do so. These relations took the form of an exchange of security information. They were to result in his assessing more closely the rising star of French policy:

M. Thiers lacks the positive information he must have if he is not to misunderstand many situations. Generally speaking, the French have little knowledge of foreign countries, and although intelligence is needed in public affairs, intelligence is not enough to derive benefit from them. Positive information is needed as well, and it is precisely this that M. Thiers lacks in respect of foreign affairs.

Those men who take sides as soon as they enter public life and whose legislative, administrative, and political education have all been directed towards this one aspect, have much to learn when they find themselves called on to handle real affairs. However talented M. Thiers may be . . . he will have to learn little by little to understand the world as it is and to forget the world of his own creation wherein he has dwelt in imagination all his life. . . . (to Apponyi, Jan. 2, 1836)

The downfall of the Molé Ministry in March 1839 opened up a period of political crisis. Metternich had estimated the opportunities and all the assets at the disposal of the two candidates most likely to succeed him:

The real difference between the two candidates for the Ministry and the existing President of the Council lies in their moral qualities. In the life of M. Molé the heart plays a part, whereas Messieurs Thiers and Guizot are guided by the head alone.

Between these two M. Guizot has the better of M. Thiers as a *man*; but in matters of *savoir-faire* the reverse is true. Guizot makes the mistake of confusing *doctrines* with principles. Thiers subordinates both to what he considers to be his interest. Thus the former gets involved in a circle of ideas many of which are faulty, judged by healthy practice; the latter leads an indeterminate existence, aiming at what is useful. Of the two, the man of substance is preferable to the man who cares about nothing. Nevertheless I regard M. Thiers as more difficult to avoid than his colleague. Travelling light and being decidedly agile, he is one of those men who slip, like a draught, through every crack. (Feb. 15, 1839. *Mémoires*, VI, p. 359)

In the end, as Metternich had foreseen, it was Thiers who won, and Louis-Philippe was obliged against his wishes to entrust the government to him in March 1840. Thiers was destined to plunge his country into the gravest of international crises over the Eastern question. This matter is too complex even to be summarized here. Let us simply recall that in August 1840 France, standing quite alone, was a prey to a crisis of jingoism inspired by the imprudent revival of Napoleonic memories. We know that once again Louis-Philippe saved the peace by compelling his fiery little Minister to resign (October 20), and Metternich concludes from this:

That man was wrong in every respect. This can only be explained by his extreme presumption, a defect which so blinds its victims that they come to look on their own nebulous individuality as the pivot on which the entire world rotates. The political course pursued by the preceding President of the Council was mad, because it took account of no nationality other than the French and of none of the influences that are and always will be exerted in a State by a diversity of interests. (to Apponyi, Nov. 24, 1840)

The task of sticking the pieces together fell to Guizot, who, under the quite nominal Presidency of old Marshal Soult, was to govern France until the revolution of February 1848:

M. Thiers wrote the novel, M. Guizot will strengthen his posi-

tion if he concentrates on writing history. At least on this level
he will be sure of meeting us. (to Apponyi, Dec. 1, 1840)

Hitherto Guizot had hardly had the good fortune to please
Metternich. Was he not one of the dishonoured tribe of doctrinaires? Could this 'ideological conservative' be trusted? Yet, after
a year and more of stability, Metternich confesses:

> The factions are right to attack M. Guizot as they do. No
> Minister since 1830 has shown his qualities (and I could easily
> extend that judgment to the Ministers of the Restoration). I
> admit that he has learnt much as he goes along, but there is merit
> in that very fact. I hope that circumstances will come to M.
> Guizot's aid and that he will be successful in that session. If he
> is, then he has a great opportunity to establish a lasting Ministry
> and that is just what France needs. (Aug. 12, 1842. *Mémoires*,
> VI, p. 621)

The Parliamentary and administrative corruption which
tarnished Guizot's long and otherwise beneficent rule, could not
escape Metternich:

> Conditions in France today are fundamentally different from
> those on which the existence of other States and of our Empire
> in particular is based. The House of Rothschild, for reasons that
> are natural although I cannot regard them as good and certainly
> not as morally satisfying, plays a much bigger part in France than
> do the foreign Cabinets, except possibly that of England. The
> great vehicle in France is money, and men who have to discount
> philanthrophy and crush criticism under the weight of money
> need a great deal of it. Corruption, that most practical element
> of the modern representative system, is discounted quite openly.
> The situation by its very nature requires it and such a force
> is irresistible. Traffic in that commodity is not welcomed here
> and this fact alone would be enough to set up a certain moral
> uneasiness between two body politics so differently organized.
> (Dec. 11, 1845. *Mémoires*, VII, p. 104)

Nor was the foreign policy of Guizot by any means entirely
satisfactory to the Austrian Chancellor, but somehow there sprang

up between the two men a feeling of trust, supported by a personal relationship. Let us hope that the history of this relationship will soon be made clear by the papers of the mysterious Mr. K. (Klindworth), who was their go-between. In this hope we will leave that aspect of the matter and pass on to the conclusion of the chapter.

The revolution of February 1848 swept Guizot and Louis-Philippe away. Metternich had not expected it, at least not at that particular time:

> I had proof that affairs in France were only resting on an insecure foundation. The Ministry indulged in many illusions about its own strength, I was quite sure on that point; the present movement is a radical, not a superficial, one, on that point there had been no doubt. Yet I could not suspect, let alone know, that things would turn out as they have. The latest event is the crisis of the July revolution, which for all the appearance of good health it was at pains to give itself, was only an abnormal product, made up of unhealthy social elements, and so a crisis was inevitable. (Feb. 29, 1848. *Mémoires*, VII, p. 594)

> You know what my opinion had been all along of the July throne: I am not surprised at its downfall. What I did not altogether expect was that France would have insufficient strength (or patience which is also strength) to wait for the death of Louis-Philippe. And so the event upset my calculations, if impressions so deserve to be called. (Mar. 1, 1848. *Mémoires*, VII, p. 568)

A few days later Metternich suffered the same fate as Guizot, and consequently his diplomatic correspondence, that broad stream in which the events of the world were reflected for forty years, suddenly disappeared into the abyss opened in Vienna by the revolution of March 12.

Epilogue

FROM 1848 onwards Metternich is nothing more than an old man in exile, a mere spectator on the balcony of history. Unlike so many statesmen once they are removed from the scene, he did not use his leisure to write his apology or even to prepare material which could be used as a monument to his glory. Perhaps his pride had reached that exalted level when one has no need of the approbation and admiration of others to be perfectly satisfied with oneself. Or perhaps this great realist was aware that the most carefully elaborated masks do not stand up to the erosion of time and the implacable curiosity of succeeding generations.

'In a hundred years' time,' he wrote one day to the comtesse de Lieven, 'historians will understand me better.' We have reached that point. Why is it that we still find ourselves faced with such a swarm of different judgments? This lack of agreement is all the more surprising because in this case we are certainly not dealing with an enigmatic character. There is no 'Metternich mystery'. His political achievement? That is accessible to all in the history of his times. His personality? Nobody was readier than he to talk about and analyse himself. Why, then, so many contradictory opinions?

It would certainly be pretentious on my part to try to pronounce judgment equitably and definitely after so many others have done so. But at least one may try to lay closer siege to the problem. Perhaps one ought to draw a distinction between the objects of reflection and appraisal: on the one hand, the achievement of the statesman, on the other his personality and his mode of action.

On the first point differences of opinion are inevitable, and in the first place for the good reason that enough is not yet known of Metternich's political work. The monumental proportions of the famous work of H. von Srbik are deceptive: close scrutiny reveals that he made only very limited use of the State archives: nor was it really possible to do anything else once it had been decided to attempt to cover the whole of such a career. What history needs now is a series of monographs exploring one particular aspect, a problem limited in time and extent, but making use of all the existing sources. In some respects, this work is well advanced. It is true, for example, of Germany, Italy, Switzerland, and also, it can be said, of the Napoleonic era as a whole. But there is still bread on the platter.

Assuming that one day all the original material is worked through, will it then be possible to formulate a generally acceptable principle? Who would dare to hope as much? Will not the opinions of future historians, like those of yesterday, be coloured by national and ideological prejudices? Would there not always be Germanic writers to condemn Metternich because he was opposed to the unity of Germany? Will the Italians be able to detach themselves completely from the tradition of the Risorgimento? Austrian historians, justly proud of their past, will always be tempted, from a spirit of revenge, to admire and to make much of the man who presided over their affairs during one of the happiest eras in their national history. And as for Soviet historiography . . . we know that it serves a higher cause, as it sees it, than that of plain, *bourgeois* objectivity. To all those who believe that democracy and the Parliamentary regime are the inevitable and beneficent end of the progress of human societies, that nationalism is a sacred virtue, the man who tried to put a brake on this evolution can only appear as a blind reactionary, whose efforts were as vain as they were harmful. Finally, let us not forget that prejudices of this kind can as easily lead to an over-estimation as to an under-estimation of the statesman. Thus for a French historian, the man who won the fight against Napoleon could only be a genius of Machiavellian proportions. Similarly, liberal history which cannot otherwise explain the setbacks suffered by so righteous a cause, and one so much in keeping with the image it has formed of popular aspirations, will always be inclined to exaggerate the ability of one who was the frequently victorious enemy. Thus it was that in 1889 an American writer, G. B. Malleson, described Metternich as 'a central, omnipotent, figure ... before whom the nations bow down ... crushing all generous aspirations and every attempt to win true liberty'. We dare to suggest, in conclusion, that the best point of view from which to judge the work of Metternich would be the very one that was also his: did he serve well the cause of the Austrian Empire? Given the elements at his disposal, could he have done better? The fact that one hesitates to reply squarely to these questions would seem to prove, if proof were needed, that the last word has not been spoken.

If the political work is likely to lend itself to discussion for a long time to come, the features of the statesman himself make up for it by appearing to be fairly clearly defined. There is certainly no need to have scrutinized his every action to see them; a serious study of a few typical episodes should enable us to recognize style, character, and personality.

Let us beware of summary judgments and remember that we are dealing with a many-sided personality. Above all let us take into account the inevitable transformations brought about by the trials and hazards of a career that spanned half a century; only then shall we understand the divergence of opinions to be found among Metternich's contemporaries no less than among historians.

It seems to us possible to distinguish three Metternichs.

The first picture to appear is that of Austrian ambassador at Paris, of Francis II's Minister before 1815, as shown in the portrait of him by F. Gérard: a full face, features still soft to the point of effeminacy, very young beneath his carefully curled hair powdered like hoar-frost. Here is the 'knight of the rose', a frivolous dandy after the manner of an eighteenth-century courtier, mixing

M.–L

political with amorous intrigue, and sometimes more preoccupied with the second than the first. Here is the 'butterfly-
Minister' whose shallowness and versatility were still exasperating Gentz in 1815. Others, greater than he, were calling the tune
at the time, but by flair and resilience, assisted also by good
fortune, he succeeded in making the best possible use of the
interests for which he was responsible.

The second Metternich is that of the triumphant period of the
great congresses, from 1819 to 1822. It is the personality given
to us in Lawrence's famous portrait: the Chancellor of State,
bedecked with embroidery, wearing all his decorations, the
'coachman of Europe' at the height of his power and glory. The
expression and the pose clearly reflect his pride at feeling that a
docile team is well in hand, at being master of events and seeing
the realization of his plans. The maturity of forty years has
sharpened the profile and made the hair recede from his temples.
The time for extra-conjugal amours is past, so too is the age of
worldly distractions. His last liaison with la Lieven is an affair of
the head rather than of the heart. The senses seem hardly to play
any part in it now.

Nothing matters any more compared with politics and the
satisfaction of being in control. The prestige of diplomacy carried
to the highest pitch of perfection masks the fundamental weakness of the situation and although one may still stoop to unworthy
measures, one can often now allow oneself to speak as the master.

The third and last Metternich is the one caught by the famous
daguerrotype of Mylius. He is in the last years of his life now,
but the picture also seems to apply to the end of his Ministerial
career: clothed entirely in black, in a meditative and professorial
attitude, his head slightly to one side, the mask nobly desiccated
by the years, on his lips the traces of a disillusioned smile. The
aged statesman has watched the mainstays of his power crumble,
stronger wills than his have brought his system to a standstill;
he knows that the future belongs to all the things that he has
loathed and fought against. All that he can do is to put off the
fatal moment, and he devotes all his experience and what remains

of his prestige to rendering harmless all over Europe the mines which might start the avalanche moving. Disappointments and mental suffering have made him more tolerant and more benevolent: increasingly paralysed in the sphere of action, he seeks to give himself and others the illusion of power by redoubling his output of professorial verbiage and interminable reflections on the past. He resembles a living encyclopedia of the politics of half a century, an encyclopedia which one consults out of habit even if one takes no notice of its oracles. And when he no longer has the responsibility of power he can still console himself with the luxury of giving free expression to his thoughts. For all his senile ramblings, this last Metternich is probably, taking all in all, the least antipathetic of the three.

Yet under these three metamorphoses he remains one and the same man. By combining them and superimposing one upon the others, one can perceive the permanent features of his personality.

The picture that emerges in this way hardly resembles that of the bugaboo of traditional liberal mythology, one made up of Lucifer and Machiavelli, of Torquemada and Matamore. It is equally far removed from that which Metternich would himself have liked to draw in his time: the infallible oracle, the serene genius floating above human defects, the champion of Truth and Right. More prosaically Metternich appears to us as a man of goodwill and as a man of good sense: an admirable judge of men and of the political problems of his age, experienced in all kinds of diplomatic finesse; much less doctrinaire and much more opportunist than he appears at first sight. Circumstances at least as much as his gifts assisted his career. His rise was encouraged by a situation in which finesse and patience were the only weapons that could be matched against power and genius; and finally the astonishing length of his reign is due in large part to the combination of circumstances which placed him, the conservative and cautious Minister *par excellence*, at the head of an empire, which, if it was to survive, needed above all peace and stability.

Everything that is known about his behaviour, the whole judgment of those who knew him well, converge on the same conclusion: in him character was not on the same high level as intelligence. There is, for example, Lord Stewart underlining 'the natural bent of His Highness's mind to be always projecting and wishing to originate, though equally slow in conveying any one point into effect. . . . Prince Metternich's desire to do a great deal and yet to put off actual decisions or doing anything until the last moment . . .' (Stewart to Castlereagh, June 17, 1817, and Aug. 24, 1818. P.R.O. F.O. 7/136 et 139)

Again, there is this remarkable, hitherto unpublished, testimony of the Czar Alexander, the man whom Metternich believed he had in his pocket: 'You must have known Metternich,' he said to La Ferronnays in 1823, 'and he is no doubt a man of great intelligence, but the moment he sees the slightest difficulty, he hesitates, stops, looks all round for a way of escape, and then if he considers that he can no longer avoid this obstacle, he plants all his friends down in front of it.' (*Arch. La Ferronnays*)

If he unquestionably appears as a great historical figure, it is because there is incarnate in him a whole aspect of the political thought and action of his age. But a whole series of other values passed him by, and because of that one hesitates to proclaim him as a great man. A man of the eighteenth century who strayed into a romantic era, he may have lacked the faculty of understanding the passions of his age and of making use of whatever might be valuable in them. Too reasonable to be really inspired, he lacked also perhaps those impulses which come from the heart, the imagination to project action forward into the distant future, that implacable will which crushes opposition and forces the hand of destiny. 'I have never been a Richelieu,' he admitted in a rare moment of modesty, and one is tempted to add: nor a Pitt, nor a Castlereagh, nor a Casimir-Perier, nor a Cavour, nor a Bismarck . . . 'It seems to me,' Louis Veuillot wrote in 1849, 'that what was principally at fault was his wisdom. . . . Constant preoccupation with the need not to undertake what is impossible and to make peace endure does not always prevent great faults, but it certainly prevents great achievements, great actions.' (*Oeuvres complètes*, XXXIV, p. 360)

BIBLIOGRAPHY

Manuscript Sources

I am far, indeed very far, from having exhausted everything, directly or indirectly, that represents the expression of Metternich's thoughts. The experts know that a lifetime of work would not be enough. There has been nothing systematic in the choice of manuscript sources which I have seriously consulted, since it corresponds, as I explained in my first foreword, to a pattern quite unlike that of the present book.

1. Metternich's Archives (Plasy Archives)

The Chancellor's personal archives were preserved until the last war in his castle of Plasy (Plass) in Bohemia. Later they were taken to Prague and are now in the fourth section of the State archives, where I was allowed to consult them. The present classification has been scrupulously respected, so much so that in order to get an idea of their contents I had only to refer to the inventory drawn up fifty years ago by Ottokar Weber, and published in the *Archivalien zur Neueren Geschichte Oesterreichs*, I (1913), pp. 140–56. It must be admitted that these personal archives are not so useful as might be imagined, and the reason is that those documents of use historically have been for the most part published in the volumes of Metternich's *Mémoires*, referred to below.

2. State Archives of Vienna

Metternich's diplomatic correspondence preserved in the archives of the State Chancellery in Vienna (*Haus-Hof-und-Staatsarchive*) supplied me with the largest number of unpublished texts. There should, in principle, be two copies of every letter: on the one hand a copy in the vaults of the State Chancellery (*Staatskanzlei-Ministerium des Aussern*), in the sub-sections corresponding to each country: on the other hand, the original, in the vaults of the embassies concerned (*Gesandschaftarchive*). In either case the documents are collected higgledy-piggledy, so to speak, in boxes the numbering of which cannot be considered reliable. That is why, in order to make the system of reference less laborious, I have simply given for this kind of document the date with the name of the person to whom it is addressed. If anyone cares to consult the originals some time he will have no difficulty in finding them at once under the heading of the diplomatic post to which that person was assigned under the appropriate date. To take only the most frequently mentioned ambassadors, the posts are: Paris for Vincent, Apponyi (from 1826) and Hübner; London for Esterhazy, Neumann and Hummelauer; St. Petersburg for Lebzeltern and Ficquelmont; Berlin for Zichy and Trautmansdorff; Rome for Apponyi (before 1826) and Lützow. Let us, however, take note of an anomaly in connection with one important document: the instructions given in 1825 to Apponyi. He had been nominated for the London post, and so those instructions are to be found in the series *England* of the *Staatskanzlei*, although the man to whom they were addressed was finally given quite a different assignment, that of Paris.

Much less numerous are the texts borrowed from other series; in the case of those a more detailed indication has been given:

3. Archives of the Foreign Ministry in Paris

The great series (Diplomatic correspondence, *Mémoires* and documents) in the Austrian sections, furnished some remarks made by Metternich to the French ambassadors and relayed by them to the Ministry.

4. Public Record Office (P.R.O.)

The correspondence of the British representatives at Vienna (=envoys), preserved principally in the series F.O.7, furnished a few useful notes.

5. Richelieu Papers

These are the personal papers of the duc de Richelieu, preserved today in the Sorbonne, Victor Cousin library.

6. Letters to Sir Travers Twiss

These forty letters written by Metternich after 1848 to an eminent British jurist and professor were acquired in 1935 by the Manuscript Office of the Bibliothèque Nationale in Paris (*Nouvelles acquisitions françaises* 12629) and have never, as far as I know, been exploited.

For those who might be interested in this correspondence, I might say that Metternich's personal archives (Plasy) contain, together with copies of Metternich's letters, the originals of those that Twiss had written to him.

7. Archives of Madame Maurice Firino-Martell

Madame Firino-Martell, a descendant of the marquis du Caraman, ambassador at Vienna from 1816 to 1828, has preserved an important part of the papers of this personage, and she was kind enough to allow me to make use of them.

8. Archives La Ferronnays

They are in the chateau of Saint-Mars-la-Jaille (Loire Maritime), where M. le comte Artus de Cossé-Brissac was kind enough to allow me to consult them.

Printed Sources

There could be no question here of providing even a cursory bibliography of Metternich. The elements of it could be found in the large work of H. von Srbik: *Metternich der Staatsmann und der Mensch*, Munich, 1925, 2 vols., and especially in the third supplementary volume published in Munich in 1954 by the Viennese professor Taras von Borodajkewycz (*Quellenveröffentlichungen und Literatur, eine Auswahlübersicht von 1925–1952*, 235 pp.). The article by Silvio Furlani: 'Gli Studi sul Metternich dal 1925 al 1952', in the *Nuova Rivista Storica*, 1955, pp. 302–9, and that by Paul W. Schroeder, 'Metternich Studies since 1925' in *Journal of Modern History*, Vol. XXXIII, September 1961, pp. 237–60, are also worth consulting.

Of the works published in France, those of J. Hanoteau (publication of letters to Madame de Lieven) and of Grunwald, mentioned below, contain useful bibliographies.

The following list includes only those publications that are referred to in the present work.

A. Metternich's memoirs and letters

Mémoires, documents et écrits divers laissés par le prince de Metternich ... publiés par son fils le prince Richard de Metternich ... Paris 1880–4, 8 vols.

This momumental collection, which has also been published in German, has always been and remains, in spite of its imperfections, the basis of every study of Metternich. Its irreplaceable value lies in the fact that it is very largely based on the Chancellor's personal archives; but it should be realized that the official documents reproduced in it represent a very minute proportion of what still remains unpublished in the vast series of State archives.

The following publications, very varied in character, have supplied letters from Metternich which had not been included in the aforementioned work:

Despatches, Correspondence and Memoranda of Field-Marshal Arthur, Duke of Wellington, London 1867–73, 5 vols.

Supplementary Despatches, Correspondence of . . . Wellington, London 1856–65, 15 vols.

Charles van DUERM: *Correspondence du Cardinal Hercule Consalvi avec le prince Clément de Metternich, 1815–1823*, Louvain–Brussells 1899, Vol. CXXV, 421 pp.

Ernest DAUDET: 'Un Roman du prince de Metternich', in *Revue hebdomadaire*, July–August 1899, pp. 31–53. *A travers trois Siècles*, Paris 1911 (*Vie de cœur d'un Homme d'Etat*, pp. 163–227).

These two publications make use of letters intercepted by the French dark-room, between July 1819 and March 1820, and thus complete the subsequent work of J. Hanoteau, which is based on a collection of letters ending on April 30, 1819. In addition some of these letters had been published in the big collection of the *Mémoires*, but without any indication of the person to whom they were addressed and with the compromising 'tu' shamelessly replaced by 'vous', not to mention other minor 'adjustments'.

Lettres du prince de Metternich à la comtesse de Lieven, 1818–1819, published . . . by Jean Hanoteau, Paris 1909, LXXIII, 421 pp.

Boyer d'Agen: *Une Dernière Amité de Metternich, d'après une correspondance inédite.* (In co-operation with Cardinal Viale-Prela, formerly Nuncio at Vienna.) Paris 1919, 125 pp.

M. A. de Breycha-Vauthier, who announced the publication in 1959 of a series of 171 letters written by Metternich to Alexander Hübner between April 1849 and February 1859, has given some interesting samples of them, first in the *Journal de Genève* of August 13–14, 1955, and secondly in an article in the *Revue générale belge*, October 1957, pp. 45–49: 'Metternich à Bruxelles'.

Narciso Nada: *Metternich e le Riforme nello Stato pontificio: La Missione Sebregondi a Roma, 1832–1836*, Turin 1957, 234 pp.

G. de Bertier de Sauvigny: 'Metternich et Decazes, d'après leur correspondence inédite, 1816–1820', in *Etudes d'Histoire moderne et contemporaine*, V (1953), pp. 60–115.

France and the European Alliance, 1816–21: the Private Correspondence between Metternich and Richelieu, Notre Dame (Indiana), 130 pp.

B. Contemporary Evidence

A certain number of persons who met Metternich have recorded his remarks, often more revealing in their spontaneity than things written on reflection.

Others expressed opinions worth committing to paper:

Fr. von GENTZ: *Dépêches inédites aux Hospodars de Valachie*, published by A. Prokesch-Osten, Paris 1876–7, 3 vols.

U. MAYNARD: *Jacques Crétineau-Joly, sa Vie politique, religieuse et littéraire, d'après ses Mémoires, sa Correspondence et autres Documents inédits*, Paris 1891, 574 pp.

Life, Letters and Journal of George Ticknor, Boston 1876. 2 vols.

Marquis de VILLENEUVE: *Charles X et Louis XIX en exil: Mémoires inédits* . . . published by his grandson, Paris 1889, Vol. VIII, 327 pp.

Joseph-Alexandre HÜBNER: *Une Année de ma Vie, 1848–9*, Paris 1891, 574 pp.

Comte de SAINTE-AULAIRE: *Souvenirs: Vienne, 1832–41*, Paris 1926, Vol. XXIV, 360 pp.

Louis VEUILLOT: 'Le Prince de Metternich à Bruxelles', in *Oeuvres complètes*, Vol. XXXIV: *Mélanges*, pp. 337–62.

C. Other Works

For the chapter on the methods of Metternich, I made use of the two remarkable studies by the Austrian archivist Joseph Karl MAYR: *Geschichte der österreichischen Staatskanzlei im Zeitalter des Fürsten Metternich*, Vienna 1935, 166 pp.

Finally a few quotations from the following biographies:

Viktor BIBL: *Metternich*, Paris 1935, 330 pp. (translation of a work which appeared in German in 1827 under the title *Metternich in neuer Beleuchtung*, the most malevolent of the works for the prosecution).

Constantin de GRUNWALD: *La Vie de Metternich*, Paris 1938, 347 pp. (The most recent and the best of the biographies written in French.)

Index

Dy 8vo Gen

Sender .... DUE .... FOR OFFICE USE ONLY
(*Mr/Mrs/Miss/Rev...... (*delete where is inapplicable)

Occupation ....

Address ....

....

On behalf of *myself/the institution below:

I wish to receive regularly your announcements of new books in
the following categories (*please tick appropriate boxes*):

GENERAL NON-FICTION ☐ Biography/history/travel/how-to/misc.

RELIGION & THEOLOGY ☐ Bible/liturgy/doctrine/pastoral/history/
biography/meditation/prayer (*C. of E./Free Church/R. Cath. ....)

LIBRABOOK paperback series ☐

Special interests ....

and level of treatment? ....

Please send similar reply-card to my friends listed inside ☐

*do/do not mention my name. I have written inside this letter ☐
(*please do not write lower than the* ✱ *sign by publisher's address*)

Signed... Date as postmark

✓ NOTED   ✓ ACTION

FOLD HERE, GUM REVERSE OF 'DARK STRIP' AND SEAL AS LETTER

TO OPEN LETTER—CUT OFF THIS DARK STRIP

CUT OFF HERE

POSTAGE
WILL BE PAID
BY
LICENSEE

NO POSTAGE
STAMP NECESSARY
IF POSTED IN
GREAT BRITAIN
OR NORTHERN
IRELAND

BUSINESS REPLY SERVICE
Licence No: S.W. 2561

M & H T

Darton, Longman & Todd Ltd

29a Gloucester Road

LONDON SW7

England

*

CUT OFF HERE